Guides, Guards and Gifts to the Gods: Domesticated Dogs in the Art and Archaeology of Iron Age and Roman Britain

Kate Smith

BAR British Series 422
2006

Published in 2016 by
BAR Publishing, Oxford

BAR British Series 422

Guides, Guards and Gifts to the Gods: Domesticated Dogs in the Art and Archaeology of Iron Age and Roman Britain

ISBN 978 1 84171 986 3

© K Smith and the Publisher 2006

The author's moral rights under the 1988 UK Copyright,
Designs and Patents Act are hereby expressly asserted.

All rights reserved. No part of this work may be copied, reproduced, stored,
sold, distributed, scanned, saved in any form of digital format or transmitted
in any form digitally, without the written permission of the Publisher.

BAR Publishing is the trading name of British Archaeological Reports (Oxford) Ltd.
British Archaeological Reports was first incorporated in 1974 to publish the BAR
Series, International and British. In 1992 Hadrian Books Ltd became part of the BAR
group. This volume was originally published by Archaeopress in conjunction with
British Archaeological Reports (Oxford) Ltd / Hadrian Books Ltd, the Series principal
publisher, in 2006. This present volume is published by BAR Publishing, 2016.

Printed in England

BAR titles are available from:

	BAR Publishing
	122 Banbury Rd, Oxford, OX2 7BP, UK
EMAIL	info@barpublishing.com
PHONE	+44 (0)1865 310431
FAX	+44 (0)1865 316916
	www.barpublishing.com

Summary

The Domestic Dog in the Art and Archaeology of Iron Age and Roman Britain

This study investigates the symbolic role of the domestic dog in Iron Age and Roman Britain through contextual analysis of their faunal remains and interpretation of their representations in iconography. Previous studies have highlighted linkages between the species and ideas about death, healing and regeneration (Jenkins 1957, Ross 1967, Toynbee 1973, Henig 1984, Green 1992). Although these connections clearly did exist in the cosmologies of Britain and the Western provinces of Rome, this detailed examination of the evidence seeks to identify reasons why this might have been so. The enquiry was also designed to highlight any previously unnoticed patterns in the dataset that might add a further dimension to our understanding of how the domestic dog was perceived at a symbolic level.

It has been established for some time that dogs appear in statistically significant numbers, compared to other species, in the special animal deposits that are a feature of certain Iron Age pits (Grant 1984, Wait 1985, Hill 1995). Dramatic evidence for ritual practice involving animals found at a Romano-British temple complex in Springhead, Kent, and comparable finds from both sacred and secular sites, suggest that domestic dogs were also a favoured sacrifice during this period. As well as analysing such archaeological evidence, this study draws on anthropological, psychological and historical writings about human relationships with the domestic dog in an attempt to forward our understanding of religious expression during antiquity.

Acknowledgements

First of all, I would like to thank my excellent supervisor Professor Miranda Aldhouse-Green for all her advice, support and encouragement throughout the production of this thesis. I am also very grateful for Professor Stephen Aldhouse-Green's faith in me as an undergraduate; without his encouragement I would not have attempted research in the first place.

During my studies I was delighted to find that the vast majority of people who I approached for information were really very helpful and forthcoming with their responses. In no particular order I would like to thank: Kate Clark, Mark Maltby from Bournemouth University, Barry Cunliffe and Martin Henig from Oxford University, Phil Andrews of Wessex Archaeology. Martin Millet from Cambridge University, Ian Baxter, Roger Jacobi and J D Hill of the British Museum, Sylvia Jones and Sally James from Lydney Park Estate, Helen Glass of Rail Link Engineering, Kirsty Stonell of English Heritage, Hannah Firth from Hertfordshire Archaeological Trust, Annie Grant from Leicester University, Robin Birley from Vindolanda/Chesterholm Museum and Sue Byrne from City of Gloucester Museum and Art Gallery.

I consider the photographs and illustrations in this book to be very important and feel that they will certainly add to the enjoyment I hope people get out of reading my work, so I would like say thank you once again to the following people and institutions who very generously allowed me to reproduce their images: The Danebury Trust, Elsevier Publishing, ULAS, T C Champion at Southampton University, Society of Antiquaries of London, Blackwell Publishing, Essex County Council, MoLAS, Cambridge Antiquarian Society, Channel Tunnel Rail Link, Wessex Archaeology, Oxford Archaeology Unit, Anne Lever, Tullie House Museum and Art Gallery, Chris Rudd, The British Museum, Hunterian Museum and Art Gallery, University of Glasgow, Peter Leach, Esmonde Cleary, Rijksmuseum van Oudheden, te Leiden, Tempus Publishing, Corinium Museum, Cirencester, Cotswold District Council, Philip De Jersey at Oxford University, Bristol's Museums, Libraries and Archives, University of Reading.

Please accept my sincere apologies if I have left anybody out.

Finally I would like to thank my friends and family for being there for me - particularly Mum, Dad and Andrew. Love always.

Contents

		Page
Thesis Summary		i
Acknowledgements		iii
Contents		v
Figures		vii
Tables		ix
Chapter 1	The Domestic Dog in the Art and Archaeology of Iron Age and Roman Britain – An Introduction to the Study	1
Chapter 2	Dog Remains from British Iron Age Settlements, Sacred Sites and Human Burials	6
Chapter 3	Domestic Dogs in the Archaeology of Romano-British Settlement Sites	14
Chapter 4	Dogs Remains from Romano-British Sacred Space including finds from Recent Excavations at Springhead, Kent by Wessex Archaeology	25
Chapter 5	Domesticated Dogs found in association with Romano-British Human Burials	36
Chapter 6	Dogs as Symbols in Roman Britain – Images, Visualities and Metonyms	47
Chapter 7	Domesticated Dogs – Companions to the God Nodens and Goddess Nehalennia	59
Chapter 8	Conclusion	71
Bibliography		75

Figures

Fig. 1	A selection of Romano-British dog femurs illustrating the marked variation in size of the species population	5
Fig. 2	A dog and horse Special Animal Deposit in a grain storage pit at Danebury Hill Fort, Hampshire	7
Fig. 3	The dog skeleton found in the boundary ditch entranceway at the East Leicestershire hoard site	9
Fig. 4	A human and dog pit burial from Broadstairs, Kent	9
Fig. 5	Grave of a young woman and associated dog burial at Maiden Castle, Dorset	11
Fig. 6	The arthritic femur of a Romano-British pet dog (left) compared to a healthy modern specimen (right)	15
Fig. 7	A knife handle from Silchester decorated with the image of a dog and bitch mating	17
Fig. 8	A Romano-British dog buried in a standing position in a pit at Silchester, *Insula IX*	17
Fig. 9	Possible termination deposit of a dog found at Rangoon St, London	21
Fig. 10	Dog tooth pendant and horse remains from Ivy Chimneys, Essex	27
Fig. 11	Diagram of the animal deposits within the subterranean shrine at Ridgeons Gardens in Cambridge	28
Fig. 12	Diagram of the arrangement of three chained domestic dogs in the subterranean shrine at Ridgeons Gardens in Cambridge	29
Fig. 13	A chained dog from the top of the 'Dog Pit' at Springhead, Kent	32
Fig. 14	Diagram of area of recent excavations at Springhead, Kent	35
Fig. 15	The burial of a woman and a dog at Ilchester Roman cemetery	39
Fig. 16	Hunting frieze on a Romano-British Bronze belt buckle found in Chapel Street, Chichester (left). The structured burial of a dog, a horse and a deer from Eastern London Roman Cemetery	41
Fig. 17	Bones from Dog Paws Pierced for Suspension from Iron Age Bramdean, Hampshire (left). A diagram of an infant's grave from Asthall, Oxfordshire (right)	42
Fig. 18	A 3rd Century AD Roman sarcophagus decorated with a small dog peering through a doorway	46
Fig. 19	Hunter-gods and their hounds – Hunter God from Southwark, London (right) and the Hunter God from Bisley, Gloucestershire (left)	49
Fig. 20	A hound and hare pen-knife handle from Lydney Temple, Gloucestershire	50
Fig. 21	Diana and hound from shrine of Apollo at Nettleton, Wiltshire	51
Fig. 22	An early issue of Cunobelin's silver coin featuring a large hound (top) and later issues featuring Diana and hound (below)	52
Fig. 23	2nd Century AD enamelled dog brooch found in Wiltshire	52
Fig. 24	Romano-British bronze dog statuette from Kirkby Thore, Westmorland	53
Fig. 25	Mother-Goddesses with infants and lap-dog from Cirencester, Gloucestershire	55
Fig. 26	Funerary monument depicting a man and a lap-dog from Shirva, Dunbartonshire, 3rd Century AD	56

Fig. 27	A Romano-British bronze statue of a canine monster devouring a human limb, Woodeaton, Oxfordshire	57
Fig. 28	A 1st Century BC stater from Norfolk depicting a wolf-like monster	57
Fig. 29	Reconstruction of Lydney Temple site, Gloucestershire	59
Fig. 30	Plan of Lydney Temple site, Gloucestershire	60
Fig. 31	The human-faced quadraped from Lydney Temple site, Gloucestershire	63
Fig. 32	Statuette of a Bronze Deer Hound from Lydney Temple, Gloucestershire	63
Fig. 33	Picture (left) and diagram (right) of a bronze plaque bearing an inscription to the God Nodens and an image of a dog	63
Fig. 34	Bronze diadem from Lydney Temple, Gloucestershire	64
Fig. 35	The mosaic from the *Cella* floor of Lydney Temple Gloucestershire	66
Fig. 36	A recent map of the Severn Estuary from Avonmouth to Sharpness with the navigation channel indicated	68
Fig. 37	The Severn Bore	69
Fig. 38	Nehalennia and her hound on an altar found in Colijnsplaat, Netherlands	69

Tables

Table 1.	Number and species of complete animal skeletons by archaeological zone in the 'Great Shaft' at a Romano-British farmstead in Warbank, Keston, Kent	23
Table 2.	Survey Results – The presence of dog remains within 18 examples of Romano-British constructed sacred space	26-7
Table 3.	Details of animal bone assemblages from Romano-British cemeteries reviewed for this study	37

Chapter 1

The Domesticated Dog in the Art and Archaeology of Iron Age and Roman Britain – An Introduction to the Study

1.1 The Origins of our Relationship with the Domestic Dog – A Brief Overview

The archaeological record informs us that *Canis familiaris*, the domestic dog, was our first domesticated animal companion. Genetic tests have revealed that dogs were most likely to have been domesticated from wolves in East Asia about 15,000 cal. BP (Savolainen et al. 2002, 1610-1613). That they shared a strong social link with humans by at least the 10th millennium BC was revealed in 1977 at the Natufian site of Ein Mallaha in Northern Israel, where the skeletal remains of a woman and a puppy were found together in a tomb dated to around 9750 BC; the woman's hand had been placed on top of the animal. There is a gap in the archaeological record of roughly another 2,500 years before any other species of domesticated animal can be identified anywhere in the world (Davis and Valla 1978, 608-610, Davis 1987, 142-152). Dogs are now found in every part of the world that we occupy; our homes are their natural habitat. It has been suggested that the behavioural similarities between humans and wolves hold the key to understanding how the affiliation between man and dog came into being. Wolves, like humans, are pack animals, the pack instinct arising from the need to hunt in teams to hunt effectively. Such a strategy relies on the ability of the individual to recognise their place, within the social hierarchy of the group and act accordingly. The similarities between human and wolf non-verbal means of communicating status would have led to the forming of an alliance between them during the Upper Palaeolithic when both species were competing for the same game. Realising the potential of the wolf as a hunting companion, humans would have begun to draw wild wolves into their groups to tame them for this purpose. The domestic dog was the product of these animals, isolated from the wild breeding population over numerous generations (Clutton-Brock 1999, 49-51).

1.2 Dog Images and Remains from Iron Age and Romano-British Archaeological Contexts – What We Know

Dog remains are frequently recovered during excavations of Iron Age and Romano-British sites, albeit in small numbers. Analysis of these bone assemblages has led archaeologists to conclude that dogs were not bred for food nor did they form a regular component in human diets during these periods. Although this does inform us that dogs were treated differently from most other domestic animals it does not prove that the animals held any special status in terms of their relationships with humans or human beliefs about them; Britons in Iron Age and Roman antiquity may simply have found them unpalatable or uneconomic to keep in larger numbers. However, there is a quite high incidence of dog bone deposits that display unusual characteristics suggesting that their carcasses were not simply 'dumped' as part of ordinary refuse disposal (Grant 1984b, 221-227, Wait 1985, Hill 1995, Fulford 2001, 199-218). There is a general feeling that the comparative scarcity of dog remains in the archaeological record should not be taken as a measure of the animal's importance in the lives of the ancient populations under discussion.

Previous studies of the archaeological record, particularly the iconography from the Western provinces of Rome, have led scholars to suggest that domestic dogs were in fact associated with spiritual beliefs surrounding hunting, healing, guardianship, death and fertility and that these ideas were in some cases interrelated. This extensive survey of the record focussing entirely on this animal, sought to reaffirm or question these ideas and identify trends relating to such beliefs across time and space. The research outlined below was designed to enable any other ideologies linked to the domestic dog to be recognised and reveal patterns in the deposition of their remains that will inform the interpretation of future finds.

1.3 The Background Literature and Origins of the Project

At the beginning of the 19th century at least ten complete and incomplete images of dogs in bronze and stone were discovered, in and around, the remains of a Romano-British temple in Lydney Park Gardens, Gloucestershire, dating to the 3rd- 4th centuries AD. Reverend William Hiley Bathurst kept a written record of these excavations on his land, which was published posthumously in 1879. His report included an enquiry into the significance of dog symbolism within a Romano-British religious context. His investigations led him to link Nodens, the deity named at the Lydney temple, with Asklepios, the Greek healer god, whose great shrine in Epidaurus is known to have housed dogs that were accorded sacred status and used in healing rituals (*Iamata* IV(2), 1.121-2, Stele I, Edelstein and Edelstein 1998). This was the first line of evidence that led Bathurst to believe the remains at Lydney were those of a healing temple (Bathurst and King 1879, 14-15).

Sir Mortimer Wheeler excavated the site again between 1928 and 1929. In his report he supported the interpretation of the site as a healing shrine, writing in detail about each of the most noteworthy votive offerings. As well as the numerous portrayals of dogs, Wheeler also drew attention to the great number of bone pins found at the site and other offerings that he considered to be markedly feminine, like the carved bone image of a woman whose abdomen was emphasised with incised lines as if indicative of pregnancy; thus the possibility of an ancient connection between dogs and fertility issues was suggested (Wheeler 1932, 40-42). The main sources of reference for Wheeler's interpretations were Classical texts and comparable continental archaeology.

In 1957 Frank Jenkins produced a paper called 'The Role of the Dog in Romano-Gaulish Religion' for the Belgian journal *Collection Latomus* (Jenkins 1957, 60-78). He looked at the myths, legends and religious beliefs of numerous ancient cultures, from Greek and Roman to Teutonic and Netherlands. He found recurrent links across time and space in the ideas associated with dogs. Not only were they apparently wide spread symbols of health and fertility but they were also connected with notions about guardianship, hunting and in particular, death and the underworld. Jenkins also looked at their representation in iconography to support these interpretations as well as considering the significance of the contexts in which images of dogs were found, like the Lydney temple.

In 1973 Professor Jocelyn Toynbee produced a book devoted entirely to the subject of animals in Roman life and art. Like Frank Jenkins, she used both material culture and textual evidence to inform her work that included a comprehensive chapter on canines. Much of the chapter was devoted to identifying the dogs described in ancient written sources in the contemporary art, but she also included a section on the ritual role of dogs, which again identified a substantial amount of evidence for their association with the afterlife, healing and fertility (Toynbee 1973, 101-124).

One obvious source of information about ancient dogs that was largely ignored until the late 1960s/ early 1970s was their physical remains in the archaeological record. Animal bones from excavations were usually dismissed as domestic waste unless they were found in a clearly unusual context. However, in 1968 Anne Ross undertook a survey of shafts, pits and wells in Britain that she interpreted as possible receptacles for votive offerings. The remains of dogs were a relatively common component amongst material recovered from these features, but no explanation was offered as to why this might be. In fact the main flaw of the work was that it failed to incorporate any criteria for the recognition of a ritual shaft, pit or well as opposed to a non-ritual example (Ross 1968, 256-285).

Ralph Harcourt carried out a study, published in 1974 that dealt exclusively with the remains of dogs in the British archaeological record dating from the Mesolithic to the Anglo-Saxon period. Using a method of estimating the shoulder-height of the animals by measuring their long-bones he was able to establish a size range for each period under discussion that is still often quoted today. Harcourt drew attention to the paucity of adequately recorded bones from excavations in Britain, concluding that a more uniform approach to the documentation of this evidence was essential if interpretative headway was to be made in archaeo-zoology. However, his study did reveal that a quite dramatic increase in the diversity of the British dog population took place in the Roman period. One notable aspect was the introduction of lapdogs, the first dogs in Britain that were too short and slightly built to have survived without human care (Harcourt 1974, 151-175). In 1987 Simon Davis illustrated the full potential of archaeo-zoological studies in his book *The Archaeology of Animals*. He clearly explained the variety of ways that faunal remains can inform a survey of the past, covering techniques to discern everything from the ancient environment to the origins of domesticates. Davis demonstrated that animal bones are often the least ambiguous form of evidence available to the archaeologist (Davis 1987).

Annie Grant's analysis of the huge animal bone assemblage from excavations at Danebury hillfort in Hampshire marked a turning point in the way studies of Iron Age animal remains from settlement sites would be approached. A new type of deposit was recognised that differed from ordinary domestic waste in a number of ways. These 'special animal deposits' were found in disused grain storage pits and were represented by three types of find; complete or nearly complete skeletons, animal skulls/horse mandibles and articulated limbs. These body parts often appear to have been deposited with special care and did not exhibit signs of butchery. Grant suggested that these could be the remains of sacrificial offerings and statistical characteristics of special animal deposits indicated that economic factors might have been taken into consideration when an animal was chosen for use in such rituals. One of the most convincing arguments used to substantiate this claim was that dogs and horses were present in special animal deposits far more frequently than would be expected given their overall numbers in the bone assemblage as a whole. In terms of primary produce these were probably the least productive animals on the site and therefore a smaller loss to the community in these terms (Grant 1984a, 221-227). Grant's conviction that the identification of animal bone deposits as symbolically charged features should not be restricted to those found in obviously religious contexts, like human burials or shrines, was reinforced in her 1989 paper in *Anthropozoologica* (Grant 1989, 79-86).

In 1985 Gerry Wait undertook a survey to test whether or not special animal deposits could be identified as archaeological features at sites other than Danebury hillfort. After surveying the contents of grain storage pits from 28 Iron Age sites he concluded that special animal deposits, as defined by Annie Grant, were indeed a valid characteristic of settlements from the period. Throughout his sample, dogs and horses appeared in statistically surprising numbers as they had in Grant's study (Wait 1985, 122-153). In the same piece of work Wait also re-examined the evidence for ritual practices involving shafts, pits and wells as investigated by Anne Ross some 17 years earlier. He redefined the criteria for identifying a ritual deposit within these features and undertook a survey of the material recovered from a number of such contexts. Dog bones emerged as one of the principal elements in ritual shafts, pits and wells from Iron Age Kent and Surrey, Roman civilian sites and Roman military sites (Wait 1985, 51-82).

Bob Wilson argued that the proposed criteria for positively identifying special animal deposits were extremely questionable, asserting that the existence of the majority of these features could be explained by mundane activities and taphonomic processes, rendering the term 'special animal deposit' unjustifiable (Wilson 1992, 341-349). In his reassessment of the evidence in the 1990s, J D Hill attempted to take a more objective view by renaming the 'Special Animal Deposits', in his study he used the description 'Articulated Bone Groups' instead. However, he concluded that a 'typical' backfilled grain storage pit in the Iron Age of Wessex did not contain articulated bone groups and that therefore those that did can be considered to be examples of "distinct, irregular, social practice" (Hill 1995, 20). Hill also noted that minority species at Iron Age settlements, dogs were given as a specific example, were often singled out for 'special' or 'different' treatment in these contexts (Hill 1996, 19).

The existence of special animal deposits or articulated bone groups at Iron Age sites is now widely accepted by archaeologists. Barry Cunliffe produced a paper speculating about the beliefs surrounding these types of deposit at Danebury hillfort (Cunliffe 1992, 69-83) and Miranda Aldhouse-Green used them as an illustration of sacrificial activity in her 1992 book *Animals in Celtic Life and Myth*. This comprehensive study brought artefactual, physical and written evidence together to provide and support theories about animal involvement in a diverse range of activities during the Iron Age and Roman periods in Britain and on the continent. Throughout the work dogs emerged as one of the most important animals in the Iron Age archaeological record, its uses and symbolic associations ranging from lowly rat-catcher to underworld guardian and healer.

In 2001 Michael Fulford produced a paper urging archaeologists to take a closer look at a particular type of deposit frequently found in pits at Romano-British settlements. These deposits included groups of articulated animal bones, collections of animal bones dominated by a particular species and complete or near complete vessels. He asserted that these could well be interpreted as evidence for the continuation of the Iron Age practice of creating 'special deposits' as discussed above. He emphasised that work reappraising the view that Romano-British society was a new 'civilised' order distinct from the rest of British prehistory should be considered an archaeological priority. Fulford felt that progression in urban Romano-British archaeology has been hindered by its focus on identification of architecture rather than examination of its context. For example, a look at the archives from early excavations at Silchester between 1890 and 1909 clearly showed that biases in the choice of material chosen for publication had contributed to the importance of the finds under discussion remaining veiled until now. The reports published in *Archaeologia* in the late 19th and early 20th centuries refer to the discoveries of only three deposits of dog remains at Silchester, in fact the museum archive revealed that more than fifty dog skulls were found in pits during these excavations. In his survey of six Romano-British settlements it became apparent that dog remains were one of the most notable characteristics of the features under study (Fulford 2001, 199-218).

The evolution of dogs (Clutton-Brock, 1987) and ethnography are also important areas of study in terms of our understanding of human relations with dogs in prehistory. *Signifying Animals – Human Meaning in the Natural World* (Willis 1994) brought together a series of papers inspired by the success of the talks on animal and human relations at the 1986 World Archaeological Congress. Contributors included not only professional archaeologists and anthropologists but also direct representatives of the cultures under discussion, offering a more intimate insight into the way that different societies perceive the animal world. These rich ethnographic perspectives are interesting and enlightening and can be used to open our minds to possible interpretations of the archaeological record. Another compendium of papers from the International Council for Archaeo-Zoology symposium held in 1998 is dedicated entirely to the subject of prehistoric dogs. In *Dogs Through Time,* edited by Susan Crockford, the number of contributors and variety of contributions made, covering everything from aging techniques to the dog symbolism of the ancient Maya, clearly illustrates the amount of interest there is about this subject worldwide (Crockford 2000). The success of the symposium led to a further two days of talks being devoted to the topic at the 2002 ICAZ annual conference in Durham, the proceedings of which will be published in the not too distant future.

1.4 The Aims and Objectives of the Study

The aims of this study are to:

i. further the understanding of the ritual treatment and symbolic perception of the domesticated dog during the Iron Age and Romano British periods, thus contributing to our overall knowledge of human perceptions of the supernatural world in European antiquity.

ii. establish whether spiritual beliefs held about the species in antiquity, as illustrated in the contemporary iconography, are in any way reflected in the archaeology of their physical remains.

iii. identify any patterns in the deposition of dog remains in a number of selected contexts that could be used to inform future interpretations of similar discoveries.

In order to achieve these aims, the following objectives were pursued:

i. contextual analysis of dog remains from selected sacred and secular sites was carried out and the results from each data set are compared and contrasted across time and space as well as analysed individually. Where relevant the remains of associated domestic animals, and humans, from the chosen sites were examined to identify any significant similarities and/or differences between features of their deposition and those of domestic dogs. Features that can inform us about the animal's treatment in life i.e. pathologies and injuries were noted as general points of interest.

ii. artistic portrayals of domestic dogs and details of contexts in which these were found, if available, were examined with a view to establishing what they might have represented, how they might have been used and to explore the wider significance of the motifs in religious iconography. Contemporary continental iconography was used as comparanda to inform the study.

The recurrence of particular images was recorded in order to reveal dominating and connected themes. Interpretations arising from analysis of the iconography were compared with those stemming from the analysis of ritual deposits, to ascertain whether or not the beliefs that appear to be associated with domestic dogs in one source of evidence could be recognised in the other.

The iconography depicting dogs and the historical writings alluding to British dogs from the periods under discussion were compared to their contemporary physical remains, to determine whether there are discrepancies between the types of dogs that appear in each case.

iii. The symbolic roles of dogs in other cultures, in both modern and prehistoric contexts, were explored. Comparable attitudes towards and treatment of domestic dogs in both art and life were used to inform interpretations of their use as symbols during the Iron Age and Romano-British periods.

1.5 The Study Methodology

To achieve the above aims the following methodology was formulated:

The research area is located, primarily, in the archaeological record of Iron Age and Roman Britain, dating between approximately 600BC – AD43 and from AD43 – approximately AD 400 respectively.

Sources of information include:

i. Published and unpublished site reports traced for inclusion in the study. Access to relevant museum collections and excavation archives was sought, so that the archaeological material itself, as well as the contextual information surrounding its discovery, could be examined if necessary.

ii. The following information, when possible, was collated via scrutiny of faunal assemblages: -
- location of deposit
- approximate age of deposit
- associated finds
- body parts represented
- age of the animal at death
- sex of the animal
- body size and proportion
- pathologies and injuries
- human interference and/or modifications to the bones

Animal remains to be included in the study were selected according to the following criteria:

- The context in which they were found has obvious ritual associations e.g. cemeteries, shrines, mortuary enclosures and associated features etc.

- The nature of their deposition exhibits characteristics that suggest "distinct and irregular social practice" has taken place e.g. structured deposition (Hill 1996, 17-32).

iii. As well as the physical remains of dogs, artefacts portraying them, and their associated site reports when available, were located and studied. This material includes items like jewellery, ceramics, glass, metalwork, coins and stone-work.

iv. Professional archaeology units, university departments, museums, specialist archaeologists and archaeo-zoologists were contacted for information, advice and opinions about the research topic. Libraries nation wide were contacted in order to complete a comprehensive review of relevant academic literature, including both factual and theoretical archaeological material and anthropological and ethnographic writings.

1.6 Iron Age and Roman Britain - An Island but Not Isolated

Although this study focuses primarily on the archaeological record of Iron Age and Roman Britain it would be erroneous to try and interpret how the art from this island functioned on a symbolic level without reference to the contemporary iconography of its continental neighbours, and without acknowledging that to, varying degrees, Graeco-Roman ideologies, cosmologies and means of religious expression permeated the culture of Western Europe during the decades leading up to and during Roman rule. Time and again scholars have clearly demonstrated that visual and epigraphic linkages exist between the art from Britain and Gaul in particular. The discussion of the symbolism associated with domestic dogs in ancient Britain in this study takes a holistic view of archaeological evidence from this time and maintains this standpoint: although, clearly, indigenous British culture did not suddenly become 'Roman' either forcibly or voluntarily after the conquest, neither did it exist as an impenetrable bubble before or after it, any more than it does today (Aldhouse-Green 2004b, 194).

The Roman invasion of Britain, however, does coincide with some quite marked changes in the physicality of the native dog population. In Harcourt's study on dogs in British antiquity it was found that most dogs had a shoulder height of 29–56cm and there was little variation in the shape of their skulls, despite the fact that faunal evidence from settlements indicates that dog populations were allowed to interbreed freely. In the very late Iron Age and after the Roman invasion the dog population became far more diverse: dwarf hounds and lapdogs appear in the record for the first time and particularly large hounds also became more common. In Harcourt's study the sample of Romano-British dog skeletons analysed produced an estimated shoulder height range of 23-72 cm (fig. 1) (Harcourt 1974, 151-175). Whether these quite dramatic physical developments in the dog population coincided with any identifiable changes in human perception of the animal is one question this study seeks to answer.

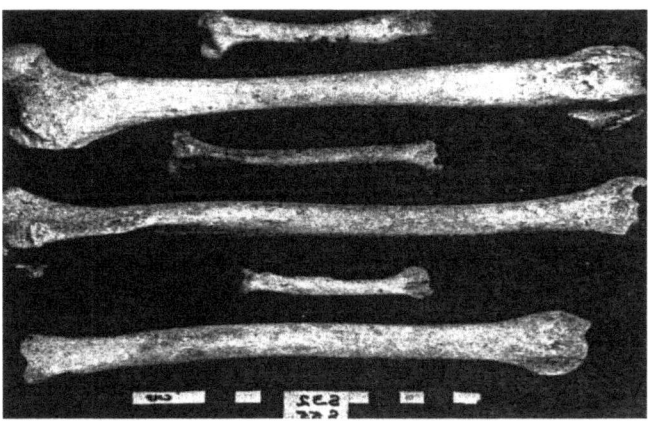

Figure 1. A selection of Romano-British dog femurs illustrating the marked variation in size of the species population. Photograph © Harcourt 1974, The Dog in Prehistoric and Early Historic Britain, *Journal of Archaeological Science*, Elsevier Publishers.

Chapter 2

Dog Remains from British Iron Age Settlements, Sacred Sites and Human Burials

2.1 Introduction

Dog remains are a common feature of the archaeology from British Iron Age sites, so too are the bones of other domesticates, particularly, cattle, sheep, pigs and horses. One way that we might gain insight into how dogs were treated and perceived by humans during this period is to compare the treatment and depositional context of their remains with those of other species. The excavations of Danebury hillfort in Hampshire during the 70s and 80s produced the largest, well documented faunal assemblage of any Iron Age settlement site in Britain. Although dog bones formed only 3% of the animal bone assemblage from Danebury, as a percentage of a collection that consisted of nearly a quarter of a million pieces, and analysis of these remains must still be considered one of the most archaeologically revealing in the country (Grant 1991a, 476, Grant 1991b, 110).

2.2 The Dog Population at Danebury Hillfort, Hampshire

The occupation of Danebury hillfort spanned some five hundred years between the middle of the 6th century BC and the middle of the 1st century BC. Dogs were present at the site throughout its occupation but appear to have been most common in the earliest phase of occupation, between 550 and 400 BC (Cunliffe 1984, 172-173). Although no neonatal bones were recovered from any phase, examination of the degree of epiphysial fusion in the sample revealed that a number of dogs had died at the age of 10 months or younger. This information, coupled with the considerable variation in the size of the animals, their femur lengths ranged from 107mm to 191mm, led to the conclusion that there had probably been several different dog populations at the site and that they had been allowed to breed with each other quite freely (Grant 1991a, 476-478).

The range of sizes suggests that the dogs could have been utilised in some of the same ways they are today, for example, as guards, shepherds and hunters. Unfortunately the nature of the evidence only allows us to speculate on such matters. Strabo, writing in the 1st century AD, recorded that British hunting dogs were one of the island's main export commodities (Strabo *Geoography*, IV.2, Jones 1923, 255). However, if we look to the Danebury excavations for earlier evidence of hunting, we find very little. The total number of wild animal bones in the assemblage is very low, so if hunting was a local activity the kill does not appear to have been brought back to the settlement for general consumption (Grant 1984a, 546). The faunal assemblage revealed that horses were not bred at the site, but were more likely to have been brought into be tamed from wild. It is possible that dogs were used to corral these animals: it has been suggested that domestic dogs were used for this purpose from as early as the Late Upper Palaeolithic because their remains were usually found in areas where contemporary horse remains were found in high numbers (Jacobi 2004 Pers. Comm.). Domestic dogs may well have survived as scavengers at Danebury, their presence was perhaps tolerated because they helped control vermin at the hillfort: dog gnaw marks are plentiful on animal bones from other species at the site and dog coprolites were found to be full of bone splinters (Grant 1984a, 525).

2.2.1 Domestic Dogs as a Source of Primary Produce at Danebury Hillfort

As a source of primary produce a dog's usefulness at Danebury appears to have been minimal. Dogs were eaten at the hillfort but only occasionally and even then their bodies were not exploited to the extent of other domesticates. For example, unlike sheep, their skulls were not split open to access the brain (Grant 1984b, 223).

The fact that some dogs were eaten at Danebury does not preclude their adoption as pets at the site. There is also evidence that some were cruelly neglected. One dog was left to suffer for weeks after the head of one of its femurs broke off in the socket. Enough time passed for a false joint to develop almost fully between the fracture before the animal was killed and butchered (Brothwell 1995, 217). Elsewhere in the world there are still cultures that keep dogs as companions and on the menu, indeed the Sioux of North America keep dogs that they name and are considered to have individual personalities, but they raise others, that they do not name, for meat and for use in sacrificial rituals (Serpell 1995, 249). Further examples of human ambivalence towards dogs can be found much closer in time and space to the occupation of Danebury hillfort. At the Iron Age settlement site of Houghton Down, Stockbridge, Hampshire a dog's skeleton was found in such a state that it seems highly unlikely that it would have been able to survive to what was described as "…limping, toothless, half blind old age…" without a considerable amount of human care and attention. The animal's remaining teeth had been infected with caries, which is very rare in carnivores and suggests that he was perhaps fed on slops that were easier for him to manage. It was felt that he had been somebody's companion. However, at the same site there is ample evidence that dogs were butchered: some of their bones displayed both chop and cut marks (Hamilton 2000, 138-139).

2.2.2 The Special Animal Deposits at Danebury Hillfort

The majority of animal bones found during archaeological excavations appear to be the residue of human activities like butchery, cookery and in some cases craft-work; their analysis can reveal a great deal of information about ancient economy. However, during the excavations at Danebury an unusual type of animal bone deposit was recognised; Dr Annie Grant termed these finds 'special animal deposits' (Grant 1984a, 533-544). Before looking specifically at the special animal deposits that included dog remains it is necessary to review the defining characteristics that make these interments special. They were usually found in grain storage pits, cut into the chalk earth. The deposits were divided into three main categories; complete or mostly complete skeletons, animal skulls/ horse mandibles and articulated limbs. At Danebury hillfort remains fitting the criteria were usually from the same five domestic animal species; sheep, cattle, pigs, horses and dogs, although there were isolated incidents of cat, goat and some wild species (Cunliffe 1983, 157). The special animal deposits did not show signs of butchery and sometimes several species of animal would be found together, which in itself is unusual as it is seems unlikely that natural fatalities would occur in two or three different animal populations at the same time (Grant 1984b, 222-223). Furthermore, the arrangement of some of the animals within the pits displayed a significant degree of human forethought.

Figure 2. A dog and horse Special Animal Deposit in a grain storage pit at Danebury hillfort, Hampshire. Photograph © The Danebury Trust

For example, a complete dog skeleton was found with a horse; the horse had two of its legs slightly displaced and its head had been removed and positioned above its own body next to the dog (fig. 2) (Cunliffe 1983, 157). These special animal deposits were found throughout all phases of occupation at the hillfort and out of the 891 pits excavated between 1969 and 1978 20% contained at least one example (Grant 1984b, 222-223). Some archaeologists argued that the proposed criteria for positively identifying a special animal deposit were extremely questionable, asserting that the majority of these features were probably the results of mundane activities and taphonomic processes (Wilson 1992, 341-349). A detailed reassessment of the evidence in the 1990s led J D Hill to conclude that a 'typical' back filled grain storage pit in the Iron Age of Wessex did not contain special animal deposits and therefore those that did can be considered to be examples of "distinct, irregular, social practice" (Hill 1996, 20). This view is now widely accepted.

Professor Barry Cunliffe speculated that the placing of special deposits in grain storage pits might have been an element of a proprietary ritual ceremony (Cunliffe 1992, 69-82). Through experiments, such as those carried out at Butser Iron Age Farm, we now have scientific understanding of why these chalk pits were such an effective means of storage (Reynolds 1980, 14-16). However, for an Iron Age Briton, placing an important part of one's livelihood in the ground may well have been an act of faith and the creation of a grain storage pit might have been perceived as an invasion into the underworld. It was suggested that chthonic deities were perhaps believed to control fertility, so placing a thanks offering into a pit after the protected seed grain had been removed would perhaps have been a natural and fitting response (Cunliffe 1992, 77-80).

2.2.3 Dogs as Special Animal Deposits at Danebury Hillfort

At Danebury dog bones appeared in 40% of the pits that contained special animal deposits (Grant 1984a, 525). They were found in these contexts far more frequently than was expected given the relatively small size of their population at the site. A survey of the pit deposits from Danebury and 27 other Iron Age settlements revealed that statistically exceptional numbers of dogs appearing in special animal deposits was not unique to Danebury (Wait 1985, 150). The rarity of the special animal deposits supports the idea that, rather than being coincidence, there was some reason why dogs were chosen over other more common domestic animals: out of the 28 sites surveyed only 400 animals were disposed of in this manner over a period of 500 years (Wait 1985, 126). It has also been noted that special deposits of dogs made up a substantial part of the most rare of the categories of special animal deposits i.e. the complete skeletons (Hill 1995, 59). Indeed, there are numerous notable examples of dogs as Iron Age special animal deposits in the British archaeological record. One quite shallow pit at an Iron Age site at Twywell in Northamptonshire was found to contain the complete skeletons of a dog and two pigs. The body of the dog had been covered in large glacial pebbles (Jackson 1975, 60), Interestingly, a number of human skeletons found in the grain storage pits at Danebury hillfort had received similar treatment (Cunliffe 1992, 77).

A group of unusual deposits was found in pit features at an Iron Age settlement site in Great Houghton, Northamptonshire. Five pits were excavated; notably none of them contained domestic refuse and the stratified layers of clean clay and limestone within them were exceptionally well defined. One of the pits contained part of a Middle Iron Age jar; in another a complete domestic dog had been interred. The animal's fore and hind limbs were drawn tightly together and its head and neck were bent backwards at an unnatural angle; it was suggested that the animal had been mutilated and trussed before its deposition (Chapman 2000, 7). The body of a similarly restrained adolescent male was found within the Iron Age defences of South Cadbury hillfort in Somerset (Alcock 1973, 102-103). The treatment of these bodies could perhaps be interpreted as attempts to weight down or restrain the subjects as part of a sacrificial ritual. Whether this was a symbolic act, an act of necessity or both is unclear.

Dr Annie Grant suggested that economic factors might have influenced the choice of animal to be sacrificed. As mentioned earlier, in terms of primary products dogs were perhaps less important to the hillfort community than sheep which were extensively exploited for their meat and no doubt their wool. However, for a sacrifice to be effective it does have to be considered a loss to the party making the offering (Grant 1984b, 221-227). The domestic dog's economic value most likely lay in its capacity to assist humans in aspects of their work, particularly guarding and shepherding. The mutually beneficial relationship that humans and dogs shared perhaps gave the species a degree of status not afforded to most other domesticates. Like humans, dogs are pack animals and sharing this instinct with us enables them to recognise human social hierarchy and consequently they can fit themselves into this system unobtrusively, even in cultures where they are not treated as pets (Clutton-Brock 1999, 50). This ability to merge with us often leads to the creation of an environment where dogs are in the unusual position of not really being considered an animal in their own right but rather "quasi-human" with "sub-ordinate status" (Serpell 1995, 254). Although it is unlikely that all dogs were put to work, the species as a whole perhaps came to symbolise this valuable co-operative bond.

2.3 Dog Remains from Iron Age Sacred Space

Iron Age constructed sacred space is far less visible in the British archaeological record than Romano-British examples. In his study of constructed sacred space Alex Smith identified 20 possible Iron Age examples (Smith 2001, 166-186). In the database of ecofacts from these sites dog bones are all but nonexistent. There is a record of their presence in the faunal assemblage from the pre-Roman phase of a shrine at Uley, Gloucestershire, but in the site excavation report Bruce Levitan interprets these as part of the non-votive assemblage; dog remains contributed less than 1% of the bones collected overall (Smith 1999, 208; Levitan 1993, 260). The same percentage of dog bones came from the pre-conquest phase at Harlow temple in Essex; the excavators were unable to draw any conclusions about how they came to be in the archaeological record from such a small sample (Legge 1985, 122-123). However, the paucity of dog remains as a feature of recognised Iron Age constructed sacred space does not indicate that they were not used in ritual activities in other contexts during this period. As discussed above, dog remains were a statistically significant presence in the special deposits recognised in grain storage pits on Iron Age settlements (Wait 1985, 150, Grant 1984b, 221-227, Hill 1995, 59). Flag Fen in East Anglia and Llyn Cerrig Bach, Anglesey are well known for the discoveries of a large number of exotic metal artefacts that were cast into water at these sites from the Late Bronze Age/ Early Iron Age to the Late Iron Age and possibly into the Roman period. These finds were interpreted as offerings to underworld gods that were believed to inhabit such realms. Both sites also produced animal bone assemblages from the same contexts as the collections of artefacts and similarly we can perhaps identify these deposits as sacrificial offerings (Cowley 1946, 97, Pryor 2001, 386-390). Dog bones were noted as being present in the Llyn Cerrig Bach assemblage. The faunal collection from Flag Fen included nine partial dog skeletons that were found during excavation of a man-made island and the trackway post-alignment that led to this platform. The lack of gnawing and butchery marks on their remains compared to other animal bones in the site collection suggests that the dogs were deposited shortly after death, which supports the idea that they were involved in sacrificial rites: natural deaths would perhaps have been more likely to have been exposed for some time with other domestic refuse (Halstead et al 2001, 330-350).

2.3.1 The Dog Remains from the East Leicestershire Hoard Site

A new example of Iron Age sacred space has recently come to light in East Leicestershire. This site is perhaps most notable for producing the largest Iron Age coin hoard legally found in this country: over 3000 Iron Age coins were found as well as a silver decorated Roman helmet dating to the early 1st century AD. Excavations at the site uncovered an area of hilltop that appears to have been used for ceremonial, ritual activities. The site was divided by a ditch with a complex entrance way. The ditch was only partly revealed during excavation so it is unclear whether it was just a partial boundary or part of a ditched enclosure, but if this was a ditched enclosure the area it enclosed was some 80m wide. Strangely, the area of land that might have been enclosed was archaeologically barren. Structural archaeology was absent from the site overall, so it appears people gathered here in the open air. Thirteen coin groups were found north west of the ditch entrance. South of the entrance two further coin hoards were discovered in a small pit, along with a large mass of silvered iron including a Roman military helmet. On the side of the ditch boundary that did contain archaeology, large deposits of butchered pig, sheep and cattle bone, covering approximately 20 square metres, were found. Radiocarbon dates from the bone indicated that the animals were killed between 50BC and AD80, so it is likely that their remains were deposited at the same time as the coins and the helmet. It would appear that specific areas of the site were allocated to particular elements of ritual activity, with sacrifice and feasting on one side and deposition of coins on the other. The helmet and the partial skeleton of a dog were found close to the ditch entrance and in the middle of the two areas, although they were not found in the same pit feature it still seems very likely that the animal was also ritually deposited (fig. 3) (Priest 2003, 13, Hill 2003, Pers. Comm.). The symbolic connection between dogs and boundaries at a number of Iron Age sites is discussed later in this chapter (section 2.6.1).

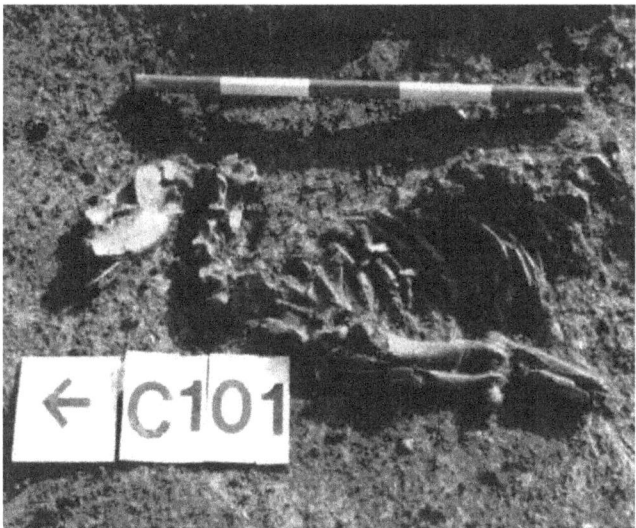

Figure 3. The dog skeleton found in the boundary ditch, entranceway at the East Leicestershire hoard site. Photograph © ULAS

2.4 Dog Remains in Association with Iron Age Human Burials

Deposits of human remains in antiquity in any context are of intrinsic interest to the archaeologist. For many years British Iron Age mortuary practice has by and large evaded archaeological perception. The remains of only a small percentage of the estimated population are thought to have been disposed of in an archaeologically visible way, even when geographical biases and excavation limitations are taken into consideration. The traditions that have been identified include pit burials, grave inhumations, cist inhumations and cremations. On occasions when animal remains appear to have been deliberately interred with a human body, the association merits investigation as the decision to include the animal in the burial is quite likely to lie beyond practicalities and represent an act of some symbolic significance.

The sites chosen for discussion in this section have either yielded burials of complete humans and dog remains in close association with each other or deposits of dog remains in the context of Iron Age mortuary features. Dates for finds have been included when they were available, but unfortunately this is not the case in all instances.

2.4.1 Associated Human and Dog Remains from Iron Age Grain Storage Pits at Broadstairs, Kent and Dibbles Farm, Christon

The deliberate and carefully executed interment of a fully articulated dog as part of an Iron Age mortuary procedure was a feature of one of the two human burials found in pits at a settlement in Broadstairs, Kent. An adult male human had been laid on his left side with his arms stretched out from his body on the bottom of a storage pit. The man's head rested upon a stone that in turn lay upon the body of a dog (fig. 4). The dog's head, still in articulation with its body, was also laid upon a stone to the west of the human skull. The pit was filled immediately after the burial took place. To glean the precise meaning of this structured deposition, if indeed one ever existed, is currently impossible but it is clear that some level of abstract thought went into the arrangement of this interment. However, if one was to speculate about the motive behind such an unusual display it is perhaps worth noting that the relatively comfortable attitude of this human inhumation is in stark contrast with another body found in a pit at the site. The second body, also male, had been placed in a space within the pit that could barely accommodate it and consequently his legs were propped against the side of the pit and his head was twisted at an awkward, unnatural angle (Whimster 1981, 214).

Figure 4. A human and dog pit burial from Broadstairs, Kent. Photograph © T C Champion, Southampton University

Dibbles Farm, Christon was occupied throughout the Iron Age. In 1970 65 storage pits were excavated and the remains of 21 individuals were identified in these features (Morris 1988, 55). Pit XLIV at the site was dated by associated ceramics to the Early Iron Age (Morris 1988, 44). In this pit two dogs were found buried, one above the other, at the feet of an adult male aged between 25 and 35 at death. Both dogs were young adults, comparable in size to modern day lurchers. No indication of how the dogs or the human had died was identified, although it seems unlikely that the animals would have died of natural causes at the same time. R E Everton who analysed the dog remains from the pit suggested that these two dogs had perhaps been lifetime companions of the dead man and this would seem a reasonable conclusion to draw about the relationship between the trio (Everton 1988, 54). However, pit burials from Southern England do not generally betray signs of Iron Age sentimentality, but in support of Everton's interpretation of the dogs as grave furnishings it is perhaps worth noting that unlike pit burials from other sites like Gussage All Saints, Dorset and Danebury hillfort, seven of the 21 Dibble's Farm burials were accompanied by personal items that could also be interpreted as grave-goods, including a complete ceramic vessel and personal items of worked metal and bone (Whimster 1981, 16, Wainwright 1979, 33-38, Cunliffe 1992, 69-83, Morris 1988, 55-73).

2.4.2 Ritual Pit Burials from an Iron Site in Andover, Hampshire

As human pit burials do appear to have been a minority rite it has been suggested that the people who were interred in these features might have been in some way different from, and out-side of, the community who buried them (Wait 1985, 119). This interpretation ties in with the idea that the burials in grain storage pits were part of a proprietary rite; perhaps humans as well as animals were sacrificed. Numerous historical writers recorded that human sacrificial victims were often chosen because of their otherness, for example, prisoners of war or criminals (Aldhouse-Green 2001, 139-160).

At an enclosed Iron Age settlement in Andover, Hampshire a number of pits were found to contain special deposits: one pit contained a complete dog skeleton and others several complete deer burials. The upper parts of four deformed human skulls were also found together in the same layer of one of the pits (Champion 1975, 22-23). It is perhaps noteworthy that unrelated, detailed investigations of the British archaeological record have reached conclusions that dogs, deer and human skulls were symbolically significant in the Iron Age. As mentioned earlier a number of studies have confirmed that dogs appear in special animal deposits in statistically striking numbers (Grant 1984a, 525, Wait 1985, 150, Hill 1995, 59). Annie Grant also noted that, of all the native wild animals, deer appear most frequently in ritual animal deposits in the British archaeological record (Grant 1989, 135-146).

Miranda Aldhouse-Green collated a large body of evidence to support the notion that ritual activities involving heads and skulls, although not common, were a widespread phenomenon across Celtic Europe including Britain (Aldhouse-Green 2001, 93-111). She also identified a trend indicating that humans with physical deformities were 'dispatched' and disposed of in unusual ways with marked frequency in antiquity (Green 2001, 157-160). Although we cannot say with absolute certainty that these interments are evidence of human sacrifice, the presence of three different types of deposit that had particular ritual significance during the Iron Age suggests that their burial at the site was far more symbolically complex than straightforward carcass disposal.

2.5 Human Remains Accompanied by Dog Remains from Iron Age Cemeteries

2.5.1 Dogs as Negative Features in Iron Age Cemeteries

An extensive study of the characteristics of Late Iron Age cemeteries in southern Britain has revealed that dogs are all but non-existent as grave accompaniments at most of these sites (Brookes 2004, 193-205). Taking the two largest sites to demonstrate this point we find that out of the excavations of 455 cremations and 17 inhumations at King Harry Lane cemetery, St Albans dogs were represented by only one solitary canine incisor in Grave 287. The majority of animal bones found in the graves came from pigs, sheep and goats and were interpreted as funerary offerings of joints of meat (Davis 1989, 251). None of the animal bones that could be identified to species in the faunal assemblage, from West Hampnett, Iron Age cemetery in Sussex were from dogs (McKinley et al. 1997, 73-77). Similarly, in the 'Arras' burials of East Yorkshire and the Durotrigian burials from southern Dorset, dog remains are conspicuous only by their absence (Whimster 1981, 253-310). As such an overwhelming negative feature we may consider that dogs were an inappropriate presence in these contexts.

2.5.2 The Thorley Dog Burial – Sacred or Profane?

A dog skeleton was discovered in an area interpreted as a mortuary enclosure from the Late Iron Age phase at Thorley, Hertfordshire. The dog was laid out in its own grave on its side. Its front and back paws were neatly crossed over each other in pairs. Alongside the body of the dog lay a large round stone. An anonymous note on the respective context sheet mentioned that the stone had indentations on it that may have been made by a dog's claws or teeth and also suggested that the stone could have been the animal's toy, referring to the canine habit of carrying such objects around (Last 2001, Unnumbered). However, the director of the excavation, Jonathan Last, concluded that the stone was not an artefact but a chance association (Last 2002, Pers. Comm.) It is certainly very rare to find Iron Age domestic dogs buried with items that appear to have been interred as grave furnishings; although at Stanton Harcourt, Gravelly Guy in Oxfordshire at least a dozen dogs, buried individually and in pairs, were accompanied by meat bones from other domesticated animals (Lambrick 1985, 108).

Despite the mortuary context, Last felt that there was no need to subscribe any ritual interpretation to the deposition of the dog or to the cattle skull and horse mandible closely associated with it. However, the only other dog bones recovered from the same phase at the site appeared to be altogether far more mundane deposits: three isolated bones from different animals were found in a ditch containing domestic refuse at the south end of the cemetery (Last 2001, 86-87).

At Folly Lane, St Albans several dog bones were recovered from the ceremonial enclosure ditch associated with a particularly rich late Iron Age cremation. Excavator, Ros Niblett, felt that these might have represented a ritual interment, but could not be sure about this because dog bones were similarly deposited in domestic contexts at the site (Niblett 1999, 327-328). A pit containing the partially articulated body of a dog and a great deal of domestic refuse was found to the south of a Welwyn style burial at Stotfold, Bedfordshire; the deposit was interpreted as rubbish disposal (Duncan 2002, Pers. Comm.). A mortuary context cannot always strengthen an argument for the ritual nature of a find, but when a deposit is also clearly structured, like the complete Thorley dog, it seems rather sceptical or overly cautious to dismiss the possibility that it might represent something more than rubbish.

2.5.3 Mill Hill, Deal, Kent

In the Late Iron Age cemetery at Mill Hill, Deal in Kent the burial of a woman aged between 28 and 35 was accompanied by an adult dog; its small bones indicate that it had very likely been a pet lapdog (Parfitt 1995, 16, Legge 1995, 46-152). Some small dogs in antiquity were probably hunting dogs rather than pets, like terriers that are used today to retrieve small kills or flush out prey from undergrowth. Furthermore, the roles of pet dog and hunter are obviously not mutually exclusive. However, the Mill Hill dog was too slightly built to have been anything other than ornamental. Very small dogs only appear in the British archaeological record in the very late Iron Age but become more common during the early Romano-British period (Legge 1995, 146-152). At this time they were likely to have been considered a status symbol, as being able to afford to keep an animal of an essentially useless nature could be read as a measure of one's prosperity (Creighton 2000, 214).

Examination of its skeleton did not reveal how the dog died. Although it is not impossible that the woman and her dog passed away at the same time it is perhaps more likely that the dog was killed for inclusion in the grave. Whether killing the dog for this purpose held any profound meaning for the executers of the burial is a purely speculative matter, it may merely have been a convenient way of disposing of a now ownerless and particularly needy animal. It was noted that the dog appeared to have been thrown into the grave with the infill; this is a stark contrast to the careful burial of an entire horse in its own grave at the same site. If the time and effort invested in the interment of this animal can be seen as a measure of the esteem the animal was held in, one might conclude that the lapdog was not held in such high regard. However, in some traditional sacrificial ceremonies the physical act of putting distance between oneself and the offering or viewing the spectacle is essential to success of the ritual and this might involve casting and burial, burning or decomposition (Kuchler 1997, 39-60)

2.5.4 Maiden Castle Hillfort, Dorset

An unusual array of animal remains were discovered in a Late Iron Age/ Early Romano-British inhumation at Maiden Castle, Dorset. The recovery of iron nails from the grave indicate that this adult female, who had died aged between 25 and 35, was buried in a coffin with a pair of boots. The headless but otherwise articulated skeleton of a lamb lay under the woman's pelvis and vertebrae, and a young dog was found close to her body (Wheeler 1943, 350). The woman and the dog lay facing each other but the animal was positioned 25cm above the body of the woman, which is believed to have placed it outside of the coffin (fig. 5). The dog may have been the deceased's pet, but the significance of the animal accompaniments may well have been more complicated than this if we assume that the headless lamb was also of some symbolic importance. Plutarch records the use of dogs in Greek purification rituals whereby a person's illness could be transferred to the animal; puppies and lambs were also used in purification ceremonies in prehistoric Hittite culture (Collins 1992, 1-6, Plutarch *Quaestiones Romanae*, LXVIII, Rose 1924).

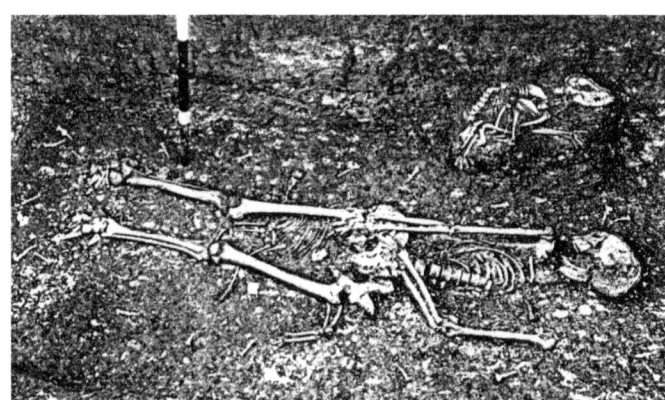

Figure 5. Grave of a young woman and associated dog burial at Maiden Castle, Dorset. Photograph © Wheeler 1943, Society of Antiquaries of London.

Another example of closely associated dog and human remains at Maiden Castle contrasts markedly with the careful interment described above. A group of four fragmentary human skeletons were found together with a dog skull and a pottery vessel. They formed part of the group of Late Iron Age/ Early Roman period burials found in an area that the excavator termed 'the war cemetery', because the skeletal remains displayed numerous wounds that could only have been caused by weapons (Wheeler 1943, 351). Interestingly contextual associations between dog remains and mutilated human remains, particularly skulls, appear repeatedly in the Romano-British archaeological record and are discussed in detail in chapter 5.

2.6 Blewburton Hill, Berkshire – A Rampart Burial

The simultaneous burial of an adult male, a small horse and a dog below a rampart ditch at the Early Iron Age hillfort at Blewburton Hill, Berkshire appears to be highly symbolically charged (Collins 1952, 30). Accompanying the bodies were a stone adze, an iron pin or rivet and sherds of black burnished pottery, a considerable number of which were from the same vessel. The discovery could perhaps be interpreted as the burial of a man with his hunting partners. However, the positioning of the bodies suggests that something of significance over and above the laying of an individual to rest had occurred. The dog and the base of a pot were placed close to the horse's hind legs. The head and torso of the man lay between the front and back legs of the horse and the man's legs appear to have been wrapped around the body of the horse. The excavator suggested that perhaps the body had been tied astride the horse and the action of casting the bodies into the ditch slewed the body around. It does seem odd that those who invested considerable time and effort creating a grave for the bodies did not bother to arrange the human in a more dignified position (Collins 1952, 21-64). However, as mentioned earlier the casting away or 'riddance' element of a sacrificial ceremony in some cosmologies may be considered central to its successful completion. Similarly, casting the body in a funerary context could have been perceived as an important factor in the successful transference of the deceased to another spiritual realm (Kuchler 1997, 39-60). If it was a respectful burial then the animals may have been intended to accompany the deceased into the afterlife. However, like the group of bodies found buried within the ramparts at Danebury hillfort and the cramped skeleton of adolescent male interred behind the defences at South Cadbury hillfort, the Blewburton bodies could perhaps be interpreted as sacrificial offerings (Cunliffe 1983, 156). The Greek historian Herodotus, writing about the Scythians in the 5th century BC, told of a custom that involved the sacrifice of fifty horses and their riders the year after the death of a king (Herodotus *Histories* IV 72-73). The sacrifice of dogs and horses on the death of their owner was also an almost ubiquitous feature of high status pagan Scandanavian ship burials from the second half of the first millennium AD (Ellis-Davidson 1982, 115-120). The Blewburton rider's animals were perhaps perceived as an inherent part of his identity that needed to be destroyed in the event of their master's death or the trio may have been a fabricated one, contrived to symbolically represent a hunting group or a man at war; Strabo recorded that the Celts used British dogs in war as well as hunting (Strabo *Geography*, IV.5.2. Jones 1923, 255). Such an offering placed beneath the rampart may have been an attempt to promote welfare and security at the hillfort. A dog was buried in the middle of the fairway of the eastern entrance of Maiden Castle hillfort; it was suggested that this was perhaps a symbolic, permanent guard dog (Wheeler 1943, 115). At Danebury, excavations uncovered four large pits beneath the counterscarp of the hillfort's middle earthwork. One pit had been dug after a period of natural silting and the remains of two dogs and a variety of other animal bones were placed in the bottom of the pit. The dogs were covered with large blocks of chalk on top of which a timber post was fixed; whether this was part of a more substantial structure is unknown; the post itself was almost 1m in diameter (Cunliffe 1984, 12, Cunliffe 1971, 240-252).

2.6.1 Domestic Dogs – Guards in this World and the Next

It seems likely that one of the original reasons that humans kept dogs was because of their instinctive territoriality: their warning barks alerting their keepers to the approach of welcome and unwanted visitors. The species' superior sense of hearing and smell give them sensitivity to the world around them that at times appears to border upon the supernatual. Working guard dogs are of course still common place in societies throughout the world today and in some cultures, the Kagoro of Nigeria for example, dogs are kept to protect homesteads against outside threats both from the living and the dead (Olowo Ojade 1994, 219-220).

One way that a subject gains symbolic value is from human experience of that thing at a secular level. The observations made are supported and embellished by the stories and beliefs of the culture for which the symbol exists (Stevens 1998, 76-89). In the light of this theory it is perhaps easy to understand why dogs appear at important thresholds in the myths and beliefs of so many cultures across time and space. Cerberus, the three-headed hound of Hades, guarded the underworld in ancient Greek mythology, preventing the living from entering and the dead from returning to life (Virgil *The Aeneid* VI 415-418, Day Lewis 1961, 129). In ancient Mesopotamia in the 1st millennium BC dog figurines were placed beneath thresholds and some of the names inscribed on them leave no doubt about the function they were intended to perform; they include 'Catcher of the hostile one', 'Consume his life!' and the rather less threatening 'Introducer of the beneficent ones'(Porter 1993, 65-75). Territorial markers in ancient Mesopotamia were also decorated with dog images. As mentioned in 2.3.1, a dog was recently found buried within an entrance in a boundary ditch that defined the accessible limits of an Iron Age ritual feasting site in East Leicestershire (Hill 2003. Pers. Comm.). At Springhead in Kent, a pit containing the bodies of at least a dozen dogs, some wrapped in chains, had been dug on one side of an entranceway cut through an Iron Age ditched boundary that demarcated the northern extent of a Romano-British temple complex.

The act of sacrifice is intended to remove the offering from this world to the realms of the spirit world and it is easy to imagine that a dog, sacrificed and placed beneath a threshold, was intended to function as a guard against disagreeable otherworldly forces in much the same way as the clay figurines from ancient Mesopotamia (Porter 1993, 65-75). The creation of a physical boundary is an acknowledgement that not all are welcome within, and the presence of a doorway within that partition can be seen as an invitation to enter or a sign of exclusivity (Stevens 1998, 244). In instances where dogs have been placed at a doorway its symbolic duality is reinforced by the associated dog symbolism: whether they are present in their bodily form or as iconography they represent a creature that fiercely guards its domain against intruders or provides an unprecedented welcome to humans they are close to. Unfortunately, there isn't any Iron Age iconography from Britain that can help support this interpretation. In fact there are very few representations of dogs from the British Iron Age at all: a few small bronze quadrapeds, interpreted as dogs, have been found in Southern Britain and the blade of an Early Iron Age dagger recovered from the River Thames was decorated with the head of a canine (Jope 2000, 228 and 265).

Dogs and doorways also compliment each other symbolically because they both represent liminality. Entrances symbolise the transition from one realm to another. For instance, the term 'rites of passage', used to describe landmark ceremonies in a person's life, is suggestive of movement through a metaphorical portal to another stage of existence. Often elaborate rituals are performed on such occasions to ensure the safety of the participant because transitional states are 'open' to danger. Actual doorways are not part of one realm or the other, but they are the all-important means of transition and when a doorway is open the inside is vulnerable to outside influences both earthly and supernatural (Kvideland 1993, 84-90). Placing a dog at an entrance may well be a means of providing the inside with protection in the first instance, but the unstable nature of a beast that seems to occupy a hinterland between human and animal worlds, as we perceive them, is also invocative of a median state of being.

2.7 Summary

The recurrence of statistically high numbers of dogs in special animal deposits in Iron Age grain storage pits has been supported by numerous academic surveys of the evidence. This phenomenon appears to indicate that the species was considered to be in some way special or high status compared to most other domesticates; this was perhaps due to their close proximity to humans in both working and living environments. Dogs were also amongst the species found in the vicinity of votive hoards of metal work that were cast into water at Flag Fen, East Anglia and Llyn Cerrig Bach. Anglesey.

In a survey of the faunal assemblages from examples of Iron Age constructed sacred spaces, dog remains were found to be surprisingly scarce. A few bones from the species were found at Uley temple but these were considered to be part of the non-votive assemblage. A dog was recently discovered within an entrance to a boundary ditch at the Leicestershire Hoard site where ritual activities involving large scale feasting and the deposition of metal work took place. Notably a number of dogs have been found buried within boundary features at Iron Age sites, suggesting that the species was perceived as a symbol of guardianship during the period.

The rather direct contact between dogs and humans in a number of burials described in this chapter perhaps suggests that a living relationship had existed between the person and the animal they were found with. The deliberate and careful arrangement of the bodies in several instances suggests that the interments were symbolically charged, perhaps for the benefit of supernatural entities or to say something about the deceased. It may also be significant that in most of the burials the dogs are found in a position that could be perceived as subservient to the associated humans: beneath a man at Broadstairs, Kent, at the feet of a man at Dibble's Farm, Christon, Somerset, outside the coffins of two women at Mill Hill, Kent and Maiden Castle, Dorset and behind the horse and rider at Blewburton Hill, Berkshire. Although, judging by the variety of different contexts and the considerable period of time that the burials span, it is unlikely that these details are any more than a coincidence. Nevertheless, it seems reasonable to suggest that the arrangements might reflect human perception of the species in relation to themselves i.e. close but subordinate.

There is insufficient data available to reveal unquestionable patterns relating to the treatment of dogs in burial contexts in Iron Age Britain, but if other examples of humans and dogs interred together emerge in the archaeological record it is perhaps worth noting that currently there are more instances of men buried with dogs than women. Unfortunately, there are also insufficient numbers of examples to allow us to identify any patterning in the size and age of the dogs included in human burials. However, it is perhaps significant that the dogs buried with the females at Maiden Castle and Mill Hill are particularly small; both these burials date to the early 1st century AD, which is when animals defined as lapdogs first appeared in Britain. Iconography from the western provinces of Rome depicting mother goddesses with lapdogs suggests that these tiny animals were perhaps favoured by women and that they became symbols of fertility.

Chapter 3

Domestic Dogs in the Archaeology of Romano-British Settlement Sites

3.1 Introduction

Evidence for the presence of dogs, usually in the form of their skeletal remains, is a regular feature of the archaeology recovered from both rural and urban Romano-British settlement sites. In practical terms domestic dogs were probably kept to work as guard dogs or herders and it seems likely that their presence as scavengers would have been tolerated to some degree as a means of pest control (Harcourt 1974, 151-175). Archaeology suggests that pets and hunting hounds were kept in Roman Britain, but there is also evidence that dogs were sometimes eaten: bones with butchery marks on them have been found at Vindolanda fort and settlement (R. Birley 2002, Pers. Comm.). In terms of other secondary products dog skins may have been used as blankets: a second century burial of a child at the roadside site of Asthall was found in association with the extremities of a dog's front and hind legs. The arrangement of the bones, close to the child's neck and feet, and the presence of cut marks on the dog's remains suggests that the boy had been wrapped in a dog's pelt. The possible symbolic significance of this is discussed fully in chapter 5 (Booth et al. 1996, 382-387). As in other areas of Europe, their skins may also have been used as parchment and dog excrement would have been used by tanners to soften leather (Waterer 1976, 179-194, Vago 1991, 18). Dog coprolites were found in a group of interconnecting tanks at Wroxeter *basilica* that appear to have been used for tanning (Goodburn 1978, 437).

This chapter focuses on some of the more unusual characteristics of dog burials from settlement sites. However, there are other traces of canine presence in the archaeological record. These glimpses of the ways the species lived and was treated adds another significant dimension to the way one might perceive their treatment after death.

3.2 Evidence for the Presence of Domestic Dogs in Print and Imprints

It is known from Classical sources that British hunting dogs were held in high regard on the continent; Strabo recorded that they were in fact one of the primary exports from the island (Strabo *Geography* IV, 5, 2 Jones 1923, 255). The Roman prefect Symmachus reports on the arrival of seven large hounds, perhaps predecessors of the Irish Wolf Hound, that caused quite a stir when they arrived in Rome from Ireland (Symmachus *Epistolae II*, 77, Toynbee 1973, 365). Less formally, written references to the popularity of hunting with hounds were recorded on a number of the Vindolanda tablets. A soldier made a note of 'dog collars' on what appears to be a fragment of an order list and in letters from one particular officer, Cerialis, the enthusiasm and camaraderie enjoyed by hunters is clearly expressed. When writing to his friend Brocchus he declares 'if you love me, brother, send me hunting nets' (A. Birley 2002, 147-149).

Dogs have literally left their imprint on the archaeology at a number of sites by stepping on to wet ceramic tiles that were subsequently fired and preserved in the archaeological record. It was found that dogs were responsible for 46% of the prints identifiable to species on foot-impressed tiles recovered during excavations of the *forum basilica* at Silchester. Similarly, domestic dogs were the most common perpetrators of such damage to the tiles used for hypocaust pillars at Vindolanda fort. Other species including cat, fox, pig, sheep/goat and even cow also left their respective paw and hoof imprints in tiles at these sites, but in far less numbers suggesting that dogs had a relatively free range (Cram 2000, 123-126, A. Birley 2002, 67).

Perthotaxia is one of seven categories of taphonomic process; these are the forces responsible for the condition in which we find archaeological bone assemblages. Perthotaxic agencies affect bones after they have initially been discarded. It is under this heading that certain activities of ancient dogs are listed by archaeo-zoologists (O'Connor 2000, 19-27). An ethnographic study of life on a Navajo Reservation in North America revealed that a dog's inclination to take bones and hide, even bury them in a place particular to themselves could well have a considerable effect on the distribution of faunal remains at certain sites. Consequently, this factor may skew subsequent interpretation of the archaeology if it is not taken into consideration (Kent 1981, 367-372).

The reduction of bones to unidentifiable pieces by gnawing is one of the most common problems posed by a perthotaxic process and this is often attributable to dogs having had access to domestic waste in antiquity: the marks left on bones by canines are easily distinguishable from those made by other animals (O'Connor 2000, 47-53). An analyst's frustration in the face of such damage to evidence, that could have had considerable bearing on the interpretation of a site is, of course, justifiable. However, such signs indicating that dogs had access to the bones before they were finally buried are interesting archaeological features in themselves, animating our perception of life at settlement sites. Around 20% of the faunal assemblage from the Romano-British levels, from an area of industrial activity, in the northern suburbs of Winchester was affected this way, which was in keeping with the faunal evidence for a quite large dog population at the site (Maltby 1987b, 11). Animal bones gnawed by dogs were even recovered from the lower layers of deep pits and wells at the site indicating that some butchery waste was initially discarded above ground before it was finally disposed of in these features. The extent of the gnawing led archaeo-zoologist Mark Maltby to speculate that scavenging may have been the species' primary source of food (Maltby 1987b, 24).

3.3 A Dog's Life

Sadly it is quite common to find pathologies on ancient dog skeletons indicating that humans physically abused them. Skull fractures, one of which undoubtedly proved to be fatal, are present on a number of dog skeletons recovered from Silchester *Insula IX* (Clark 2002, Pers. Comm.). The animal bone assemblage from the Romano-British phases of Greyhound Yard, Dorchester contained fifteen dog limb bones showing signs of healed fractures and other traumas; 12 out of 23 dog skeletons found during excavations at Chichester Cattle Market had been damaged in life, in ways ranging from multiple breaks to snapped teeth that appear to have been kicked out (Maltby 1993, 328, Levitan 1989, 265). Ralph Harcourt's view that the average dog in ancient Britain was something of a pariah left to fend for itself and only tolerated as an aid to pest control is perhaps a fair summary of the evidence from Romano-British towns discussed in much of this chapter (Harcourt 1974, 151-175). Indeed the reality of life for the average dog living in Roman Britain appears to have been a far cry from that of the athletic hounds engaged in hunting activities portrayed in the art of the period, like the animals eternally chasing hares around the bodies of a number of late 2nd century – early 3rd century Castor ware pots found at Verulamium (Toynbee 1962, 189-190). It is also apparent from their physical remains that elegant contemporary iconographic images are by no means a realistic representation of the actual dog population. Harcourt noted that the defining feature of Romano-British dogs was their physical variability (Harcourt 1974, 151-175)

There is some physical evidence to suggest that certain dogs may have been lucky enough to find themselves in the position of nurtured pet. Harcourt was asked to examine the remains of a small dog found in association with late Romano-British pottery at an unnamed site in Suffolk. The pathologies visible on the skeleton indicated that the animal had suffered with advanced osteoarthritis in both front and back legs (fig. 6). The severely diseased limb joints would have been very painful, perhaps crippling and it seems unlikely that the animal would have lived to the age indicated by tooth-wear analysis had it had to fend for itself. Harcourt concluded that this animal had very likely been a housedog (Harcourt 1967, 521-523). This particular specimen was of a size comparable to a modern day fox terrier, so had it been in good health it would perhaps have been physically robust enough to fend for itself. However, as mentioned in chapter 2 it was during the Late Iron Age - Early Romano-British period that lapdogs appear in the archaeological record for the first time; the term lapdog referring to creatures of such slight proportions that it is hard to envisage that they would have stood any chance of survival without human aid (Harcourt 1974, 172).

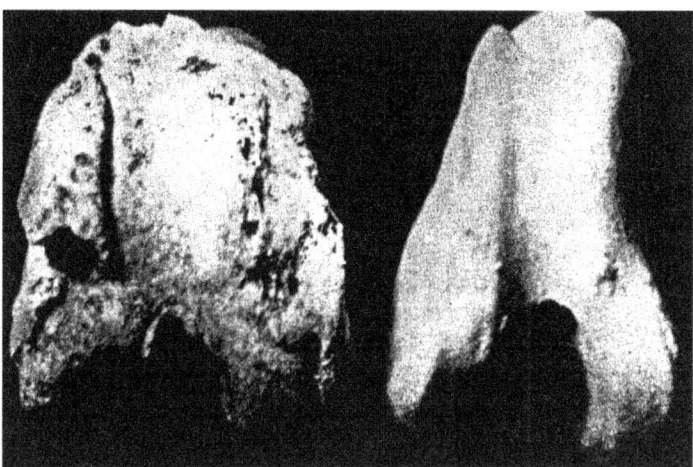

Figure 6. The arthritic femur of a Romano-British pet dog (left) compared to a healthy modern specimen (right). Photograph © Harcourt 1967, Osteoarthritis in a Romano-British Dog, *Journal of Small Animal Practice*, Blackwell Publishers.

3.4 Dogs as a Feature of Special Animal Deposits in the Roman Britain

Identifying spiritually motivated ritual activities, like animal sacrifice, at sites that cannot be readily identified as sacred, is a well-known archaeological problem. However, because of extensive analysis of certain features at Iron Age sites it is now widely accepted that the deposition of groups of animal bones that exhibit specific characteristics are best explained as the result of ritual practises of a non-secular nature during that period (Grant 1984b, 221-227, Wait 1985, 122-153, Hill 1995, 54-60). Recently Michael Fulford has examined the possibility that, along with other types of artefacts, the ritual practice of placing animal remains into human-made holes in the ground at settlement sites continued into the Romano-British period. He looked at the relevant archaeology from six towns in southern Britain, namely Porchester, Silchester, London, Neatham, Baldock and Verulamium, and found that this very likely was the case (Fulford 2001, 199-218).

Surveys of ritual animal deposits dating to the Iron Age have shown repeatedly that statistically dogs appear in pit features far more frequently than would be expected given their relatively small numbers at sites overall, as indicated by analysis of bone assemblages. Interestingly, Fulford found a high incidence of dog burials to be a notable characteristic of the Romano-British archaeology from comparable contexts (Grant 1984a, 522-525, Wait 1985, 150, Hill 1995, 103-105, Fulford 2001, 212-216). There is an alternative school of thought that considers the large numbers of dogs found buried at some settlement sites during the Romano-British period to be evidence for the collection and disposal of dog corpses in convenient holes in the ground (Levitan 1989, 266, Maltby 1993, 326-329). No doubt some dog burials represent exactly this: their bodies were rarely processed for food at this time, therefore their remains are more likely to turn up in the form of complete and near complete skeletons than those of other animals.

3.5 Archaeological Interpretation of Shafts, Wells and other Human-Made Holes in the Ground at Sacred and Secular Sites

There is evidence from historical texts that the Romans perceived certain human-made holes in the ground as conduits to the realms of the gods through which offerings could be made; writers Ovid, Plutarch and Tacitus all record the use of a pit, known as a *mundus*, into which offerings were placed during urban foundation rituals (Ovid *Fasti* IV, 821, Plutarch *Life of Romulus* 36, Tactitus *Histories* IV 53, Rykwert 1976, 58-59). In the same way natural water sources and bogs were widely used as receptacles for sacrificial offerings across Celtic Europe. Finds from Llyn Cerrig Bach on Angelsey, which included animal remains as well as fine metal artefacts and the body of Lindow Man from Lindow Moss are perhaps testament to such beliefs in ancient Britain (Stead et al. 1986, Fox 1946, Cowley 1946, 97).

For a sacrificial offering to be accessible to the gods it has to be removed from circulation in the earthly domain (Aldhouse-Green 2001, 19-25). In antiquity one of the ways in which this was accomplished within areas of constructed sacred space was to create a shaft or pit to receive offerings: the Iron Age pits within the central space of the sanctuary at Gournay-sur-Aronde in Gaul are known to have been used for this purpose (Brunaux 1988, 13-16). There are also a number of remarkable shaft deposits from later Romano-British sacred sites such as Springhead, Kent, Folly Lane, St Albans and Ridgeons Gardens, Cambridge that were undoubtedly used in this way. The archaeology from the shafts at these British sites is characterised by a number of features including infant burials, deposition of complete and near complete vessels, articulated groups of animal bone, high concentrations of dog skeletons and/or dog skeletons sometimes found in association with human remains (Niblett 1999, 85-90, Alexander and Pullinger 1999, 52-58). The nature of these finds from sites dedicated to spiritual activity is remarkably similar to the archaeology recovered from shafts, pits and wells that Michael Fulford identified as evidence of ritual practice at Romano-British domestic sites (Fulford 2001, 199-218). It would appear that in all likelihood, even in a secular arena, pits were considered to be valid receptacles for sacrificial offerings.

3.6 Dog Burials as a Feature of the Archaeology from Shafts, Pits and Wells at Settlement Sites in Southern Britain

To investigate further the role of domestic dogs in ritual animal deposition at Romano-British settlements a survey of bone assemblages from pit features at seven settlements in southern Britain, including both rural and urban sites, was carried out for this study. The aim of the study was to assess the commonality of dog burials that fulfilled Fulford's definition of ritual activity i.e. the empirical evidence should be both of a repetitive nature and display 'irrational' characteristics (Fulford 2001, 201). The sites included are Owslebury, Hampshire; Little Somborne, Hampshire; Chichester Cattle Market, Hampshire; Winchester Northern Suburbs, Hampshire; Greyhound Yard, Dorchester, Dorset; Winnall Down, Hampshire and Silchester, Hampshire (Fasham 1985, Collis 1968, Maltby 1987a, Maltby 1987b, Maltby 1978, Maltby 1993, Down 1989, Fulford and Clarke 2002, Kennedy 2002, Woodward et al. 1993). Apart from their position within the survey area the sites were chosen for inclusion in the survey because of the level of detail about the animal bone assemblages available in the published reports.

3.6.1 The Skeletons from a Romano-British Industrial site at Chichester Cattle Market, Hampshire

Excavations at Chichester cattle market uncovered an archaeological site that appears, for the most part, to have been dedicated to industrial activity: evidence indicates that iron forging, milling and the stockading of animals was taking place at the site at various times during the Roman occupation of Britain. The excavated area was situated outside the east gate of the Roman town of *Noviomagus* (Down 1989, 55-83).

The animal bone assemblage from the site is remarkable in that 45 partial and complete skeletons from various domesticates were recovered during excavation of features dating from the late 1st century to the late 4th century AD. More than half of the skeletons belonged to adult and juvenile dogs. Most of these deposits were found in pits and wells although a small number of examples came from post-holes and ditches. Evidence of butchery was recovered from all phases of occupation, however, only one of the carcasses under discussion possibly bore a cut mark. The cause of the animals' deaths was not visible as pathologies on their skeletons, which might have indicated that the animals were discarded in a partially articulated state because they were diseased and therefore inedible. Besides dog, sheep/goat and pig, the collection included two complete skeletons of cattle of veal producing age; the disposal of these meat-producing animals is at odds with any economic rationale (Levitan 1989, 261-266). The animals may have died of natural causes, but the large numbers of dogs that were found buried in cesspits and wells, in groups of two or more, seriously undermines the validity of that explanation, as it is unlikely that so many animals would have died at the same time. Bruce Levitan who analysed the assemblage suggested that the carcasses of dead dogs might have been periodically collected for disposal in these features (Levitan 1989, 265-266). However, considering the unusual nature of the associated bone groups from the site as a whole a purely functional interpretation is perhaps a rather restrictive view of the nature of the archaeology. That the ritual deposition of animals, frequently dogs, deliberately killed for this purpose was taking place at this site is at least an equally valid interpretation.

3.6.2 Dog Burials from Silchester, *Insula IX*, Hampshire

For much of the last decade Reading University's excavations at Silchester have focused on an area known as *Insula IX*. The structures uncovered at the site appear to have been a mix of the workshops and homes of craftspeople and traders. Numerous dog burials from the site display characteristics indicating that symbolically charged, structured interments were being made in this busy urban environment (Fulford and Clarke 2002, 364-369).

Three of the burials were of two dogs buried together. Pairing appears to have been an important element of some depositional ceremonies in Iron Age and Roman Britain. As well as its occurrence in numerous Romano-British dog burials, other examples of pairing include the deposition of two bronze cauldrons in a lake at Llyn Fawr, Mid-Glamorgan around 650-600BC (Savory 1980, 58-59). Two shallow bowls, two terracotta lamps and two cooking pots were found in matching pairs, placed at regular intervals, in a Roman ditch in Orpington, Kent (Merrifield 1987, 22-58). One can only speculate about the significance of pairs in these rituals, however, there are many symbolic concepts that are commonly associated with 'two' that might have contributed to this aspect of depositional practise. Two is often perceived as the feminine or maternal cardinal number relating to duplication and separation, but also to balance. This perception of two is reinforced by the many dualistic aspects of nature like male and female, night and day, life and death so elevating the symbolism of pairs to a cosmic level (Becker 2000, 312). It is perhaps significant that one pair of dogs at Silchester was found in association with a knife, the ivory handle of which was carved in the form of a dog and a bitch mating. The exotic nature of this artefact suggests that it was an imported luxury item; a single dog figurine, one of four bronze dog representations found with a hoard of coins at Llys Awel, Abergele is similarly styled (fig. 7) (Kennedy 2002, Blockley 1991, 127). The image on the knife handle in association with the double burial perhaps implies that the deposit was associated with a fertility rite. It is certainly rare for such potentially revealing iconography to be found in direct association with dog burials. Dogs have been linked with fertility through iconographic images from Britain and Gaul during the Roman period, in numerous pieces of art they are depicted with mother goddesses and hunter gods; both kinds of divinities were connected with beliefs in rebirth and regeneration, this is fully discussed in chapter 6 (Jenkins 1957, 60-78, Green 1992a, 197-203). It has also been suggested that the link between the species and fertility may have arisen in response to observation of canine sexual behaviour (Hill 1995, 104). Indeed, in some societies today women are prescribed concoctions that include dog flesh as an ingredient to promote conception because the species is perceived as overtly sexually dynamic (Olowo Ojade 1994, 219). Another dog skeleton at *Insula IX* was found together with an infant burial. Deposits of very young children have also been interpreted as symbolic offerings associated with fruitfulness when found in sacred and secular contexts because the body of a child encapsulates the promise of a new life and spirit of regeneration (Scott 1991, 115-121).

Figure 7. A knife handle from Silchester decorated with the image of a dog and bitch mating (top). Photograph © University of Reading.

Arguably the most remarkable dog burial from *Insula IX* is the interment of one beast in an upright position as if standing on all fours; the earth in the pit had been tightly packed around the body to support it in this position (fig. 8) (Kennedy 2002, Fulford and Clarke 2002, 364-369). The skeleton is believed to be the remains of a bitch comparable in size to a modern Labrador but with an incongruously small, terrier like skull (Clark 2002, Pers. Comm.). The burial was one of a number of deliberately

Figure 8. A Romano-British dog buried in a standing position in a pit at Silchester, *Insula IX*. Photograph © University of Reading.

placed deposits found in the numerous pits cut into the floor of a large building recorded as House 1. Other interments in these pits included the Silchester Ogham stone, a beef joint and a number of complete and near complete ceramic vessels and none of the pits contained fills of ordinary domestic refuse. It was suggested that these burials might have been associated with the desertion of the building: the pits were cut through the remains of the house indicating that the deposits post dated its occupation. Five radio carbon dates from several of the artefacts confirmed that they were Romano-British, dating to sometime between the 3rd and 5th centuries AD (Fulford and Clarke 2002, 364-369). Rites of termination were perhaps practised with the aim of regenerating the abandoned land, so again the dog may symbolise fertility.

This animal had not been a stranger to brutality in life: traumas to the skull had been sustained on a number of occasions. One substantial blow to the muzzle had forced the nasal bones downwards and consequently realigned the dog's teeth. The dog survived another blow to the head but died before it had fully healed. Pathologies along the animal's spine indicate that she had also been beaten along her back. Indeed the most striking feature of Kate Clark's analysis of the dog remains from the site, from a purely physical point of view, is the number of severe pathologies on their skeletons. An immature dog from Silchester had suffered a fractured humerus that consequently became infected, and another animal had sustained a blow to the neck. One dog found buried in a pit had also received several blows to the head including a fatal blow with a cleaver-sized blade. After its death there appears to have been an aborted attempt to decapitate the animal (Clark 2002, Pers. Comm.). These indications of gratuitous violence are comparable with the evidence for overkill seen in the remains of a number of humans who appear to have been the victims of ritual sacrifice. For example, Lindow man was not simply drowned but rather he was garrotted, his throat was slit and he was bludgeoned twice before being submersed in a bog (Turner and Briggs 1986, 144-161). As mentioned in chapter 2, a number of the bodies that had been buried in pits or within the earthworks of Danebury Iron Age hillfort in Hampshire, had been severely mutilated either at or shortly after their death (Cunliffe 1992, 77). This comparable treatment of humans and dogs in what appear to be sacrificial acts is suggestive of surrogacy; perhaps their strong social link provided enough similarities between the species to allow a dog to take the place of a human offering. Furthermore, the domestic dog's inferiority to humans within social order would also be in-keeping with the concept of human sacrificial victims as being outside of mainstream society in terms of status, which was recorded by a number of historical writers (Aldhouse-Green 2001, 139-160).

However dogs were regarded in life, the evidence from this study suggests that they were still considered to be appropriate offerings in what appear to be quite elaborate sacrificial rituals. A feeling of ambivalence towards one's native dog population appears to be timeless and widespread. For example, the Teenek Indians of Mexico, for example, keep companion dogs but treat them with disdain. Furthermore, the dogs are given names in Spanish, which is the language spoken by the tribes' bitter enemies. It seems that their dogs symbolise a less dignified and unsavoury type of humanity. However, in Teenek folklore the same species is portrayed as noble and heroic (De Vidas 2002, 531-550). As mentioned in 2.2.1, at the Iron Age settlement site at Houghton Down, Stockbridge in Hampshire there is evidence that great care was taken of certain dogs whilst others were skinned and eaten (Hamilton 2000, 138-139). These somewhat conflicting attitudes towards the species perhaps tell us as much about the human psyche as it does about the nature of the animals themselves. It has been suggested that such ambiguity towards the species may have arisen out of our discomfort at canine instincts reflecting the 'animal' within us. Alternatively we may simply be responding to the fact that dogs genuinely do have many endearing qualities and many disgusting habits (Serpell 1995, 245-256).

3.6.3 Dog Burials from Greyhound Yard, Dorset

The remains of at least 93 dogs were recovered during excavations of one of the central *insulae* of the Roman town *Durnovaria* at Greyhound Yard, Dorchester in Dorset. If we cannot be certain of anything else, we can feel fairly confident that dogs were quite a common presence in the town during the Roman occupation of Britain. A considerable percentage of the dog bones found belonged to puppies, which led to speculation about high infant animal mortality rates at the site and possible population control (Maltby 1993, 326-328). However, osteoarchaeology aside, the archaeology associated with the dogs and the remains of the animals themselves exhibit features that cannot be explained in terms of simple functionality.

Although the area excavated was occupied from the 1st to the 4th centuries, the dog burials to be described date to the post-conquest period and before AD200. In the lower layers of one of a group of pits, situated along the eastern frontage of the *insula*, the partial skeletons of at least eleven dogs were found together with a complete black-burnished vessel and large fragments from a number of other pots; another layer contained an intact human cranium. Another pit in the same area appeared to have been divided into two halves by a layer of chalk. Beneath the chalk layer the pit contained mixed pottery, including complete vessels and animal bone. In the four layers immediately above the chalk the remains of seven puppies and four adult dogs were found. Two of the adult dogs had been decapitated before deposition and the other two appear to have been tied together at the throat. In two layers of the pit traces of wood and iron nails were found. In both instances these features were closely associated with the body of a dog. Another contemporary shaft in the central area of the *insula* was found to contain the remains of at least twenty mainly adult dogs. In the top layer of another pit in this area a further eleven dogs were found with a large amount of late 2nd century pottery (Woodward *et al.* 1993, 31-54).

Peter and Ann Woodward have recently suggested that the central position of these pits in the town may have been influenced by Roman ritual practices associated with the establishment of a new town, and therefore the contents are perhaps best interpreted a ritual foundation offerings. A number of historical sources refer to such ceremonies. Varro described a ritual that involved taking auspices before town boundaries were defined by a ploughed furrow (Varro *De Lingua Latina,* VII (Varro De Lingua Latina VII, Kent 1938). Livy recorded details of another ritual that would be carried out to determine the orientation of a town's roads. The priest used a curved staff, known as a *lituus,* to cast shadows and so define the field of vision from which the auspices would be taken. A decision about the bearing of the town's layout was made according to portents witnessed within this area (Livy, 1.18. Creighton 2000, 210). As mentioned earlier in the chapter, several ancient sources refer to the creation of a ritual pit or *mundus* in the centre of a newly established town, into which sacrificial offerings to the gods were placed (Ovid *Fasti* IV 821. Plutarch *Life of Romulus* 36, Tacitus *Histories* IV 53, Rykwert 1976, 58-59, Woodward and Woodward 2004, 68-86).

The Woodwards noted that, like Greyhound Yard, a number of the Silchester pits containing dog remains, and the subterranean shrine at Ridgeons Gardens, Cambridge, the contents of which are outlined in 3.6.3.3, were all situated very close to the main cross-roads at the centre of the towns, further supporting the theory that dedicatory rites similar to those described by Roman writers were practised in Roman-Britain (Woodward and Woodward 2004, 68-86, Fulford 2001, 199-218, Alexander and Pullinger 1999, 35-47).

3.6.3.1 Comparative Archaeology from Other Sites in Roman Britain

It is notable that the most outstanding characteristics of the Greyhound Yard deposits appear repeatedly in this study of the symbolic use of dogs in Roman Britain, both at settlement sites and sacred sites. Taking the evidence given below into account it seems increasingly likely that these features are part of some sort of suite of sacrificial offerings that were particularly significant at the time. Examples of archaeology comparable to that associated with the dog burials from Greyhound Yard from both settlements and sacred sites are outlined below.

3.6.3.2 Human Skulls and Dog Bodies

Numerous examples of human skulls and dog bodies in close association have been recovered from both sacred and secular sites. At Folly Lane, St Albans a human skull covered with almost 100 cut-marks and a young dog were sealed in the bottom layers of ritual shaft dating to the 2nd century AD (Mays and Steele 1995, 155-161). A human skull, found with canine remains was recently recovered from a ditch at Vindolanda Fort; both the human and the dog had received blows to the head (R. Birley 2002, Pers. Comm.). In a feature known as the legionary ditch, at Colchester Roman fortress, a dog was found buried along with human remains including parts of six skulls, two of which had been brutalised (Crummy 1984, 93-98). The bodies of two dogs, a human skull and a large number of pottery fragments from flagons and amphorae were found in a wooden box at the base of a well near Cannon Street, London (Rowsome 1983, 277). At Alveston near Bristol a large bone assemblage was recovered from the bottom of a swallet hole that opened into an underground chamber. Accelerator Mass Spectrometry dates for the remains indicate that the deposits date to the mid 1st century AD. The remains included the bones of at least six dogs; a human skull that had received two violent and no doubt fatal blows; human bone from a victim of Paget's disease, a condition that causes physical deformities due to the softening and consequent bending of bone tissue, and a human femur displaying traits indicative of cannibalism. Miranda Aldhouse-Green suggested that the rather grisly contents of the shaft could perhaps be interpreted as evidence of human sacrifice and insult cannibalism, whereby people deemed offensive or dangerous for one reason or another were murdered and then placed in the hands of the chthonic forces. The inclusion of the dogs may have been a means of thanking the underworld deities for taking social outcasts into their realm and ensuring that the deceased would no longer be a danger to the living (Aldhouse-Green 2004b, 193-218).

Animal remains may be found with human remains for a number of reasons; they may represent offerings to deities to ensure the welfare of the deceased in the afterlife, alternatively a joint of meat could be a food offering for the gods or sustenance for the dead on their journey to the next world. Some animals may have been companions that were killed to enable the pet to join its mistress or master in the afterlife (Green 1992a, 105-108). In a considerable number of cultures both ancient and modern dogs are believed to guide humans to the afterlife: this idea was associated with the Greek goddess Hekate and it is still part of the Zoroastrian faith practised mainly in Mumbai, India (Clark 1998, 114-117). However, none of these explanations really seem to sit comfortably with the evidence for dogs' skeletons found with lone human skulls.

It is notable that the majority of the human skulls found with dog remains have been deliberately wounded in some way. It has been suggested that if a person met their end in a way that was considered to be spiritually dangerous in Roman Britain, perhaps through an act of tyranny or a judicial punishment, their bodies may have been decapitated to prevent their soul rising up and harming the living (Henig 1984b, 203). Indeed if this was the case it seems plausible that the dogs were interred with the deceased to guard over them as a further precautionary measure.

The fact that examples of the association between human skulls and dogs' skeletons have been identified at both sacred and secular sites supports the theory that, as appears to have been the case in the British Iron Age, ritual activities in Roman Britain were not confined to the realms of constructed sacred space even though there is a notable increase in the erection of purpose built religious complexes during this period.

3.6.3.3 Control and Restraint

The forcible restraint suggested by the discovery of two dogs that appear to have been tied together around the neck in a pit at Greyhound Yard is particularly interesting for a number of reasons, firstly, because this binding confirms the likelihood that these two animals met their end at more or less the same time, which significantly decreases the likelihood that they died of natural causes. Secondly, dogs bound around the neck and body have been found at two 2nd century sites of a recognisably sacred nature in clear association with ritual activity. The dogs in the lowest and highest layers of the Springhead dog pit, which is fully discussed in chapter 4, were bound in chains. In an unusual subterranean shrine at Ridgeons Gardens in Cambridge the bodies of three small hunting dogs were laid out in circular formation, with iron chains radiating from their necks. A number of other animals including the complete skeletons of another dog, a sheep, an ox and a horse were found with the canines at the shrine. (Anon 1978, 57-60, Alexander and Pullinger 1999, 35-47).

The chains around the dogs' necks at these sites can perhaps be interpreted as a potent symbol of the control that humans usually have over the species. The ability to train and tame these natural hunters may well have given the people responsible for the burials a sense of power over nature and this feeling perhaps manifested itself in the use of ties and chains. A large collar is a common attribute of the domestic dogs portrayed in Romano-British iconography. The bronze model of a deer hound from the Lydney temple, Gloucestershire wears a thick collar, so too do the dogs gazing expectantly upward at figures believed to representations of Diana on reliefs from the shrine at Nettleton, Wiltshire and the temple at Bath, Somerset (Toynbee 1982, 136-137, Wheeler 1932, 88-89, Cunliffe 2000, 70). Interestingly, it has been suggested that the marked contempt towards dogs notable in early monotheistic religions, including Judiasm, Islam and Christianity, might not have been solely related to perception of them as pollutants, but may also have been the result of concern amongst religious leaders that this relationship between man and beast might lead to a loftiness in human beings that was considered incompatible with doctrine based around subservience to one divine being (Menache 1997, 1-14).

3.6.3.4 Possible Cenotaph Burials

The traces of wooden artefacts and iron nails that appear to have been deliberately placed adjacent to or below dog skeletons in two areas of a pit at Greyhound Yard supports the theory that the deposition of the animals was part of choreographed and perhaps episodic ritual acts rather than a random acts of disposal. Unfortunately, any trace of what may have been inside these boxes, if indeed that is what they were, was not identified during the excavations (Woodward et al. 1993, 47-49). A number of wooden boxes containing unusual objects were found buried at the side of a road dating to the earliest Romano-British phase of the recently excavated Springhead temple complex. One of these features had held a neonate burial and two others held large pottery vessels containing cremated human bone. Another box contained two empty pottery vessels, one of which was similar to the examples that had held cremated remains. The body of a small dog and a bird had been placed together directly outside this particular box. If the wooden features identified at Greyhound Yard were burial containers it seems very odd that traces of the wood would survive in the record but not the human bone. However, it has been suggested that the deposition of dogs above an empty coffin at the Romano-British cemetery at Lankhills, Hampshire, interpreted as cenotaph burial, was meant to attract the soul of the deceased person for whom the grave was intended. This measure may have been influenced by the Classical belief that if a body could not be afforded a proper burial for some reason the soul of the absent person would be condemned to walk in limbo for one hundred years (Virgil *The Aeneid* VI 323-330, MacDonald 1979, 421-423). Similar beliefs about attracting life force to the empty grave of an absent individual could also explain the burial of the dogs next to apparently empty wooden vessels at Greyhound Yard and the presence of the bird and dog outside the only box at Springhead that did not contain human remains in some form.

3.6.4 Ritual Practise and Practical Ritual – Dog Population Control in Romano-British Wessex

Groups of newborn and infant dogs buried together are not an uncommon occurrence in the British archaeological record and they are often interpreted as possible evidence of litter control, which may well have been the case in some instances. At the rural site of Little Somborne, Hampshire three puppies were found in the upper layers of one of a group of wells dating to around 3rd - 4th centuries AD. A considerable number of bird skeletons and the partial skeletons of two horses were also found in wells at the site, as were three near complete cattle skulls. Mark Maltby who analysed the faunal remains pointed out that the well shafts would have been convenient places to dispose of parts of animal carcases that were not butchered for some reason (Maltby 1978, 10-11). He gave a similar explanation, regarding carcase disposal and population control, for both the remains of at least 17 dogs and a further 200 disarticulated puppy bones recovered from the lowest layers of two late 3rd - mid 4th century well features at the extra-mural site at Winchester Northern Suburbs, Hampshire and for the remains of at least seven adult dogs and thirty puppies recovered from an Early Romano-British shaft at the rural site of Owslebury, Hampshire (Maltby 1987a, 5-6, Maltby 1987b, unnumbered, Collis 1968, 28). These interpretations are sound and logical, however, it is understood that animal sacrifice and economic considerations were not entirely divorced from each other in the ritual activities of British antiquity (Grant 1991b, 109-114). A practical solution could also have been taken as an opportunity to make an offering to the gods. Sacred and secular experiences were not mutually exclusive events in the polytheistic beliefs of ancient Europeans, rather they were inextricably entwined to form a singular spiritual way of life (Finn 1997, 50). Given the frequency with which considerable numbers of adult and infant dogs are found in Romano-British shafts, pits and wells it is important that archaeologists are open to the possibility that acts interpreted as 'discard' or 'dumping' may represent more than a simple means to a simple end regardless of whether or not the site is regarded as sacred or secular.

3.6.5 Evidence for the Continuation of Ritual Animal Deposition in the Romano-British period from Winnall Down, Hampshire

Winnall Down, Hampshire produced some of the most compelling evidence for the practice of ritual deposition in pit features, within the settlement areas, in J D Hill's study of the phenomenon in Iron Age Wessex. Perhaps the most notable animal deposits at the site were those from Pit 6595: this assemblage included an unusually dense concentration of butchered cattle and horse bones together in one layer and in another the bodies of a sow and a bitch were found buried beneath a compacted layer of deliberate infill. The archaeology from the pit has been interpreted as the remains of an extravagant feasting event (Hill 1995, 127). A considerable number of human burials and articulated groups of unbutchered animal bone dating to this phase were recovered from pits across the site, including the complete skeleton of another adult dog and the articulated remains of four neonatal or foetal puppies (Fasham 1985, 25-26, Maltby 1985, 103).

During the Romano-British period settlement activity at Winnall Down focused around a number of linked enclosures to the west of the earlier open Iron Age settlement. Several infant burials and deposits of articulated horse limb bones and horse vertebrae dating to this later period were found situated close to, indeed sometimes immediately above Middle Iron Age burials. It would seem quite likely that the existence of the earlier burials must have been communicated in some way over a considerable period of time perhaps suggesting that earlier ritual practices were being acknowledged at this time and retained significance at some level. (Fasham 1985, 18-37, Maltby 1985, 97-112). The burial of a complete dog, in what appears to have been a deliberately dug grave was also found within one of the Romano-British enclosures (Maltby 1985, 108).

3.6.6 Pervasive 'Ritual' Behaviour in Roman Britain

It is quite clear that the deposits from pits, ditches, shafts and wells from domestic and sacred sites share more in common than can be attributed to pure coincidence. If these deposits are viewed in temporal isolation they are undoubtedly a phenomenon of the Romano-British archaeological record in their own right. However, considering the acceptance of special deposits in the Iron Age it is difficult to imagine that the two patterns of behaviour were completely unrelated.

3.7 Dogs as a Feature of Termination and Foundation Deposits

Dog burials in Roman Britain are sometimes found beneath the foundations of a property or appear to coincide with the disuse of a nearby structure. After being partially destroyed by fire, a building at Newgate Street, London was reconstructed and the body of a small dog was placed beneath the main east wall of the building (Roskams 1980, 406). The skeleton of a dog and several whole pots were found in backfilled ditches thought to have been part of an early Roman field-system at Rangoon St, London (fig. 9). It was suggested that these deposits were associated with a phase of upheaval and redevelopment in the late 2nd century AD when the area became enclosed by the city wall (Bowler 1983, 13). A well that supplied water to a Romano-British villa at Welton in East Yorkshire was abandoned and deliberately sealed around the middle of the 2nd century AD (Mackey 1999, 24-26). The lowest layers of the feature contained the remains of 68 animals including 15 dogs and 28 cats; the remaining 28 metres of the well were then infilled with assorted soil and debris. As discussed above, a 'standing' dog burial, an Ogham stone and several complete pottery vessels were all found in a group of pits in a disused building in Silchester *Insula IX* (Fulford and Clarke 2002, 364-369). In light of the evidence it seems quite likely that rites of termination were practised in Roman Britain (Merrifield 1987, 48-50). These offering were perhaps a means of giving thanks to the gods for a feature's prior use and to ensure that the land might one day be successfully regenerated after deliberate or accidental destruction.

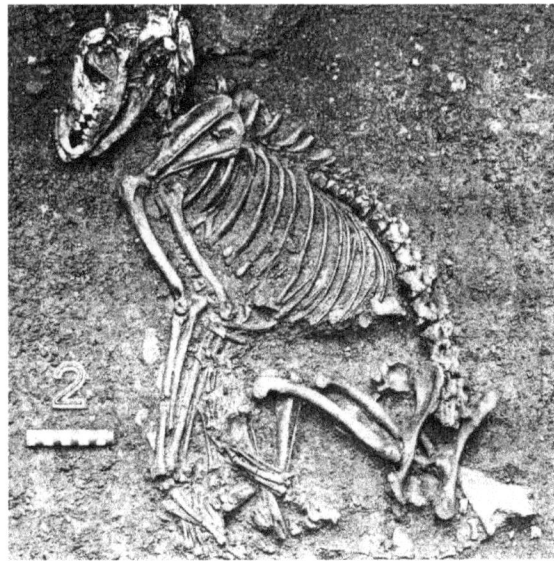

Figure 9. Possible termination deposit of a dog found at Rangoon St, London. Photograph © MoLAS

The enactment of foundation rituals perhaps explains the astounding deposition of over 100 complete dogs in the area of a *mansio* in Godmanchester, Huntingdonshire. The large inn was constructed within the area of the original Roman fortress in the early 2nd century AD. Public baths and a small temple were also built next to the *mansio* during this phase of redevelopment. The excavator, Michael Green, noted that there appeared to have been a delay in the completion of the *mansio* and baths, at which time a series of pits were dug amongst the foundations of the buildings. In the basal layers of many of these pits the bodies of pairs of dogs had been deposited and one feature contained 20 canine skeletons. When Ralph Harcourt analysed these remains the sizes and shapes of the dogs were found to encompass almost all previously known domestic canine skeletal variants dating to the Romano-British period, which in terms of femur length, for example, could range from 86mm to 234mm (Harcourt 1974, 151-175). Two pipeclay 'Venus' figurines that may have had a votive function were also recovered from these features. Although Michael Green interpreted the contexts in which the bodies were found as rubbish or cesspits he did consider that the dog burials were probably ritual sacrifices, particularly in view of the repetitive pairing of the animals. Interestingly several pairs of hares were also found in the pits (H. J. M. Green 1977, 6-18, H. J. M. Green 1986, 29-55). In the light of the recent interpretations discussed in this chapter, particularly the pits from Greyhound Yard, Dorchester, it seems quite possible that the pits were in fact dug to receive foundation offerings in the first instance (Woodward and Woodward 2004, 68-86).

The foundation of a structure, its disuse or redevelopment is a transitional period, the end of one era and the beginning of another. In some instances human perception of these occasions is comparable to the way certain societies view life-changing events, like marriage, birth or death. Anthropologists have termed such interim phases in the life of a person 'rites of passage' and the concepts surrounding them can also be applied to the lifecycle of a building. Although these transitory occasions may be cause for celebration, they are also a time of uncertainty (Huntington and Metcalf 1979, 1-17). The Romano-British evidence of dog burials and other deposits being placed within or close to a building, during its foundation or after its disuse, suggests that these junctures were perceived as being vulnerable to negative, outside influences and consequently propitiatory sacrificial offerings were made to the numinous forces that influenced the outcome of the transformations (Merrifield 1987, 22-57, Huntington and Metcalf 1979, 1-17).

As animal symbolism often develops out of observation of a creature in an everyday environment, it is perhaps not surprising to find that, as an emblem, the naturally territorial domestic dog is often associated with doorways or thresholds: as noted in chapter 1 domestic dogs have been found buried within the entrances and boundaries of a number of Iron Age sites in Britain, including the hillforts at Danebury, Hampshire and Maiden Castle, Dorset (Stevens 1998, 76-89, Cunliffe 1984, 12, Wheeler 1943, 115).

3.8 Evidence for Ritual Dog Burials in Kent

E W Black noted the recurrence of unusual dog burials in the Romano-British archaeological record in 1983 (Black 1983, 20-22). Two of the examples he cited in his report were found within Roman villas at Darenth and Farningham in a small area of Kent (Payne 1897, 62, Meates 1974, 7-8). Each of these burials comprised a single complete animal within the foundations of the villas themselves; at Farningham a group of ceramic vessels had also been placed under the floor of the building. Finds from two other sites; Warbank, Keston, Kent and Upchurch Marshes, Kent were also amongst those catalogued by Black. None of these sites are further than twelve miles from the Springhead temple complex where perhaps some of the most compelling evidence to support the species' extensive use in cult practices in Britain has been found (see chapter 4 for a full discussion). All of these sites are believed to date to between the late 1st century - late 2nd century AD.

The burials of dogs and other animal interments at Warbank and Upchurch Marshes are particularly interesting because, as will be discussed, they display characteristics that blur the interpretative boundaries between structured deposition at sacred sites and those of a predominantly secular nature.

3.8.1 Puppy Burials on Upchurch Marshes, Kent

A group of seven Romano-British *ollae* were found buried on the Upchurch Marshes, Kent in the 1950s. Each vessel contained the remains of a puppy aged about three weeks old at death and charcoal from burnt twigs and small branches. They were buried in a line running north-south at uniform intervals and depths. Although these burials are undeniably remarkable it is becoming increasingly clear that the association between deposits of dogs and complete or near complete vessels is not as unique as it once seemed: the burials were unparalleled in Britain or on the continent at the time that the excavator Ivor Noel Hume published his findings in the late 1950s (Noel-Hume 1957, 160-167). Noel Hume looked to Classical mythology for a possible explanation for the burials, suggesting that these animals could have been offerings to the chthonic goddess Hekate who was said to favour sacrifices of puppies (Plutarch *Quaestiones Romanae*, LXVIII, Rose 1924, 148, Noel-Hume 1957, 163). She was also believed to have power over fishermen and this connection to the sea might have attracted people living near the low-lying Kent marshes to her cult (Noel-Hume 1957, 163, Cary *et al.* 1961, 407). Six of the *ollae* appear to have come from the same kiln. The combination of this apparent common source for the *ollae* and the inclusion of the charcoal and twigs, which perhaps represented kiln fuel, led to speculation that it was perhaps the pot manufacturer who actually made this ritual offering. The wood was certainly burnt before it was placed in the pot, and the choice of burial situation within the clay earth of the marshes might also be seen as reference to the trade (Noel-Hume 1957, 160-167).

Possible motives aside, it is the remote nature of these burials that might be of particular significance in terms of the way archaeologists interpret similar finds at other sites. It is apparent that complete and near complete vessels are repeatedly found in association with dog burials at both sacred and secular sites. However, categorising sites this way has quite frequently led to otherwise comparable archaeology from both types of site being pigeon-holed in the same way. The Upchurch Marshes in Kent do not clearly fall into either site category, but the similarity between these deposits and ritual interments outlined elsewhere in this study is unmistakeable. The marked similarities between the unusual dog and pottery interments at Silchester *Insula IX*, the Springhead temple complex and Upchurch Marshes, Kent clearly suggests that certain ritual practices in Roman Britain were not governed by differences in location as we view them.

3.8.2 The Ritual Shafts at Warbank, Keston, Kent

Excavations carried out by Kent Archaeological Rescue Unit in an area of Warbank, Keston, Kent uncovered evidence of site occupation dating from the Late Iron Age to some time in the 5th century AD. Between AD50-160 the site appears to have been a large farmstead characterised by two enclosures, a ditched boundary, kiln debris, black-smithing debris, quarry-pits, shafts and a small cemetery; in later years the area was redeveloped as a villa site. As well as providing a wide range of evidence for domestic occupation, archaeology from the site might also broaden our understanding of ritual deposition in Roman Britain. The only plausible explanation for eight large shafts and their contents at Warbank is that the features were dug specifically to receive votive offerings. The Keston shafts certainly could not have functioned as wells because they would not have reached the water table (Philp *et al.* 1999, 14-35).

The contents of one of these shafts, a feature known as the 'Great Shaft', are no less remarkable than any ritual deposits found at any temple site in Britain. This feature was 4.88m deep and 3.25m across at its widest point. It was filled over a period of between 30-50 years from early in the 2nd century AD (Philp *et al.* 1999, 14-35). The layers of the shaft were divided into six zones of archaeological deposits labelled A to F by the excavation team, with F being the primary deposit. A total of 34 complete animal skeletons and a considerable amount of pottery were found in the great shaft; the distribution of the animal species is given in Table 1 (Locker 1999, 148).

The archaeology from Zone D is particularly notable. It contained the skeletons of three dogs, two horses and an ox. The dogs and other faunal remains had been pushed to the side of the shaft to make room for the larger animals. The fact that the two horses and the ox had been arranged in a nose to tail configuration may have particular significance as this distinct patterning has emerged elsewhere in Britain: as mentioned above the deposit of three small dogs from the 2nd century

Table 1. Number and species of complete animal skeletons by archaeological zone in the Great Shaft at a Romano-British farmstead in Warbank, Keston, Kent (after Locker 1999, 148)

Zone	Ox	Horse	Sheep	Pig	Dog	Total
A	1	-	1	2	1	5
B	-	-	1	-	7	8
C	-	-	1	1	3	5
D	1	2	-	-	3	6
E	-	-	-	2	-	2
F	-	-	5	-	3	8
Total	2	2	8	5	17	34

subterranean shrine at Ridgeons Gardens, Cambridge were arranged similarly as was the 1st century burial of a dog, horse and a deer found in Eastern cemetery, London (Alexander and Pullinger 1999, 35-47, Barber and Bowsher 2000, 318-320, Philp et al. 1999, 14-35). One might consider that the circle that their bodies formed was intended to symbolise the cyclical nature of life, death and regeneration so important in the beliefs of pagan Europeans at this time.

Shaft 'B', which was excavated by Nancy Piercy Fox in the 1960s, and the 'Great Shaft' share a number of interesting structural characteristics. Firstly, they are both 4.88m deep. Secondly, they both appear to have originally been divided into upper and lower chambers. This is made apparent in Shaft 'B' by a chalk ledge that protrudes from the circumference of the shaft at a depth of 2.3m. It is thought that this once may have supported a floor of some kind. The cremated remains of two small dogs were found in the section of the shaft that would have been beneath this surface if it existed. Their remains had been gathered into a pile in the centre of the shaft and seven sherds of red ware pottery had been placed on top of them, before they were finally covered by an even layer of chalk and fine brown powder (Piercy Fox 1963, 1-1i, Piercy Fox 1968, 184-190, Philp et al. 1999, 19-21). When excavated in the 1980s the sides of the Great Shaft's upper layers were found to have collapsed inwards due to weathering. At a depth of 1m the character of the shaft changed becoming a narrow and jagged vertical passage 1.4m long before finally opening out into a lower chamber. The numerous pick marks that remained on the walls of this area suggested that people had taken considerable trouble to smooth these surfaces. On the west side of the shaft was part of a chalk ledge similar to the perimeter shelf in Shaft 'B'(Philp et al. 1999, 24-34).

It is unlikely that either of the shafts were filled over night: as mentioned above, evidence suggests that the Great Shaft took between 30-50 years to fill. Unfortunately, damage to Shaft 'B' caused by 4th century quarrying has meant that similar information is not available for this feature (Philp et al. 1999, 24-34, Piercy

Fox 1963, 1-1i). However, it seems quite possible that for some time the lower chambers of these shafts, situated in the grounds of a fairly prosperous farmstead, functioned as subterranean shrines. What the evidence from Warbank can tell us for certain is that the creation of purpose dug ritual shafts was not restricted to areas of constructed sacred space.

3.9 Summary

The majority of evidence we have for the presence of dogs at Romano-British settlement sites is in the form of their skeletal remains, but there are also a number of references to British dogs in historical writings. Canine gnawing marks on animal bone and dog paw prints set into ceramic tiles are also indicative of their presence. In terms of provision of secondary products there is some evidence to suggest that dogs were occasionally eaten, their pelts were sometimes used as blankets and their coprolites were used in tanning. Overall it would appear that the average British dog at this time was a rather inelegant mongrel and something of a scavenger who was often roughly treated.

Despite appearing to lead quite unremarkable lives domestic dogs were quite often buried within Romano-British settlements with a considerable amount of ceremony. Michael Fulford recently observed that acts of ritual deposition involving certain animals and objects, particularly dogs and complete and near complete pottery vessels was taking place at settlements at this time. A survey of the archaeology from seven sites in southern Britain carried out for this study supports this theory. Certain archaeologists have interpreted multiple dog burials as evidence of litter/ population control, however, it should be noted that a practical outcome does not necessarily rule out spiritual motivation.

Although the minutiae of the dog burials differed considerably from site to site in the survey, there is sufficient evidence to suggest that the choice of particular items for ritual deposition at different sites was not coincidental. These items include complete animal skeletons, particularly dogs; complete and near complete pottery vessels; infant burials and human skulls. Perhaps significantly combinations of similar objects are also quite often found in human-made holes at sites of a fundamentally sacred nature, which are discussed in detail in chapter 4. The main difference between deposits at sites of constructed sacred space and those at most settlements is that at the former it is clear that the shafts were purpose dug to receive these offerings. However, there is clear evidence from sites in Kent that quite elaborate ritual activities were not limited to temple complexes.

There are also a considerable number of dog burials in Roman-Britain that indicate that they were used as foundation and perhaps termination offerings within buildings. The domestic dogs perceived role as an intermediary between the animal world and the human world, and its fiercely territorial nature perhaps gave rise to its symbolic association with liminal space in both time and place.

Chapter 4

Dog Remains from Romano-British Sacred Space, including finds from Recent Excavations at Springhead, Kent by Wessex Archaeology

4.1 Introduction

Over the last twenty years there has been much debate about the difficulties of recognising ritual practices involving animals in the archaeological record (Grant 1984a, Wait 1985, Wilson 1992, Hill 1995). How can one begin to differentiate between a bone assemblage created as consequence of an everyday meal or a funerary feast? The matter is further complicated by the fact that in pre-Christian antiquity native Britons probably did not differentiate between the sacred and the profane the way that most of us do in the Western world today. The two realms we perceive as spiritual and earthly may have been inseparable in the human psyche of the time. It is an interesting fact that a number of African tribes today do not have a word for 'religion' in their vocabulary for this very reason. In the past anthropologists claimed that such people did not practise any form of worship because such spiritual unification was so alien as to be completely unrecognisable to them (Turner 1971, 6). It is possible that all meals held spiritual significance in Roman Britain; as pointed out by Annie Grant, who gave the Friday evening meal of Orthodox Jews as an example, religious activity can take place in a domestic setting (Grant 1991b, 109). Conversely within an identifiably religious context in Roman and pre-Roman Britain we must be aware that butchered animal bone could still represent the remains of an 'ordinary' meal. The author acknowledges these issues but they remain unresolved; this study is based upon the information that is currently available and working hypotheses outlined in relevant scholarly texts.

4.2 Methods of Identifying the Symbolic Use of Animals in Areas of Romano-British Constructed Sacred Space

In his hypothesis for the recognition of religious activity within constructed sacred space in southern Britain during the Iron Age and Romano-British periods Alex Smith stated that:

> *The ritual use of animals will be indicated by bones showing evidence of species selectivity.*

In other words, if a bone assemblage is dominated by a certain species or if certain animals, that were common in the area, are conspicuously absent this suggests that deliberate choices were being made in accordance with formal rules applicable in the temple context.

> *There will be a pronounced difference between articulated unbutchered animal bone deposits and butchered waste bone.*

Unbutchered bone at a shrine is likely to represent a ritual act where the entire animal is offered as a sacrifice, whereas butchered bone may represent sacrifice followed by ritual feasting. The two different types of bone assemblage are likely to be found in different contexts at the site under investigation (Smith 2001, 29-30).

4.3 Dog Remains within Romano-British Sacred Space

4.3.1 A Survey of Dog Remains from the Animal Bone Assemblages of Romano-British Temple Sites

A survey of 18 Romano-British temple sites, chosen for inclusion in the study because their reports recorded details of the animal bone assemblages recovered during excavations, revealed that dog bones had been identified at ten of them (see Table. 2). Although dog remains are present at a considerable number of the sites, a closer look at the reports reveals that their bones rarely occur in numbers that allow archaeologists to establish how they came to be part of the record. It is probably worth noting that although dogs were eaten during the Romano-British period, as mentioned in chapter 3 evidence of their consumption was found at the Roman fort of Vindolanda near Hexam (R. Birley 2002, Pers. Comm.), none of the dog bones from these sacred sites exhibit signs of butchery. This provides an interesting contrast with finds from a number of the continental shrines including Epiais-Rhus, Gournay-sur-Aronde and Ribemont-sur-Ancre in Gaul where there is clear evidence that dogs were slaughtered in the same way as more familiar meat bearing animals (Meniel 1987, 25-31, Meniel 1989, 87-97, Green 1992a, 111-113). A collection of bronze tablets from Iguvium, (modern day Gubbio in Italy) a province allied with ancient Rome, describe in stomach churning detail the sacrifice, butchery process, serving and consumption of dogs on an appointed day known as Hondia. The earliest of these inscriptions dates to the 1st century BC (Poultney 1959, 179-189).

Table 2. Survey results - the presence of Dog remains within 18 examples of Romano-British constructed sacred space

Name of Site	Chronology of Site	Presence of Dog Bones	Features of the Assemblage
Pagan's Hill, Somerset	Late 3rd – 5th century AD	No	Fragments of ox and sheep bone found in a well at the site.
Chedworth, Gloucesterhsire	Prob. 2nd century – 4th century AD	No	Bones from red deer found in the ambulatory of a pit that also contained human remains.
Caistor-St Edmund, Norfolk	Late 2nd – 3rd/4th century AD	Yes	Dog bones present amongst small plough soil bone collection that also included horse, pig, cow and sheep/goat remains.
Harlow, Essex	1st century – late 4th/early 5th century AD	Yes	Dog bones were present in all phases at the site but did not form more than 1.5% of the bone collection from any one period. Number of animal bones present by species, total for all phases; sheep/ goat 3015, pig 361, cattle 145, dog 32, horse 22 and others 51.
Uley, Gloucestershire	1st/2nd – late 4th/ early 5th century AD	Yes	Dog bones present in all phases of but form less than 1% of the animal bone assemblage overall. Interpreted as non-votive in the excavation report. Percentage of mammal bone by species for all phases; sheep/goat 88%, cattle 8.3%, pig 2.2%, horse 0.2% and small mammals 0.1%.
Muntham Court Sussex	Later 1st/2nd – 4th century AD	Yes	A large number of dog skeletons were found in a deep well associated with the temple. The assemblage is widely believed to be the result of religious ritual activity. An ox skeleton was found within the remains of a Romano-British circular building and deer antler was found in a storage pit at the site.
Weycocks Hill, Berkshire	Late 3rd – late 4th century AD	Yes	Dog bones present in the fill of three wells/shafts associated with the temple. Excavator concluded that there was no indication of ritual activity. Other species present; horse, pig, cow and sheep/goat.
Nettleton Scrubb, Wiltshire	Late 1st/ mid 2nd – mid/late 4th century AD	No	Number of animal bones per species; horse 8, ox 180, sheep 263, pig 27, birds, 37, small mammals 29 and fish 4.
Cambridge, Cambridgeshire	2nd century AD	Yes	Clear evidence of ritual activity involving dogs and other species of animal including cattle, horse, and sheep. See 4.3.4.
Bourton Grounds, Buckinghamshire	Late 2nd/mid 3rd – late 4th/ early 5th century AD	No	A small animal bone assemblage was recovered, species present; ox, sheep, pig and horse.
Ivy Chimneys, Essex	3rd century – early 5th century AD	Yes	Dog remains from a number of features associated with the use of main religious precinct. Including a group of dogs' teeth that appear to have once adorned a necklace. See below. Total animal bones by species for all phases; horse 1628, cattle 9641, sheep/goat 1924, pig 744, dog 156, cat 2 and wild animals 23.
Verulamium, Herts	Early 2nd – late 4th/5th century AD	No	Animal species present included: small ox, sheep, pig and horse.
Caerwent, Monmouthshire	Prob. 3rd – 4th century AD	Yes	A dog skull was found beneath the apse of a temple. It was associated with a bronze snake's head and a birds head carved from bone. No other animal remains noted.
Caesaromagus, Chelmsford	Early 4th – late 4th/ early 5th century AD	Yes	Dogs formed less than 1% of the animal bone assemblage in each phase of each area of excavation. The excavators claimed that a partial dog burial from a pit containing Samian Ware, brooches and other small bronze objects was possibly of a ritual nature. No information to support this interpretation was given. Number of animal bones present by species; cattle 600, sheep/goat 1399, pig 184, horse 42, dog 31 and wild animals 4.

Lydney, Gloucestershire	Late 3rd/ early 4th - late 4th/ early 5th century AD	No	Animal bones present by species; ox, pig, sheep/goat, horse, bird, red deer and fish.
Great Chesterford, Essex	1st/2nd – 4th/early 5th century AD	No	Animal bone assemblage 99.8% sheep/goat.
Hayling Island, Hampshire	1st century – late 2nd century AD	No	Percentage of mammal bone by species; cattle 1.1%, 55% sheep/goat, pig 43.9% and horse 0.2%.
Bath, Avon	1st century – late 4th century AD	Yes	Dog bones were present at the site in very small numbers and distributed widely throughout the occupation layers. No evidence of butchery. 9000 animal bones were identified to species. Almost half came from cattle and just over a quarter were from sheep. Other species present were pigs, birds, cats, horses, hare, deer and fish.

Table 2 References - Top to Bottom: (Rahtz and Harris, Goodburn 1979b, Gregory and Gurney 1986, France and Gobel 1985, Levitan 1993, Smith 2001, Cotton 1957, Hall 1982, Alexander and Pullinger 1999, Turnbull 1975, Wheeler and Wheeler 1936, Ashby et al. 1910, Luff 1992, Watson 1932, Miller 1995, King and Soffe 1998, Grant 1985)4.3.2 Dog Remains from Ivy Chimneys, Witham, Essex.

The archaeological site at Ivy Chimneys, Witham was occupied continuously from the beginning of the Iron Age to the end of the Romano-British period. In the 3rd century AD a large structure, believed to be a temple building, was constructed at the hilltop site along with a man-made pond. In the early 4th century AD another temple building was built and items interpreted as possible votive offerings were recovered during excavation of a shallow pit feature next to this structure. Dog bones, including three partial burials, were found in various contexts at the site and dated to all phases, but particularly the Romano-British period. The most notable of these deposits was a line of dog canine teeth laid out in a row as if they had at one time formed a necklace. The teeth were found in association with a group of animal bones in an early 4th century ditch. The arrangement of the bones suggested that some care had been taken in their deposition and it was suggested that the act might have held some religious significance. The dogs' teeth were found next to the torso of a sheep that had been placed partly inside the jaws of a horse skull (fig. 10) (Turner 1999, 47).

The dogs' teeth from Ivy Chimneys could represent an offering of jewellery and the material it was made from need not have been significant. However, it is perhaps worth considering that amulets and talismans frequently made from animal parts have been a ubiquitous part of material culture throughout world history; such ornaments are often believed to have totemic or apotropaic qualities (Budge 1930, 1-33). A number of dogs' teeth have been found in unusual contexts dating to British antiquity. A perforated canine was found in association with a human mandible and some pottery fragments in an Iron Age pit at Wavendon Gate in Milton Keynes (Dobney and Jacques 1995, 203-236). At the Butt Road cemetery, Colchester dating to the 3rd century AD, an amber pendant, a dog's tooth, a copper phallus, a copper bell and two perforated coins were found in an early inhumation grave (Henig 1984, 244).

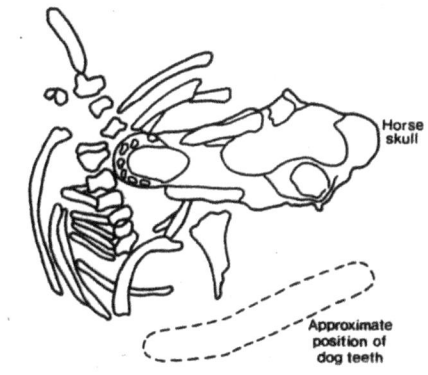

Figure 10. Dog tooth pendant and horse remains from Ivy Chimneys, Essex. Diagram © Turner 1999, Essex County Council.

Dog and horse remains are quite often found together in unusual deposits in both Iron Age and Roman Britain (Green 1992a, 102-103). This could also support the idea that the dog's teeth themselves and not simply the necklace were symbolic at Ivy Chimneys. As mentioned in chapter 3 the interment of a dog, a horse and a deer dating to the early 1st century AD were found together in the Eastern London cemetery (Barber and Bowsher 2000, 318-324). As discussed in detail in 3.8.2, two complete horses and one ox skeleton, arranged head to tail and a large number of dog skeletons, dominate the bone assemblage from a ritual shaft discovered at a farmstead site at Keston, Kent, dating to the 2nd century AD (Philp et al. 1999, 30-34). The fact that horses were brought to the Ivy Chimney's site to be butchered and consumed in fairly high numbers certainly suggests that the species may have held a cult status at the site, as such practice is relatively uncommon in British antiquity. Therefore, the dog tooth pendant's close association with the skull of a horse increases the likelihood that the deposit was symbolically charged (Aldhouse-Green 1999b, 255-258).

4.3.3 The Findon Well, Muntham Court, Sussex

A Romano-British temple at Muntham Court was excavated in the 1950s. Despite poor recording of finds from the site it is clear that several of its features produced noteworthy archaeology. A considerable number of small artefacts were recovered from a mound of earth positioned just outside the temple, the context and the nature of these finds suggests that they may well have been votive offerings. They included a small bronze plaque of a boar, a decorated military horse-harness buckle and an inlaid enamel bridle toggle. A well of 4th century date close to the temple was found to contain what has been recorded as 'a large number' of dog skeletons. This assemblage is believed to be the result of ritual activity (Bedwin 1980, 192-193, Smith 2001, 250). The presence of the dogs and the votives, which included a clay limb, perhaps suggests that the temple was dedicated to a healing deity, but that may only have been one element of the cult. The presence of the dogs, the bronze boar and the horse equipment could suggest that the god or gods worshipped at the site were associated with both hunting and healing. However, these interpretations are rather tentative due to a lack of direct iconographic or epigraphic evidence to support them.

Large quantities of dog remains from wells are a relatively common feature of Romano-British archaeology and the sites where these features are found do not appear to share any other notable characteristics that might enable us to explain their existence or link them with one particular cult or deity. Five dog skulls were found in a well in the Roman town of Caerwent in Monmouthshire (Ross 1968, 262). Beneath an infill of building debris, an Antonine well in Market Square, Staines, Surrey was found to contain 16 dog skeletons (Merrifield 1987, 47). Five small dog skeletons were recovered from the bottom layer of a well of Romano-British date at Asthall, Oxfordshire (Ross 1968, 259). When Gerry Wait carried out a survey of Romano-British shaft and well deposits from 31 sites, dog bones emerged as one of principal characteristics of the fills (Wait 1985, 79). Undeniably, some of these remains probably represent the convenient disposal of a corpse. It is also undeniable that in Britain deposits of complete dogs and dog skulls in human-made holes in the ground are so numerous and so often plainly distinguishable from the usual rubbish deposits, that whether one believes the motivation behind them was spiritual or not, they are a significant characteristic of Romano-British archaeology in themselves as this study clearly illustrates.

4.3.4 The 2nd Century Finds from Ridgeons Gardens, Cambridge, Cambridgeshire

The 1970s excavations at Castle Street in Cambridge uncovered a small, civilian Romano-British settlement dating to the 2nd century AD. Unfortunately, finds from the cluster of identical one room houses found at the site did not provide any clues about the nature of the beliefs that inspired the quite remarkable ritual activities that took place at a large subterranean shrine built in their vicinity.

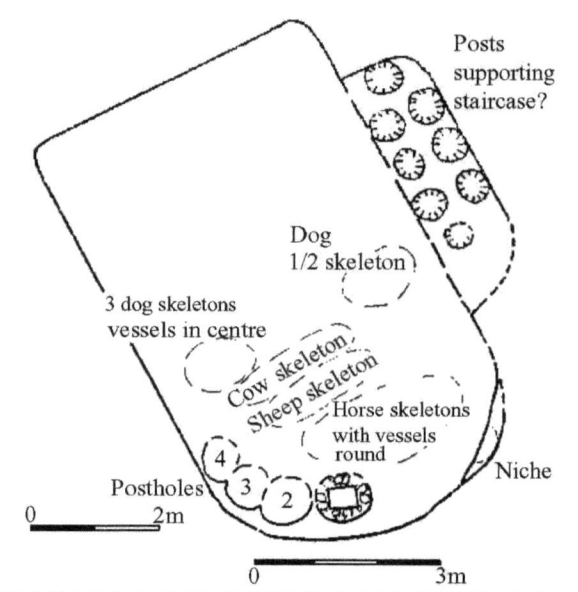

Figure 11. Diagram of the animal deposits within the subterranean shrine at Ridgeons Gardens in Cambridge. Diagram © Alexander and Pullinger 1999, Cambridge Antiquarian Society.

The shrine was rectangular with an apse at one end (fig. 11). On the left hand side of the apse was a recess in the wall that might have contained a cult statue. Large post-holes around the shrine suggest that a substantial timber superstructure had once existed. Underneath the gravel floor of the *cella* the body of a dog and the skull of an ox were found, a large square stone had been placed upon the neck of the latter. At a later date in the same century the superstructure was burnt down. The wood ash remains of the temple were pushed into a pile about 2m high in the area of the *cella*. The structured animal deposits placed within the ash are arguably the most unusual to be found in a Romano-British temple context. In the area of the apse an entire horse skeleton had been buried and carefully surrounded by seven complete vessels. The complete skeleton of a bull with the body of a sheep between its legs lay close to the horse. Half of an articulated dog skeleton was also found near these remains as were a group of three small dogs. The latter were arranged in a circle, with the heads of two overlapping and the third lying across their paws. Iron chains radiated outwards from the iron collars they wore around their necks and the rounded and smoothed bottom of a pottery vessel was placed in the centre of the group (fig. 12). The remains of hundreds of high quality pottery vessels and oyster shells were then placed on top of the ash pile (Anon 1978, 57-60, Alexander and Pullinger 1999, 35-47). The animal deposits and subsequent feasting were perhaps a spiritual response to the destruction of the shrine; the dogs serving as one element of the sacrificial offering of domesticated animals. It is perhaps significant that the horse and the group of three dogs were associated with the structured deposition of pottery; this extra detail could have been an acknowledgement of the close relationship between humans and these species. Similarly, the careful arrangement of the dogs' chains may have been a symbolic act, perhaps alluding to the level of human control over the species. In the art from the Western provinces of Rome domestic dogs are frequently portrayed wearing collars whether they were accompanied by a human companion or not, as if it was important that these constraints on the animal were illustrated; even in a representation of a harmless lamb being carried by a young pilgrim from Fontes Sequanae, the animal clearly wears a collar and lead (Aldhouse-Green 1999a, 13-15).

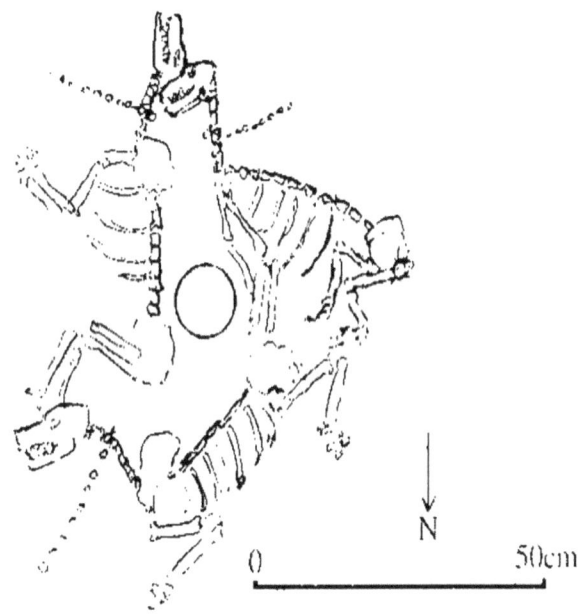

Figure 12. Diagram of the arrangement of three chained domestic dogs in the subterranean shrine at Ridgeons Gardens in Cambridge. Diagram © Alexander and Pullinger 1999, Cambridge Antiquarian Society.

44 The Romano-British Temple Complexes at Springhead, Kent

4.4.1 Excavations at Springhead

The archaeologist William Penn carried out extensive excavations in the area of Springhead, Kent during the late 1950s and 1960s, uncovering a substantial religious complex that would have fronted on to Watling Street (Penn 1958 - 1968). The complex was in use from at least late 1st century AD to the 4th century AD, although evidence of intensive activity in the area around the middle of 1st century AD perhaps suggests that the site may have been a recognised area of sacred space for some time before the temples were built (Smith 2001, 207). The finds included two temples, a series of ancillary buildings and numerous other features that appear to have been the focus of cult activities at the site (Penn 1958 - 1968). The most remarkable evidence of ritual practice at the site was the discovery of four structured infant burials within the foundations of Temple IV. The babies had been buried in pairs, opposite each other in different layers of flooring, but it is clear that the presence of the first two burials was known to the executors of the later rite: the later burials were positioned in different corners of the temple from the first two and as part of each burial event one of the babies had been decapitated (Penn 1961, 121-122). Artefacts revealed little about the exact nature of the cult practised at the site, but a number of Venus figurines and a bronze votive arm and hand suggests that fertility and healing rituals may have taken place. Only a small quantity of animal bone was found and in most cases patterns reflecting their use in ritual practices could not be verified, although deliberately placed ox skulls were found at the base of some excavated post-holes (Smith 2001, 101-106).

On the opposite side of Watling Street from Penn's temple complex and west of the spring itself, recent excavations uncovered a substantial area of Romano-British occupation that appears to have been devoted to industrial activity. Furthermore, on the east side of the spring another temple complex was revealed, it appears to have been established around AD 120 (fig. 14) (Smith 2001, 207).

In the light of the established link between natural springs and healing complexes in ancient Europe it is perhaps reasonable to suggest that this temple complex may have been dedicated to a healing cult. However, the director of the excavations for Wessex Archaeology, Phil Andrews, asserts that none of the artefacts recovered from the site could be considered to directly support this interpretation (Andrews 2003, Pers. Comm.). Wessex Archaeology supplied the following details of the finds from the Springhead temple complex with the permission of their clients Channel Tunnel Rail Link; they represent an interim statement in advance of full analysis and publication.

4.4.2 The Iron Age Features at Recently Excavated Springhead Temple Complex

Excavations at the site took place over a large area of a steeply angled bank. In antiquity a natural spring swelled at the bottom of the bank forming a lake that would have been deep enough to be navigated by small flat-bottomed boats. During the Iron Age a track-way was built on the crest of the rise. Phil Andrews speculated that this might have been used for ceremonial processions; it certainly does not appear to have been utilised as an animal drove-way. The view of the lake at the valley bottom would have been restricted on this approach, perhaps adding to the sense of expectation people would have experienced as they travelled along this route. An area of Iron Age activity was uncovered at the end of the track-way. One of the earliest dog burials at the site was found in one of a group of pits dug into an Iron Age enclosure on the east side of the track-way; these pits also contained a considerable amount of imported pottery. To the west of these features a ditch, also of Iron Age date, was cut into the hillside deliberately sectioning off a large area of land close to the spring. That the spring may have held some spiritual significance at this time is supported by the fact that, unlike the area to the east of the ditch, the area demarcated by the ditch and the water's edge itself was completely lacking in Iron Age features, perhaps activity in this area was restricted for some reason; although Iron Age coins were found in the lake area.

4.4.3 The Earliest Roman Phase at Springhead

The earliest Roman phase at the site, dating to the middle of the 1st century AD, is represented by a road that led down to the spring and up to a bounded area. As mentioned in chapter 3, a number of wooden boxes containing unusual interments were found buried at the side of this road; staining evidenced the presence of the boxes. One of these features had held a neonate burial and two others held large pottery vessels containing cremated human bone. Another box contained two empty pottery vessels, one of which was similar to the examples that held cremated remains. The body of a small dog and a bird had been placed together directly outside this box.

4.4.4 Features from the Main Phase of Roman Activity at Springhead

The main phase of Roman activity in this area of the Springhead site took place from around 120AD and ended around the end of the 2nd century, although coin deposition continued around the springs until the end of the 4th century. The enormous number of finds dating to this period attest to the existence of a very busy environment, particularly in the area that appeared to have been out of bounds during the Iron Age. The excavation of the spring area itself produced hundreds of Roman coins and brooches. As a temple was constructed close to the edge of the spring during this period it seems reasonable to interpret these artefacts as votive offerings to the deity or deities worshipped at the site.

During the Roman occupancy the ditch that had defined the apparently restricted Iron Age area was used to demarcate one side of the temple complex and associated features, which included several large human-made terraces cut into the side of the hill in prime positions overlooking the temple itself. Hearths and butchery waste were found on these terraces suggesting that these features were perhaps viewing platforms where food could be prepared and consumed.

Several single dog burials were found in association with the temple complex features. A pit on one of the terraces contained a dog's skeleton and food debris. A bakery was built next to the temple and between this round structure and a beam slot feature, interpreted as a boundary fence, a dog burial was uncovered. Another dog was found beneath the temple in a pit that pre-dated its construction. Although the excavator felt that there was not sufficient evidence to suggest that these three canine interments were the result of any thing other than a secular acts of disposal, one should perhaps be cautious about interpreting any of the deposits of dogs in this area as insignificant, particularly when the burial of dogs in other features closely associated with those mentioned are so obviously of a ritual nature.

The temple itself had a colonnaded façade and was remodelled at least once, possibly being changed from a timber to a stone structure. Adjacent to this building at least 15 pits were cut into the chalk earth. The largest of these formed pit alignments that in conjunction with the Iron Age ditch on the far side of the area appear to have created a boundary around the temple complex. Horse and cow skulls were found in two of the boundary pits, three others contained various skeletal elements of domestic canines including a complete skeleton, a skull and a group of disarticulated bones. The upper fills of the shafts may have been used for rubbish disposal and the positioning of the animal bone alone does not support an interpretation of ritual deposition, but again there are several factors that suggest that one should keep an open mind about the possibility that the deposits in the boundary pits held some symbolic significance. Firstly, partial and articulated dog skeletons dominate the articulated animal bone assemblage at Springhead. The rest of the collection is made up of one entire bovine skeleton, the skulls of several large animals and very small-unidentified animal bones. This is a particularly unusual collection: at archaeological sites in southern Britain dog remains rarely contribute more than 1% - 4% to the entire animal bone assemblage (Grant 1984b, 114). We should also take into consideration the sacred nature of this site and that most of the dog skeletons were quite clearly deposited as part of an elaborate ceremony.

All kinds of human-made Romano-British holes in the ground, from disused wells to cesspits, have yielded unusual animal deposits. As discussed fully in chapter 3 a case study of six Romano-British sites conducted by Michael Fulford revealed that dog burials were a salient characteristic of pit deposits at these settlements, along with the deposition of complete and near complete pottery vessels. He noted that this practice was reminiscent of the Iron Age custom of the placing of special deposits in grain storage pits and he suggested that this was perhaps a reworking of that behaviour, possibly motivated by similar beliefs. If this was the case it is interesting that dogs appear to have gained an even more prominent role in these practices over time. It was noted that in Iron Age storage pit deposits dog remains appeared with statistically significant frequency, given their relatively small numbers on sites compared to other domestic animals. However, in Romano-British pits dog burials appear to have actually become one of the defining features of these special deposits. Although the Springhead deposits are made within sacred space they are otherwise characteristically similar to the examples from Romano-British settlement pits identified by Fulford at Porchester, Neatham, Baldock, Silchester and London (Fulford 2001, 199-218). Conspicuous amounts of complete and near complete pottery vessels were also found in the pits at these sites and also in the pits at Springhead. As highlighted previously, the fact that comparable deposits were being made in both sacred and secular arenas perhaps tells us something about the nature of Romano-British religion: as appears to have been the case in the British Iron Age the distinction between sacred and secular space remained blurred. We can only speculate about the beliefs behind such deposits and no doubt they changed overtime, but it is perhaps worth noting North American Inuits place animal bodies into holes in the ice as thanks and proprietary offerings to divinities (Saunders 1995, 54-55).

4.4.5 The Springhead 'Dog Pit'

As mentioned above, during the Roman period the Iron Age ditch was utilised to form part of the boundary enclosing the rear side approach to the temple. An interruption in the length of the ditch formed an entrance into the religious compound. On the south side of this entrance a large pit was dug 4.5 metres into the chalk. When this pit was excavated it was found to contain some remarkable deposits, including the remains of an estimated 20 dogs. Pottery dating appears to confirm that the pit was dug and infilled during the second half of the second century AD. At the very bottom of the pit lay an entire bovine skeleton and the position of the remains suggested that the body had been thrown into the pit rather than lowered into it. Also in the basal deposit, just above the body of the cow/ ox, were the complete skeletons of four dogs; some of them had chains around their necks and one of them was a bitch in pup. A number of near complete pottery vessels were also associated with the animal remains. The next two layers contained the following deposits; several complete dog skeletons and the skulls of a cow, a dog and two horse jawbones in a sub-circular arrangement. Again these were associated with some near complete, large pottery vessels. Interestingly, there was virtually no natural silting between any of the layers in the pit so the deposits could be interpreted as evidence of a single ritual event or perhaps the pit was covered in some way between depositional activities. The next layer was formed by deliberate backfilling. Above the backfill the body of a very large dog, the jawbone of a horse and a male human skull were found.

4.4.5.1 The Human Skull from the Springhead 'Dog Pit' and Comparable Finds from Other Romano-British Sites

The human skull was unusual in that the jaw was still in its correct anatomical position, indicating that flesh was probably still holding it together when it was deposited. Another striking feature, further adding to the puzzle, was that none of the cervical vertebrae was present, which one wouldn't expect to be the case if a head was freshly decapitated. The nature of the skull's peculiarities suggests that the head had been subjected to a considerable degree of handling before its final interment.

The archaeology from this layer is particularly interesting because of its similarity to finds from another 2nd century AD shaft at Folly Lane, St Albans, mentioned in chapter 3. Shaft AET was one of a number of ritual shafts dug into the side of the hill that was crested by the well-known Folly Lane burial chamber and associated features that date to the mid 1st century AD. At the bottom of shaft AET the skull of an adolescent male was uncovered beside which lay the bones of a young dog. Part of a face pot and a small knife blade were found just above these deposits. The rest of the shaft was deliberately in-filled with hundreds of disarticulated cattle bones and industrial waste associated with metal and leather working. The Folly Lane skull displayed a number of unusual features, like damage to the foramen magnum that led the excavator to suggest that the skull might have been attached to the top of a pole of some sort prior to its burial. Like the Springhead skull, it had been completely separated from the rest of the skeleton. Furthermore, their were four holes in the cranium of the Folly Lane skull which had been created at the time of death or just after and it was found to have been covered with almost 100 cut marks; this excessive interference has been interpreted as a group murder/sacrifice perhaps intended to disperse and diminish the blame for the death (Mays and Steele 1996, 155-161). At the Roman military site of Vindolanda, near Hexam, recent excavation of a 2nd century ditch uncovered a battered male human skull beside which lay the body of a small dog that had also sustained severe head injuries (R. Birley 2002, Pers. Comm.).

These finds immediately raise questions about who these men were, why were they decapitated and why were they buried with dogs? We might consider that the dogs were pets of the deceased who were seen as an integral part of their identity that had to be disposed of with them. Dogs found in ancient graves have been interpreted as lifetime animal companions that were killed so that they could accompany the deceased to the afterlife. Grave furnishings were usually intended to function in the next world as they did in this, in which case if a grave required a guardian, a domestic dog was perhaps the natural choice (Philpott 1991, 204, Green 1992a, 107). Taking this idea further, they were perhaps physical symbols of actual perceived 'spirit helpers', beings that liaised with the other world on behalf of the living and the deceased: in shamanic beliefs every person has at least one guardian spirit that supports and protects them and these often take the form of animals (Cottrell 1994, 4-8, Price 2001, 3-16). Conversely their deposition with the dead humans, in some instances, could perhaps be read as an attempt to ensure that certain human spirits did not return from the underworld. Dogs have also been found in close association with the graves of decapitated and mutilated bodies at a number of Romano-British cemeteries including one at Cassington cemetery, Oxfordshire, two others in association with a decapitation and a rare cenotaph grave at Lankhills cemetery Winchester and two more with decapitated and mutilated bodies at Alington Avenue cemetery in Dorchester, Hampshire. All these cemeteries date to between the 2nd and the 4th century AD; the dog burials are fully discussed in chapter 5 (Harman et al. 1981, 145-188, Clarke 1979, 83, Davies et al. 1985, 101-110).

Figure 13. A chained dog from the top of the 'Dog Pit' at Springhead, Kent. Photograph © Channel Tunnel Rail Link

Like Cerberus, the three-headed dog who guarded Hades in Greek mythology, dogs in the beliefs of many cultures both modern and prehistoric have been employed as guardians to the entrance of the underworld, ensuring that the living did not gain access to the realm of the dead and that the dead did not get back out once they had been led there (fig. 18) (Schwartz 1997, 94-95, Virgil *The Aeineid* VI 417-423, Day Lewis 1961, 129). In the light of this it is interesting to note that at Springhead the five layers above the human skull were deliberately filled with rubbish and so too was the layer immediately below it. It is possible that the layer that contained the human skull was deliberately isolated from the other deposits because it was deemed to be in some way supernaturally radioactive. Similarly, at Folly Lane the initial interment of the human skull and dog remains were covered by two huge deposits of butchery waste, mainly from cattle (Niblett 1999, 86-87). There was one final deposit in the 'dog pit' at Springhead. In almost the very last archaeological layer at the top of the pit the body of a small dog with chains around its neck was found. Two layers of rubbish then sealed the pit. This dog was perhaps a final attempt to enclose the spirit of the decapitated man for good (fig. 13).

4.4.6 A Connection Between the Dog and Infant Burials at Springhead

A considerable number of neonate burials were uncovered during the recent excavations at Springhead, particularly in the terrace areas that overlooked the main temple complex. Their association with a site that has yielded such a large number of dog burials opens up a very interesting archaeological can of worms. As mentioned above, in the 1950s and 1960s William Penn carried out excavations in another part of Springhead, uncovering a major religious complex made up of two temples and at least six other structures. The most remarkable archaeology from the site, other than the buildings themselves, was the discovery of no less than 18 infant burials within the temple complex. None of the children were more than a few months old (Penn 1964, 176). The highly structured and ritualised nature of the four infant burials, described in 4.4.1, led to speculation that these infants were perhaps sacrificed in an attempt to placate forces behind a high incidence of neonate fatality in the vicinity (Penn 1964, 176-177). All 18 of the infant burials are believed to date to a short period of time in the 2nd century AD, although the site as a whole was in continual use from the middle of the 1st century AD to early in the 4th century AD. Overall the most intense period of activity took place at the site in the 2nd century AD; this is concurrent with the limited length of time the recently excavated temple complex was in use (Smith 2001, 101-106).

There is a small but fascinating body of comparable archaeological evidence that suggests that the dog sacrifices at Springhead were perhaps in some way connected with the infant deaths. During the 3rd and 4th centuries AD an area close to the site of the Cambridge subterranean shrine, discussed above, continued to be used for ritual activities. An alignment of ritual shafts, up to depths of at least 3.5m, were cut into the natural chalk to the north of the shrine. In the bottom of each of the shafts the burial of a dog was found in association with at least one, and in most cases two, infant burials; the latter were identifiable for the most part as stains on the wicker mats or baskets. The estimated size of the babies suggests they were all less than 10 days old at death (Alexander and Pullinger 1999, 52-58). Three burials of babies aged between a few weeks and nine months old were found interred with the skulls of two dogs and a sheep at Barton Court farm in Abingdon, Oxfordshire. Another 23 infant burials were found at the site but these were of neonates who were buried alone (Miles 1984, 15-16). At Silchester an infant and a dog were buried together in one of six unusual canine burials discovered in a group of Romano-British pits (Kennedy 2002).

4.4.6.1 The Lugnano Infant Cemetery in Italy

William Penn's suggestion that the ritualised baby burials in Temple IV at Springhead might have been part of sacrificial ceremony beseeching the resident deities to bring an end to a spate of infant mortalities is perhaps worth reconsidering in the light of discoveries at Lugnano in Italy, dating to the 4th century AD. Lugnano in Teverina overlooks the Tiber and is situated 70km north of Rome. The excavations to be discussed took place at a villa site that was occupied from around 10BC until about AD200, where after habitation became sporadic until finally ceasing early in the 5th century AD when it came to be used as an infant cemetery. In five rooms of the villa a total of 47 infant burials were found. Subsequent scientific analysis led the excavator David Soren to the conclusion that the dead were the victims of a malaria epidemic in about AD450. In circumstances similar to those at Springhead, all the bodies were buried during a brief period of time. Most of the infants were premature or newborn but six were aged between 5-6 months and one was 2-3 years old (Soren and Soren 1995, 43-48). A number of the finds associated with the Lugnano burials suggest that unusual and complex rites had taken place during the creation of the cemetery. The presence of honeysuckle, a limbless and headless doll and a raven's claw amongst the burials suggested to the excavator that pagan rituals had been carried out at the site, despite the fact that the region of Lugnano would have been Christian by the 5th century AD. High infant mortality perhaps led the population to resurrect old pagan ways out of desperation (Soren and Soren 1999, 527). Also found close to the infant burials were the bodies of 14 puppies, and a considerable proportion of the animals had been decapitated, another one had been severed in two (Soren and Soren 1999, 547-550). The choice of puppies in this ritual, obviously associated with the child burials, is perhaps significant; a corollary between the relevant ages of associated humans and animals has been noted in certain archaeological contexts. Young or small dogs also accompanied a number of the young pilgrims portrayed in the iconography from a healing shrine Fontes Sequanae at the mouth of the Seine (Aldhouse-Green 1999a, 11-13). Mother goddesses from the western provinces of Rome were sometimes depicted with infants and also diminutive lapdogs and it seems likely that both were intended to symbolise fertility and dependency: one example from Cirencester depicts three mothers, each one with a male infant and the central mother also holds a lapdog (Green 1995, 107-111). However, where the information has been made available, this pairing is not a feature of Romano-British burials of dogs and children: all the animals buried with the infants in Cambridge, discussed in the previous section, were mature individuals at death.

David Soren speculated that the severance of the puppies had perhaps been an act of purification to rid the district of a plague. Plutarch wrote that such practices were still being carried out in Greece in the 1st century AD (Plutarch *Questiones Romanae* LXVIII, Rose 1924, 148). Soren noted that rituals of purification involving severance, particularly of puppies but also of other creatures, including humans, were carried out by a considerable number of cultures in the ancient world, most notably by the Hittites (Soren and Soren 1999, 619-631, Collins 1992, 1-6). As this idea seems to have been wide spread across both time and space, one might consider that the decapitation of two of the neonates from Temple IV at Springhead was intended to function in the same way. The deposit of the human skull plus other indications of dramatic ceremony at the 'dog pit' perhaps suggest that, like at Lugnano, rather desperate measures were being undertaken to gain some control over natural events taking place. Furthermore, the aborted development of the religious complex on the banks of the spring towards the end of the 2nd century AD, was perhaps a significant spiritual gesture.

David Soren speculated that beliefs in the Classical goddess Hekate might have influenced the ritual activities that took place at Lugnano. Dogs and puppies were the goddess' animal consorts and together they looked after the souls of the prematurely dead and aided their passage to the underworld (Soren and Soren 1999, 623). Hekate may have her origins in Greek mythology but we cannot be certain that her cult did not infiltrate British consciousness: she was worshipped in Roman Rhineland. It is a well-established fact that Roman and British deities frequently merged identities and furthermore we know that Roman religion was influenced by the beliefs of people from places as far-flung as Persia and Egypt (Green 1976, 17-36, Harris and Harris 1965, 1-109). Even if the cult of Hekate was not present in Britain in an immediate form the ritual concepts relating to her cult could well have found expression in Romano-British religious activities, perhaps at Springhead.

4.4.6.2 Dogs and Infants – The Ideal Sacrifices?

Both infants and dogs may have represented the closest thing to an adult human sacrifice in antiquity; a powerful sacrifice associated with powerful beliefs. Although obviously important, infant lives were not as highly valued as adult human lives. Infant mortality was so high at the beginning of the 1st millennium AD that the Greek writer Plutarch recorded that babies were perceived as being more like a plant than a person until they shed their umbilical cord at about one week old (Plutarch *Questiones Romanae* CII, Rose 1924, 163). It has been suggested that during the Iron Age children were not thought of as fully human until they were around five years of age, when they might be considered to have developed an individual personality. Before this age, a child's death would have been viewed as unfortunate but not a tragedy (Woolf 1997, 68-74). A study of infant burials that compared age distributions from Roman Britain, Medieval Britain and modern data led Simon Mays to conclude that infanticide was almost certainly practiced in Roman Britain (Mays 1993, 883-888). Although adult human sacrifice was outlawed under Roman rule, sacrifice of a newborn infant might have been acceptable or the death of a newborn infant could perhaps have been utilised as an offering.

Dogs are one of the only animals to have become domesticated by means other than enforced servitude (Lorenz 1964, viiii). As arguably humans' closest and certainly earliest animal companion, dogs may also have been perceived as a very powerful sacrifice in antiquity. Dogs are often perceived as liminal creatures, not belonging fully to either the human or the animal world. Although they are part of the animal world their voluntary alliance with humans places them on a sort of boundary between the two realms. Furthermore, their natures are polysemous: they are hunters but also guards; they are associated with healing but also with pollution through scavenging. Their occupation of this conceptual no-man's land appears to have led to an almost universal ambiguity towards dogs. In the western world we are often flattered by their adoration, but on the other hand many people are repulsed by some of their rather less charming habits. The 'dog' as a symbol of folklore of some peoples' culture, for example the Yurok Indians of California, embodies all that is faithful and noble, but in reality the animals are not allowed close to the human habitation. However, within the same tribe if a hunting dog is killed it is sometimes given an elaborate ceremonial burial (Serpell 1995, 243-256). Similarly, as mentioned in chapter 3, the Teenek Indians of Mexico name their ill-treated pet dogs in the language of their enemies in a show of disdain. However, according to their indigenous cosmology a person should respect and look after their dog because when they die the animal will be responsible for guiding their soul to the afterlife (De Vidas 2002, 531-550).

Being a creature that is partly revered and partly loathed within the same group of people, even within the mind of the same person, has perhaps led the dog into many a sticky situation. As a high status animal/ low status pseudo-person they make the perfect sacrifice: they are a relatively unproductive domestic animal, in terms of primary produce, but they are imbued with the positive symbolism of traits such as loyalty and humility. Furthermore, the dogs' liminal position in reality has led to its association with the concept of a liminal space between life and death. Dogs are often perceived as intermediaries between these two worlds. Even in the modern day folklore of East Anglia the sighting of a large black dog known as Shuck is seen as a warning against or portent of death (Westwood 2001, 101-116). It appears that as such intermediaries an inbuilt justification for hurrying hounds along to the afterlife existed in British antiquity, where they were perhaps considered to be equally at home.

4.5 Summary

In any archaeological context, it is often difficult to distinguish between the remains of an animal that has been killed as a sacrifice and one that has died naturally or has been butchered for secular consumption. The dog remains described in the case studies in this chapter match both Alex Smith's criteria for recognising rituals involving animals within constructed sacred space and Michael Fulford's recent definition of ritual practice, which is 'an act of a repetitive nature that also displays irrational characteristics'.

Dog bones were present in the bone assemblages from over half of the 18 Romano-British temple sites surveyed for this study. They were usually found in small numbers and perhaps significantly no incidence of butchery was noted. However, in instances where dog remains are present in considerable numbers, characteristics of their deposition reflect the importance of their role in orchestrated rituals at these sites. In particular, incidences of dog skeletons being found in association with human skulls, infant burials and complete or near complete pots are notable at Romano-British sites of both sacred and secular nature. That associations between these objects are not coincidental, but rather represent part of suite of objects commonly used in ritual activities, is demonstrated quite irrefutably by discoveries made during recent excavations at Springhead, Kent, particularly those from the 'dog pit' that was dug at an entrance way to the temple area. The finds from the 'dog pit' included the skeletons of at least ten dogs, some wrapped in chains, numerous pottery vessels and a human skull. The lack of natural silting between layers in the pit suggests that these deposits might have been part of one depositional event.

One of the most fascinating aspects of the association between dog skeletons and human skulls is the fact that the latter have, in most cases, been brutalised in some way. Whether this Springhead skull and the numerous other examples given above were sacrificial victims or were killed as an act of judicial punishment is a matter of speculation, as is the significance of the accompanying dog or dogs skeletons. However, one might imagine the inclusion of the dog as a safeguard, an attempt by the living to ensure that a potentially dangerous spirit remained entombed.

The infant burials, found at both Springhead temple complexes, might also be the remains of sacrifices. Studies have shown that it is highly likely that infanticide was practiced in Roman Britain and its incidence perhaps doubled as an opportunity to make a high status offering. A number of factors perhaps contributed to domesticated dogs also being a preferred choice of sacrificial victim, including their close proximity to humans and their positive symbolic role in contemporary iconographic images. The latter is particularly visible in their association with hunting deities and mother goddesses. For example, a large dog is portrayed in a united group with its master and prey in a stone statue found in a Roman well at Southwark cathedral, London. Passive lapdogs appear as an attribute of mother goddess iconography, for instance a seated mother goddess with an accompanying lapdog was found in Canterbury, Kent (Merrifield 1986, 85-92, Jenkins 1953, 131-133). For a full discussion about such representations see chapter 6.

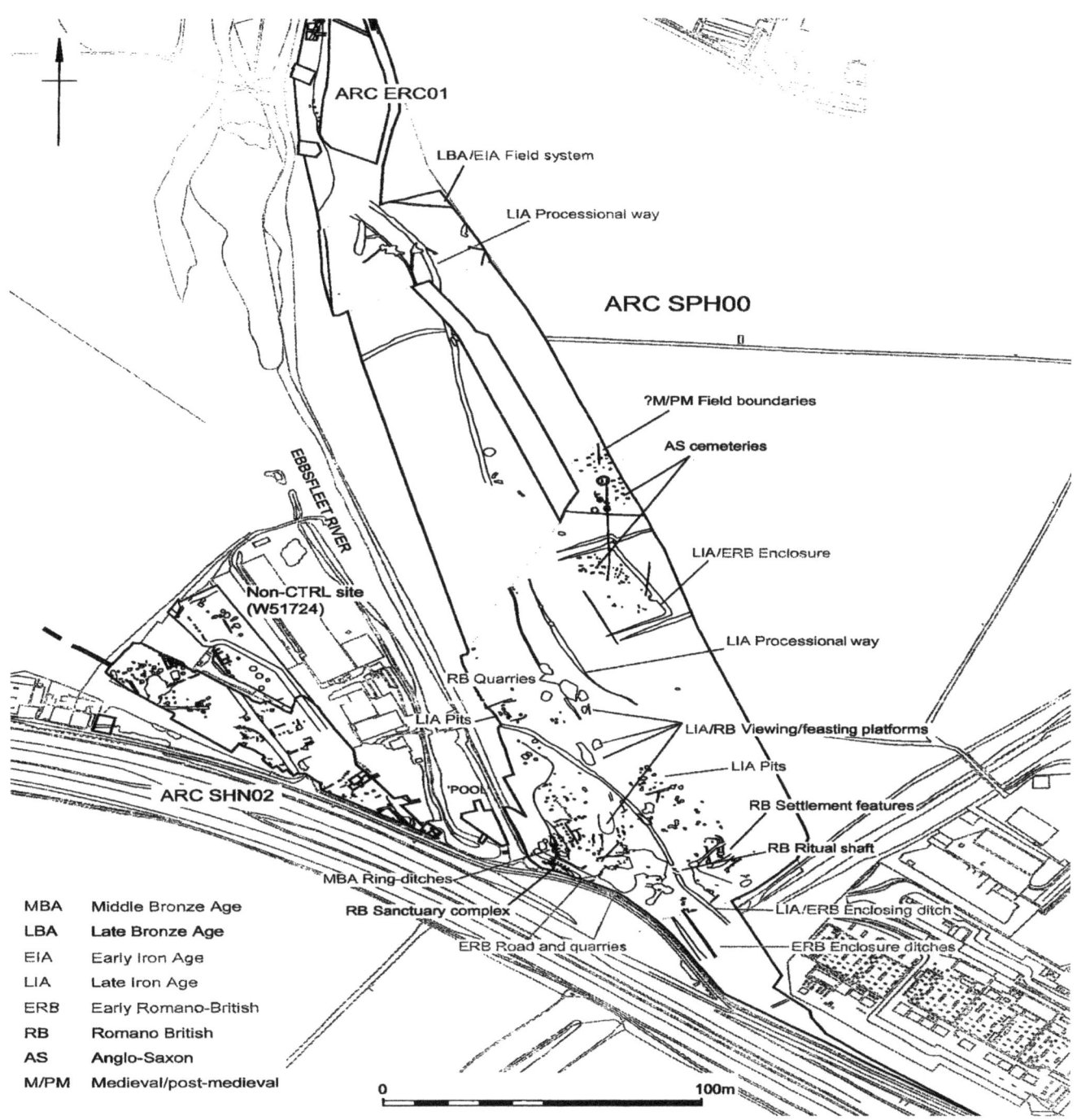

Figure 14. Diagram of the area of recent excavations at Springhead, Kent© Channel Tunnel Rail Link. Note: Scale = 200m, not 100m as shown.

Chapter 5

Domesticated Dogs found in association with Romano-British Human Burials

5.1 Introduction

There are numerous reasons why animal remains are found within human burials. They could represent food offerings to ancestors or deities to ensure safe passage to the afterlife for the deceased. Joints of meat might be included in a burial to sustain the dead on their journey to the next world; they could also represent part of an animal that was eaten at a funerary feast where the deceased was supplied with food because they were believed to be spiritually present (Green 1992a, 107). From the physical remains alone it is impossible to tell which of these beliefs provided the motivation for an interment. Animals may also be included in burials as a demonstration of wealth or power: pagan Scandinavian ship burials often contained large numbers of domestic animals, including dogs and horses, as well as exotic artefacts to reflect the high status of the deceased (Ellis-Davidson 1982, 113-132). An animal skeleton in a human burial might also be the remains of the person's lifetime animal companion. This chapter focuses on the remains of domestic dogs found accompanying Romano-British human burials and discusses possible interpretations for some of the unusual finds from this fascinating area of the British archaeological record. The animal bone assemblages analysed for this chapter came from eleven Romano-British cemeteries and numerous isolated human burials. These sites were chosen because dog bones were found to be present. The table 3 below outlines details of the animal bones found at the cemeteries.

5.2 Dog Burials from Romano-British Cemeteries and Comparable Finds

5.2.1. Dog Burials as Food Offerings

Animal remains interpreted as food offerings have been found in human graves dating to the Romano-British period with the regularity of other common contemporary grave furnishings like coins and hob nailed boots (Philpott 1991, 200-207, Woodward 1992, 81-97). Information about the animal bone assemblages from Romano-British burials where dog bone was present were examined for this study. From these collections only one dog bone was encountered that displayed a cut-mark attributable to butchery, rather than skinning. The mark was on a right mandible found within the infill of a grave from a roadside cemetery at West Tenter Street, London, dating to between the early 2nd and mid 4th centuries AD (Whytehead 1986, 64-65). As even this specimen was not found in immediate association with the burial it seems reasonable to conclude that dogs were rarely, if ever, interred as food offerings in Romano-British graves; similarly there is little evidence for their consumption as part of the everyday diet of the time.

5.2.2 The Canine Remains from Grave 400 at Lankhills, Roman Cemetery, Winchester - Associated Finds and Comparanda

One of the most fascinating examples of canine presence in a human grave at a Romano-British cemetery was found in association with Grave 400 at Lankhills, Winchester. A young adult domestic dog, comparable in size to a modern Labrador, was found lying on its back, on top of an empty human size coffin in the deepest grave at the cemetery. The dog bones were extremely well preserved, as were the other skeletons in the cemetery, which led to the conclusion that there had never been a body in this coffin. The partial remains of another fully grown dog, discovered in the in-fill, add to the complexity of Grave 400; the ends of the animal's vertebrae had been tied together to form a circle (Clarke 1979, 83). Neither of the dogs appears to have had any extraordinary, natural skeletal features (Harcourt 1979b, 244-245).

It has been suggested that Grave 400 was in fact a cenotaph burial, where the dog was buried in place of an absent person, perhaps its owner. The provision of a cenotaph might have been influenced by Roman beliefs in Classical mythology. In *The Aeneid*, Virgil wrote that if a person did not receive a proper burial they would be doomed to walk in limbo between the living and the dead for 100 years (Virgil *The Aeneid* - V1. 323-330, Rushton Fairclough 1918, 529). The presence of large areas of dark earth in the in-fill, interpreted as lumps of turf, might support the cenotaph theory: writing in the last century BC, Cicero, the Roman statesman remarked on the importance of the use of good turf in burials carried out under unusual circumstances and cenotaph rites. It has been suggested that that the grass sods within the fill of Grave 400 were included to encourage the vitality of the deceased to their allotted resting place. Similarly, the sacrifice and dismemberment of the dog in the in-fill was perhaps linked to ideas about regeneration and life-force through the spilling of its blood on the ground (MacDonald 1979, 421-423).

The presence of an animal alone in a human style grave is unusual, but not unique in the Romano-British archaeological record. At a cemetery at York Road in Leicester the body of a small, robust dog was found alone in the centre of a human sized grave and in association with a group of three 4th century human burials. Perhaps significantly the backfill of the dog burial contained several pieces of human cranium. However, there is a possibility that these were not deliberate deposits, but rather intrusive elements from later gully features that truncated the burial (Baxter 2002, Pers. Comm.). A stone-lined human inhumation grave was found next to a 4th century precinct wall at the site where Stanwick Roman villa in Northamptonshire once stood. A stone cist containing the bones of a small dog was found close to the burial (Frere 1986, 397). In the grounds of King's School, Worcester another dog burial was found with sherds from a single ceramic vessel and iron fragments. The burial was associated with seven human graves that date from some time between the 3rd and 4th centuries AD (Brown and Wichbold 1991, 1-8).

Table 3. Details of animal bone assemblages from Romano-British cemeteries reviewed for this study

Cemetery	Date as Described in Report	Number of Human Burials Excavated	Animal Species Present in Burials
Dunstable, Bedfordshire	3rd – 5th centuries AD	50 human burials in ditched boundary.	4 horses * 1 dog *
Lankhills, Winchester	4th century AD	In access of 450 human graves.	2 dogs * 4 bank voles * 1 sheep bone 5 birds*
Yarnton Worton Rectory Farm	Late Roman	22 human burials	1 dog*
King's School, Worcester	Late Roman	10 human burials	1 dog*
Cassington, Oxfordshire	3rd – 5th centuries AD	72 human burials	1 dog*
York Road, Leicester	4th century AD	91 human burials	1 dog*
Alington Avenue, Hampshire	Late 2nd – Early 4th centuries AD	58 human burials	743 animal bones from grave fills. 10 examples interpreted as possible grave furnishings - 2 dogs * 1 sheep 6 domestic fowl * 1 fish
Little Spittle, Ilchester, Somerset	4th century AD	43 human burials	1 bird * 1 dog * 1 horse 1 sheep
Northern Area of Railway Station, York, Yorkshire	2nd – Late 4th century AD	Exact figures not supplied. Described as groups and series.	1 horse * 2 dogs *
Asthall, Oxfordshire	2nd – 4th century AD	13 human burials	35 dog paw bones
Eastern Cemetery, London	Romano-British	255 human burials	46 cattle bones 7 sheep/goat bones 13 pig bones 22 horse bones 1 horse* 4 dog bones 1 dog* 1 deer* 1 cat bone 8 domestic fowl bones 1 duck bone 4 fish bones

*Key * = Complete animal skeletons or substantial articulated bone groups*

Grave 400 at Lankhills appeared to have been undisturbed since it was originally dug in the 4th century AD, although another separate burial Grave 427 cut it, using the empty grave's northern and eastern sides as its own. Grave 427 contained the body of a young man who had been decapitated (Clarke 1979, 421-422). Decapitation was not a very unusual feature of contemporary burials, but their association with domestic dogs is not commonplace. However, there are enough examples of this combination to cause pause for thought, particularly when one considers how often this pairing occurs elsewhere in the Romano-British archaeological record. Details of the numerous examples from sites, including Sprinthead, Kent; Folly Lane, St Albans; Vindolanda Fort, Hexham; Colchester Roman fortress, Essex; Alveston, Bristol; Greyhound Yard, Dorchester and Cannon Street, London have been given in chapters 3 and 4. Although these examples alone do not sufficiently support the theory that the dog from Grave 400 at Lankhills and the decapitated burial in adjacent Grave 427 were associated elements in the same funerary ceremony, as mentioned above mutilated and decapitated corpses buried with dogs have also been found at a number of other Romano-British cemeteries. Excavations at the Romano-British cemetery at Alington Avenue, Dorchester uncovered 58 adult inhumations, two of which were interred with the canine bodies. One man had been buried without his head and the body of a small dog had been placed next to his coffin. Elsewhere on the site, the remains of a badly mutilated male were found buried in a prone position. A large part of his right arm was missing, his left arm and skull were badly damaged and a dog had been placed alongside his legs inside the grave (Davies et al. 1985, 101-110). Initially it was thought that the dog had also been decapitated because its head was slightly displaced from its body. However, the archaeo-zoologist Mark Maltby has since suggested that this anomaly most likely occurred through post depositional disturbance because the cervical vertebrae did not exhibit cut marks (Maltby 1988, 11). A decapitated male from Cassington Roman cemetery, Oxfordshire was also found with the body of a dog. It has been suggested that in pagan Romano-British burial rites bodies were decapitated or laid prone as a final act of indignity for some offence committed during life (Philpott 1991, 84-88). The killing of a companion animal closely associated with them was perhaps further insult and a means of destroying part of their perceived identity. A late 4th century prone burial was recovered from a ditch at a Roman cemetery in Dunstable and a dog had been placed just above the body (Matthews 1981, 22).

As mentioned in chapter 4, decapitation as a Romano-British burial rite has been interpreted as an attempt to stop the dead walking and harming the living, which was believed to be a possibility if a person died under circumstances considered spiritually dangerous, perhaps through sacrifice or an act of tyranny or judicial punishment (Philpott 1991, 84-88). If this was the case, in these instances the addition of the dogs to guard over the deceased may have been a further precautionary measure. Undoubtedly, the majority of dead described above had been subjected to extremely violent treatment, one might even say overkill. In Miranda Aldhouse-Green's study on the subject of sacrifice it was found that excessive brutalisation of the victim or material offering was a salient characteristic of such rituals. Whether a sacrifice was animate or inanimate, the brute force applied in its destruction appears to have been an important part of its successful ceremonial transference to another world (Aldhouse-Green 2001, 50-56). That these skulls belonged to victims of sacrifice is certainly a possibility worth considering; in some cases this may have been a response to the unsettled political environment of the 1st century AD, that would ultimately have affected all areas of life, including the spiritual (Aldhouse-Green 2004b, 195-198).

The key difference between the mutilated and decapitated humans with canine interments from varied contexts and those from Romano-British cemeteries is the chronology. Whereas all of the former date from between the 1st century AD and the early 3rd century AD, the examples from cemeteries date from the 3rd century onwards: this time lapse perhaps accounts for the change of situation. When the Swedish archaeologist Lars Larsson examined the evidence for mortuary practice at the Late Mesolithic site of Skateholm, in Southern Sweden, he was struck by the variety of ways that dog remains appeared in the human cemeteries. Some dogs were buried in richly furnished graves of their own, others were carefully buried with humans, some were thrown haphazardly into human graves and still more were found dismembered in the infill of graves. Larsson speculated that one explanation for the variation in treatment of the animals was that the symbolic language used in the funerary ceremonies had changed over time. Symbolic language develops and changes through time in the same way as the spoken word and similarly the root of a symbol can become lost, although its presence in conversation/ ceremony is still deemed essential. Larsson also highlighted that symbolism always has shades of meaning for those who experience it; some elements of ceremony and ritual would have been coherently understood by everybody and other parts may have been pertinent to just a few. These factors perhaps contribute to the way that treatment of dogs in burial practices appears to change at Skateholm; unfortunately accurate dating information was not available to support these hypotheses (Larsson 1991, 33-38). Decapitation and the need to place a dog with the victim may have found its way into later Romano-British burial practice in formal cemeteries, but the original purpose for doing so may have become distorted with time, leading to variation from earlier practices. Somewhat bizarrely Larsson also noted that, at Skateholm, a considerable proportion of the dead who were buried in the same graves as complete dogs had been killed violently or dismembered. The independent development of these two undeniably similar burial practices involving dogs, over a period of several thousand years and a distance of several thousand miles, although intriguing, is beyond the scope of this thesis.

In his study of burial practices in Roman Britain, Robert Philpott looked at concepts surrounding sacrifice as transference of life-force for an explanation of decapitation; this may be a useful area to explore regarding the role of the dogs in these burials. Sacrificial acts were often intended to transfer life-force from the victim to the supernatural realms and in exchange life-force from the supernatural realms would be transferred to a beneficiary on Earth. Philpott suggested that the decapitation of a corpse might still have been considered a suitable sacrifice in terms of transference of life-force that was intended to benefit another deceased person. He argued that if we consider that death was probably perceived as a journey with different stages, rather than a single event, then the recently deceased may have been held to retain sufficient vitality to offer the gods in exchange for the safe passage of another deceased person to the afterlife (Philpott 1991, 84-88). However, if the newly dead really were believed to be in a transient state between this world and the next, and still in possession of a degree of life-force, there seems to be no reason why the decapitation of a dead person should only be of benefit to another deceased person. The intended recipient could still be amongst the living, perhaps someone sick that just a small degree of life-force might save. The sacrifice of the dogs alongside the decapitation was perhaps an attempt to regain the correct balance of life-force for the mutilated corpses; in Graeco-Roman belief violent, unusual or untimely death was believed to hinder ones journey to the afterlife and it seems likely that ante- or even post- mortem decapitation would fit this category (Philpott 1991, 84-88). Why a dog would be considered a fitting substitute for human life-force under these circumstances cannot be said for certain, but could possibly be due to their close relationship with humans and/ or a perceived role as guardians or guides in the after-life.

5.2.3 Other Dog Remains from Human Burials in Romano-British Cemeteries

Not all the dog and human burials from Romano-British sites appear to be quite as sinister as those described above, but one cannot discount the possibility that the acts were similarly motivated. A dog was found within a human grave at the small Roman cemetery at Worton Rectory Farm, Yarnton (Hey 1991, 86-92). Unlike the burials discussed so far it appears both the animal and the person were complete and articulated. A burial of a woman and an adult dog, dating to the late 4th century AD, was found at Ilchester's Roman cemetery, in Somerset (fig. 15). The deliberate arrangement of their bodies was particularly notable as it could be described as sympathetic, perhaps suggesting that there was a relationship between the two in life and in the event of its mistress' death the animal was killed so it could accompany her in the next world. The dog lay on its left side in the grave, alongside and facing the woman's legs and its front limbs had been folded one over the other. The woman was laid supine with her arms folded across her chest and her head was turned in the direction of the dog (Anon 1975, 83, Everton 1982, 263-267). According to Pliny the Elder sacrificing companion animals was practised during the period under discussion and in *The Iliad* two of Patroclus' pet dogs were placed on his funeral pyre for this purpose (Pliny *Natural Histories* XI: 150, Toynbee 1971, 50, Homer *The Iliad* 200-208, Kirk and Fitzgerald 2004). Numerous representations of people with dogs, that were quite possibly their actual pet, feature on Roman funerary monuments. These images often portray a very affectionate bond between the two subjects (Toynbee 1973, 108-121).

Figure 15. The burial of a woman and a dog at Ilchester Roman cemetery. Photograph © Peter Leach.

5.2.4 Structured Deposition of Dogs and Horses at Romano-British Cemeteries

Annie Grant recognised a phenomenon she termed special animal deposits in the fills of a considerable number of the grain storage pits from Danebury Iron Age hillfort in Hampshire. For a full discussion on this subject see chapter 2. Dog and horse bones only accounted for a very small percentage of the overall faunal assemblage from Danebury, but despite this both animals appeared in special animal deposits in statistically high numbers. Furthermore, they were found together in these ritual deposits far more often than might be expected (Grant 1984a, 533-543). Placing structured deposits in human made holes in the ground as part of a sacrificial ceremony is thought to have continued in Roman Britain, although the preferred choice of species and animal parts appears to have changed (Merrifield 1987, 22-57, Fulford 2001, 199-218). A survey of bone assemblages from Romano-British settlements in the Hampshire area was carried out for this study (see chapter 3). Amongst other things, it revealed that complete dog skeletons became one of the most prominent characteristics of special deposits in the Roman period, whilst horse bones become even more of a rarity. However, there are a few occasions where both species have been found together in Romano British cemeteries. In *Eboracum*, Roman York, numerous burials thought to date to between the 2nd and 4th centuries AD were found on an area of land close to the present day railway station. One burial of a human and a dog was found close to the coffin of a woman who had been coated with gypsum. More remarkable still were the bodies of a man, a horse and a dog found together. They were buried beneath a mass of puddled clay that is thought to have been the core or the base of a monument that had been erected directly above the deposit. Although these animals may have been the man's companions it may also be significant that these animals were of the two species allied with humans in the hunt; the presence of the monument suggests that the burial may have been symbolically complex, particularly given its proximity to a large number of other graves (Anon 1962, 85). Hunting was not simply a popular sport during the Roman period, it was also a spiritual act associated with fertility and regeneration. The positive symbolism of the hunt was perhaps further enhanced by its origin as an essential act of human survival (Webster 1986, 43-51).

The Eastern cemetery of Roman London was found within an area defined by linear ditches and gullies that may have originally been used for agricultural purposes. As mentioned in chapter 3, a large pit at the site was found to contain the skeletons of a dog, a horse and a young red deer, arranged nose to tale in a circular formation (fig. 16). The burial cannot be accurately dated, but it was certainly the earliest feature in a stratigraphic sequence that was cut by a number of Romano-British burials. It was suggested that the animals were sacrificed to prepare, in some way, the ground for the human inhumations (Barber and Bowsher 2000, 17-21). Again, it does not seem unreasonable to suggest that this interment was intended to invoke the more complex levels of hunting symbolism.

The significance of the circular arrangement of the animals' bodies might have been as important as the choice of species. As symbols, for obvious reasons, circles are universally connected with continuation and consequently cycles of birth, life, death and new life or rebirth. Circularity also serves to deny hierarchy and to emphasise interdependence; the perception of the chase as a reciprocal act between hunters and hunted in European antiquity is perhaps illustrated by the hunting friezes on some Early Iron Age pots, such as one from Matzhausen, Germany (Green 1992a, 48). A similar scene is the theme of an engraving on a Romano-British bronze belt plate found with several pieces of military equipment during excavations at Chapel Street, Chichester; it is believed to date to the 1st century AD (fig. 16) (Wilson 1970, 302-303). Circles have cosmic connotations regarding the passage of time, the inevitable rising and setting of the sun and annual cycles of animal and crop fertility, that human life ultimately depends on (Green 1991, 61, Becker 2000). For example, solar wheels were a feature of sun symbolism, which was associated with fertility and regeneration in the Western provinces of Rome (Green 1989, 75-86). It is plausible that the circular, eternal chase represented by the tri-part animal burial in the Eastern cemetery, London symbolised regeneration on a number of levels, which would explain its presence at a cemetery site and throw light on a number of other similar Romano-British animal deposits found in clearly spiritually charged contexts.

As discussed fully in chapter 4, one of the structured animal deposits found in a 2nd century subterranean shrine at Ridgeons gardens in Cambridge comprised three small hunting dogs. Each of the animals' heads was in contact with the head or back paws of the one in front, creating a circle with their bodies. Furthermore, each dog wore an iron collar with a link chain that was arranged radiating out from the skeletons, forming a swirling spiral pattern on the floor (Alexander and Pullinger 1999, 45-47). A number of shafts at a 2nd century farmstead at Keston in Kent appear to have been deliberately dug to receive votive offerings (see chapter 3 for details). In one of these features, named the Great Shaft, the complete skeletons of two horses and an ox were arranged nose to tale in a circle formation; the bodies of domestic dogs were found in the same level, placed against the shaft wall (Philp et al. 1999, 14-35). Although there is perhaps not enough evidence to suggest that these circular arrangements of animal skeletons are a non-coincidental trend they are certainly worth noting in terms of the interpretation of future finds.

5.2.5 Domestic Dogs with Romano-British Cremations

Although rare in the Romano-British archaeological record, dog remains have been found with human cremation burials. Fragments of unburnt dog bone were found in an adult, probably male, human cremation from one of two burial pits discovered in Grange Road, Winchester in the late 1960s. The grave, believed to date to the late 1st century AD, also contained ceramics, jewellery and several unburnt bones from a large ruminant (Biddle 1967, 224-250). A late 1st century or early 2nd century AD chalk burial pit containing a human cremation was found in Red Church Field, Linton, Cambridgeshire; the remains were accompanied by dog bones, pottery and a metal stud decorated with the mask of a lion. The stud was one of a type that were often used to decorate boxes, but it was postulated that it may have come from the dog's collar, which had since perished in the grave (Liversidge 1977, 15-38). It is notable that in both of these instances the dog bones themselves were not cremated, indicating that the despatch of the animal and the cremation itself were two separate elements of a multi-phased funerary ceremony.

5.2.6 A Dog Pelt Blanket from a Romano-British Inhumation Grave

A small cemetery dating from at least the 2nd century AD was found at the Romano-British roadside settlement of Asthall, Oxfordshire. In one of the graves a number of the small bones from a dog's front paws and one back paw were found lying close to the shoulders and feet of a child, aged between four and six years old at death (fig. 17). The cut marks on the animal bones were comparable with those associated with skinning. The evidence suggests that the child had been wrapped in a dog skin blanket when laid to rest (Booth et al. 1996, 382-387). The burnt phalanges of a bear found amongst the human remains of an adult male cremation from Welwyn Garden City, Hertfordshire, were similarly interpreted as the residue of an animal skin shroud; the burial dated to the Late Iron Age (Collis 1998, 172-173). There is some written evidence for the use of dog skins in Western Europe during late prehistory: Diodorus Siculus recorded that the Celts dined seated on wolf or dog pelts (Diodorus Siculus V. 28.4, Green 1992a, 99). In Britain, cut marks that are believed to be the result of skinning were found on a number of dog bones at sites excavated during the Danebury Environs Programme, including, the Iron Age enclosed settlements at Nettlebank Copse, Suddern Farm and New Buildings, Hampshire (Hamilton 2000, 109).

The fact that the dog skin was included in the grave at all suggests that its deposition held a degree of significance for those who buried the child, but whether or not the choice of particular animal or species symbolised something in itself is unclear. One might speculate that its presence as a secondary product may have some how diminished the animals usual potent symbolic value. Against this, it is perhaps worth considering that dogs'

teeth pierced for suspension have been found in spiritually charged contexts dating to the Romano-British period on several occasions. As discussed in chapter 4, number of dog's teeth, that appear to have been strung together to form a necklace, were found in a 4th century ditch feature at the religious complex at Ivy Chimney, Witham, Essex. The dog teeth were found next to the skeletal torso of a sheep and a horse skull; the arrangement of the bones suggested that some care had been taken in their deposition (Turner 1999, 49). A single pierced dog's tooth was found with a number of amulets made from different materials in a 3rd century inhumation grave at Butt Road cemetery, Colchester (Henig 1984a, 243-246). Interestingly, two pendants made from a number of dog paw bones were found in pits within an Iron Age enclosure at Bramdean, Hampshire (fig. 17) (Perry 1982, 57-74). These dog remains could of course simply represent offerings of jewellery and the material need not be of significance. However, talismans made from animal parts have been a ubiquitous part of material culture throughout world history; such ornaments are often totemic, representing qualities of the species itself (Budge 1930, 1-33). Writing in the 1st century AD, Pliny the Elder recorded numerous uses for canine amulets including keeping childish terrors at bay and remedying certain fevers (Meaney 1981, 135). We might consider that the Asthall dog's pelt was intended to function as a form of protection.

Figure 16. Hunting frieze on a Romano-British bronze belt buckle found in Chapel Street, Chichester. The structured burial of a dog, a horse and a deer from the Eastern Roman Cemetery, London. Photograph © MoLAS.

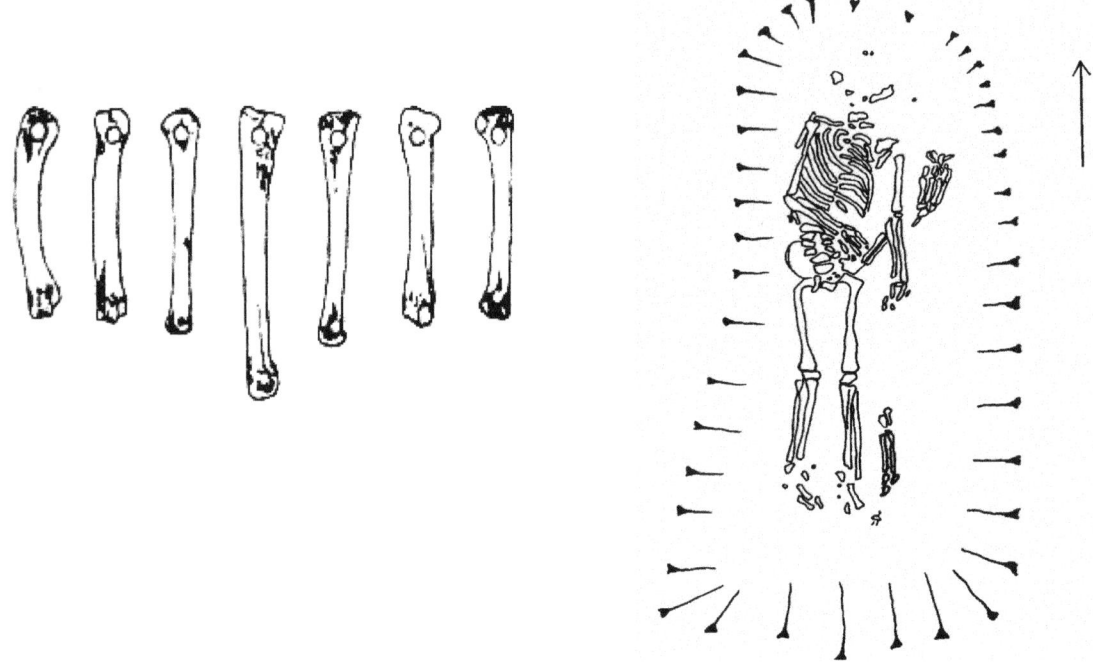

Figure 17. Bones from dog paws pierced for suspension from Iron Age Bramdean, Hampshire (left) *After* Perry, Proceedings of the Hampshire Field Club Archaeological Society 1984, 69. A diagram of an infant's grave from Asthall, Oxfordshire (right) – the child's body was wrapped in a dog skin blanket.
Diagram © Oxford Archaeological Unit

5.3 An Association Between Domestic Dogs and Infant Burials in Roman Britain

Although they are not a feature of Romano-British cemeteries, the number of infant burials found in association with structured dog burials is a notable feature in the archaeological record of the period. There are several reasons why this connection may be of significance in terms of our understanding of the spiritual beliefs and ritual practices of the time.

Infants were frequently buried within the boundaries of Roman settlements rather than formally designated burial areas: there is some evidence from historical texts that Roman newborns were not perceived as being fully human until they reached a certain age and therefore were perhaps not deemed to be entitled to, or considered to be in need of the same burial rites as their elders (Plutach *Quaestiones Romanae* CII, Rose 1924, 163). Ethnographic studies carried out in the 20th century revealed that this attitude is by no means unique to the time or location that Plutarch describes (Ucko 1969, 262-280, Esmonde Cleary 2000, 127-142). Furthermore, as mentioned in chapter 4, although infant mortality would have been far higher than it is today, a survey of the evidence that compared age at death profiles of infants from Roman Britain, medieval and modern contexts suggests that infanticide was being practised in this country during the Roman period. In view of this the dogs may have been sacrificed in expiation (Mays 1993, 883-888). At Silchester *Insula IX* one of the numerous structured dog burials was found with the body of an infant (Kennedy 2002). During excavations of one corner of a paddock system at Barton Court farm, Abingdon in Oxfordshire at least 26 infant graves were found. Two of the children were interred with dog skulls and a third was associated with the skull of a sheep. As these three infants were older than the others, who were all new newborn, it was suggested that their ages had perhaps contributed to the decision to include the animals in the graves (Miles 1984, 15-16). In Cambridge, a group of at least thirteen 3rd century ritual shafts were found to contain stains and remains from newborn infants, buried in wicker baskets. Small hunting dogs, comparable in size to modern fox terriers, were found in the southern corner of each of burial shafts. Some of the baskets containing the infants were placed immediately above one another, suggesting that their deaths had occurred during a limited period of time (Alexander and Pullinger 1999, 53-58).

As discussed in chapter 4, although the despatch of unwanted infants and dogs may have been considered a practical act on one level, their execution may have also been taken as occasion to make a sacrificial offering to the gods. Although an infant's life was not as highly regarded as that of an adult, it seems likely that they would have been perceived as having a higher status than animals because of their root in humanity. Similarly, domestic dogs may have been considered, in some way, superior to other beasts because of their close and generally unfettered proximity to humans. Perhaps infant and dog burials have repeatedly been found in association with each other because they were both considered to be high status sacrifices and therefore deemed to be particularly appropriate offerings in certain types of ceremony. Eleanor Scott noted a connection between infant burials and corn driers at Romano-British settlements and speculated that the interments may have been linked to fertility rites. A baby's form obviously represents human fertility, but also symbolises fertility *per se* and their deposition may have been intended to encourage the regeneration of crops and animals (Scott 1991, 115-121). During the Roman festival of *Robigalia* rusty coloured suckling puppies were sacrificed to the deity Mildew or *Robigo* in order to protect the crops from blight. A ritual known as *sacrum canarium* or dog sacrifice was carried out by priests in Rome around the same time of year as *Robigalia*. In this ceremony the canine offering was intended to appease Sirius, the dog star, before the onset of the potentially agriculturally destructive 'dog days' in August (Columella De Re Rustica X. 342-343, Forster and Heffner 1954, Ovid The Fasti IV. 907, Frazer 1929, Jenkins 1957, 60-78).

In iconography from the Western provinces of Rome representations of infants were amongst the fertility emblems commonly associated with mother goddesses, as were corn, fruit and lapdogs. An example from Cirencester, Gloucestershire depicts three women seated together, each one accompanied by a small boy and the central mother also holds a small dog (Green 1995, 105-116). Fertility symbolism was perhaps created with the physical remains of infants and dogs in Roman Britain, as well as with conventional artistic materials. There is further evidence from historical texts that dogs and infants were sometimes closely associated with the same deities and fertility rites. In the 1st century AD Plutarch recorded that because of the ease of the creatures' labour Romans sacrificed bitches to Geneta Mata and Eilioneia, goddesses who were associated with childbirth (Plutarch *Questiones Romanae* LII, Rose 1924, 142). In Classical Greece the goddess Hekate's sphere of influence encompassed the well being of children and monthly purification ceremonies performed in her honour involved the consumption of dogs' flesh (Plutarch *Questiones Romanae* LXVIII, Rose 1924, 142, Jenkins 1957, 60-78, Ovid *The Fasti* I.389, Frazer 1929, 414, Tertullian *De Anima* 57, Scott 1999, 118).

Although geographically remote from Roman Britain, it is interesting to note that large numbers of dogs and infants have been found together on several notable occasions elsewhere in the European archaeological record. As discussed in chapter 4, at Lugnano in Italy 47 infant skeletons, the majority of which were either premature or new born babies, were found buried amongst the remains of a villa. The skeletons of 14 puppies, a number of which had been beheaded, were found in close association with the newborns' skeletons (Soren and Soren 1995, 43-48, Scott 1999). In Athens, Greece 85 near complete dog skulls and the bones of 175 newborn infants were retrieved from a well dating to the 1st century BC. Mass starvation was offered as a possible explanation for such a dramatic loss of lives (Preston Day 1984, 21-32).

5.4 Dogs and Death – A Timeless and Worldwide Connection

Associations between dogs and death have arisen in the spiritual beliefs and myths of societies everywhere from modern East Anglia to ancient China (White 1991, 161-179, Westwood 2001, 101-116). Domestic dogs placed within the burials of Romano-British humans were perhaps present in the same capacity as other grave furnishings: they were intended to function in the afterlife as they did on earth. However, the psychology behind the choice of this animal in particular may be far more complex than this simple explanation allows. There appear to be multiple independent linkages between dogs and death, and because there is more than one conceptual thread it is quite easy for them to become tangled. Perhaps the most important thing to note, when attempting to unravel the resultant knots, is that world myths associated with dogs and death generally fall into two categories, either dogs are portrayed as guides or as fierce guards; although ultimately these two concepts are interrelated as both involve authority or helping symbolism (Schwartz 1997, 94).

The symbolism attached to many earthly objects is believed to stem from our worldly experience of the subject (Stevens 1998, 22-35). We see dogs as both guides and guards because we are aware of their keen senses, loyalty and often, particular affiliation to one person and also their capacity for aggressive territoriality. The existence of dual symbolic roles for the domestic dog, in association with one facet of existence, is in-keeping with everyday human ambivalence towards the species that has been observed in many modern and ancient societies. In the same society, even in the mind of an individual, dogs can be loved at one moment and abhorred the next; there are many ethnographic examples of this ambiguity towards the species but we do not have to stray from Western culture to find a simple illustration (Serpell 1995, 246-256). In America homeless, unwanted and dangerous dogs can be taken to a place referred to as a humane shelter to be destroyed. The result is that thousands of dog carcases need to be disposed of each year. An enterprising businessperson from Korea, where dogs are a part of the daily diet, offered to buy the bodies from the humane shelters to be sold as meat in their own country. The proposition was turned down flat by humane society representatives and the somewhat confused Koreans were left wondering why dogs that were apparently treated with such little regard should suddenly become so precious (Katcher and Beck 1991, 265-278). For some, the consumption of a 'companion' animal is viewed as similar to cannibalism, which is, and has been, considered the ultimate taboo in many societies past and present, because not only is the victim's identity destroyed through mutilation, they are reduced to just a piece of meat, a source of power for enemy and ultimately to human waste (Aldhouse-Green 2001, Harris 1991, 147-166). For other people such sensitivity about animals is almost as incomprehensible. Human perceptions of domestic dogs in beliefs about the supernatural world are often equally equivocal.

5.4.1 Dogs as Guards and Guides to the After-Life

Hades' three-headed guard dog, Cerberus, from Classical literature is perhaps the most well known canine sentinel of the underworld (Graves 1960, 514-520). Native American Indians the Huron also tell of a savage dog who guards the final river crossing to the next life, whilst the Aztecs believed that a certain breed of small yellow dog would wait to meet their lifetime owners on the 'other-side' to help them across yet another watery boundary. In some traditions, for example, the North American Delaware and the Tualipang of Guiana, dogs do not merely guard the entrance to the afterlife, they actually stand in judgement of humans according to how they treated their animals during their life-time (Schwartz 1997, 93-124). Another confusing element of dog and death symbolism is our subjective view of a guard of a portal, who can be perceived as either a threat or a welcome, and a protector of those on the inside or on the outside (White 1991, 1-21). The domestic dog's role as an earthly guardian was recognised in the Latin writer Columella's work on agriculture dating to the 1st century AD: he devoted a passage to praising the domestic dog as an avenger and defender (Columella *De Re Rustica* VII. XII. 1-3, Forster and Heffner 1954, 305-307). It is interesting to note that guide dogs and guard dogs do not confront each other in these visions of the after-life; the animal's role is usually one thing or the other. However, when the German goddess Holle or Holla guides the dead to the underworld, her canine companion helps out by snapping at the new arrivals, rather than gently directing them (Menache 1997, 1-14).

The dog's role as a hunter/ killer and carrion eater also directly connects the species with death. From historical texts and contemporary portrayals of the sport in the art and iconography from Britain and the continent during Roman rule, we know that their hunting role was certainly not viewed as a negative one in antiquity. In fact it would appear that being a vehicle for the transition between life and death in the chase contributed to its symbolic association with regeneration and healing; this is fully discussed in chapter 6 (Arrian *Cynegetica* - 33-35, Phillips and Willcock 1999, 123-125, Green 1992a, 196-203). On the other hand, in Homer's *Iliad,* dogs were repeatedly described as corpse eaters, the devourers of those not deemed fit to receive proper funerary honours, although this might also be viewed positively as they rid battlefields of putrefaction (Homer The *Iliad* I.4-5, XVII. 127, XXII. 354, Kirk and Fitzgerald 2004). Their scavenging and gluttony has been targeted as a downfall of catastrophic consequence in the mythology of the Beng from the Ivory Coast of Africa: death for humans is said to be a direct result of a dog's failure to convey a message to the gods because it was sidetracked on its errand by scraps of food (Gottlieb 1968, 479). Amongst the Melpa, from the New Guinea highlands, grave robbing cannibals are believed to exist and they are said to take on the appearance of dogs when they dig up fresh corpses. The anthropologist, Andrew Strathern, suggested that the cannibal witches take on this form because dogs steal food and eat raw flesh, and similarly to Western societies, the Melpa see dogs as partially human or part of their owners' identity and therefore they are a tainted but potent representation of humanity (Strathern 1982, 111-133).

Intimidating spectral dogs are also portrayed as harbingers of death. In Vedic India two four-eyed dogs were said to be the messengers of Yama, the god of death (White 1991, 263). It has been suggested that a dog's growl might contribute to this facet of its symbolism in that despite no words being spoken the threat is clearly conveyed (Lincoln 1979, 273-285).

Dogs have been used in the funerary practices of numerous societies. The Chinese Miao kill a dog to place alongside a dead human; pieces of paper are attached to both the bodies as a sign that the former should lead the latter to their resting place. In ancient China, Shang emperors were buried with their watchdogs, whilst Han emperors were buried with dog figurines. Straw dogs were also part of the paraphernalia of ancient Chinese funerary ceremonies and are still used by the Solon of Manchuria in these rites; they are believed to lead the deceased through the underworld (White 1991, 171-174). Clay dog figurines have also been found in Gaulish graves dating to the period of Roman occupation; they may have been purely ornamental but it has been suggested that their spectral appearance is an indication of a deeper level of symbolism (Jenkins 1957, 62). Dog representations quite often appeared on ancient Roman funerary monuments (fig. 18); they also appear on several gravestones from Roman Britain (Toynbee 1973, 108-122). On one example from Shirva, Dunbartonshire a small dog is perched on a couch beside the legs of a bearded man. It has been suggested that the scene portrays the deceased in attendance of their own funerary banquet (Keppie and Arnold 1984, 41-42). Unfortunately, it is not always clear whether these are portraits of animals that did in fact exist or whether their form in general was being utilised as a funerary symbol. One quite rare canine find, at least from the context of a Romano-British burial, was the discovery of a clay tile at the head of a woman's grave at Newarke cemetery in Leicester. Two paw prints from different dogs were embedded in the tile (Harvey 1996, 73-74).

It is not just dead and mythical dogs that have been said to commune with the spirit world. The Kagoro of Nigeria believe that a dog barking outside a family's house, early in the morning, is a portent of one of the residents' death (Olowo Ojade 1994, 215-221). Dogs play a very important role in Zoroastrian mortuary practice, in a rite known as Sagdid. After a person has died and their body has been ritually dressed and purified, they are laid out in a building called a bungli where people say prayers for them for three days and nights. During this time a dog is brought into look upon the corpse and in doing so confirm their death; at that point the soul of the deceased, which is believed to wait by the body until this time, will move on to the after-life (Clark 1998, 114-117).

5.4.2 The Liminal Nature of the Domestic Dog and its Association with Death

In many societies, both ancient and modern, the domestic

dog's perceived place in the world order has perhaps contributed to the symbolic link between the species and death. They naturally ally themselves with humans and in doing so set themselves apart from most other creatures. Nevertheless, they retain instincts and behaviours that we class as animal, as something separate from ourselves. They also blur the distinction between wild and domestic because of their likeness to wolves and their hunting instincts. Straddling real and conceptual boundaries, we imagine, is natural for dogs. This perception quite likely influences both the view of dogs as guides aiding human transition to the after-life and their position as guards on the threshold to the next world.

Death is as mysterious as it is inevitable and fear of the unknown, of something other than the natural order we have created, is a primal human fear (White 1991, 1-21). That many cultures have included a protective canine in death's symbolic repertoire is perhaps a consequence of this insecurity. Ethnographic studies have revealed that the belief that the deceased have to undertake a journey to their final resting place is widespread and in many societies the path to eternal life is fraught with danger, as if we need the challenges to prove we are worthy of the reward (Huntington and Metcalf 1979, 1-20, Schwartz 1997, 93-103). That a familiar companion animal, whose senses are far more acute than ours, will be by our side on the other side appears to be comforting for many people. Notably, in many cultures horses are as close to humans as dogs but they have not become symbols of death to the same extent. Ironically, it is perhaps the fact that dogs are natural born killers that we often find a degree of comfort in the idea that they protect us on route to a final resting place. By creating realms of the dead to comfort ourselves, we have exposed our souls to the threat of further danger, even after we have died.

One might also consider that there are similarities between human perception of dogs and death. Throughout the world both dogs and death are part of everyday life, but the darker side of the animals' nature and death's indiscriminate actuality are put to the back of our minds for most of time, nevertheless it can be costly to completely ignore the threat of either. Like our awareness of death, dogs for many people are part of everyday life and similarly to death we do not tend to dwell on their more threatening side as an immediate hazard, although the possibility that we could be confronted by it at any time is always with us at some level.

5.5 Summary

The aim of this part of the study was to examine the archaeological record for evidence that domestic dogs were being used symbolically in Romano-British human burial contexts. Although undoubtedly some of animals mentioned above were interred with their master or mistress because they had been their lifetime companions, other burials exhibit features that make the presence of the dogs more difficult to fathom. A considerable number of the human skeletons from Late Roman cemeteries found in association with dogs were mutilated in some way, often decapitated. In view of the number of examples of domestic dogs found in association with disarticulated and damaged human skulls from earlier Roman contexts at both sacred and secular sites, it seems quite possible that the symbolic language conveyed by the interments from both periods shared a common root, although the precise understanding of the emblematic syntax may have changed over time. It has been suggested that the geographically and temporally widespread symbolic role of dogs as guides and guardians to the afterlife motivated these interments. This symbolism most likely stems from observation of their natural guiding and guarding instincts but might also be connected to our ambivalent feelings towards the species.

Another aim of the study was to establish whether the symbolic roles in which domestic dogs appear in the iconography of the Western provinces of Rome were also visible in characteristics of their physical deposition. There is some evidence to suggest that regenerative themes, perhaps associated with hunting and hunter gods, were alluded to in the arrangement of their bodies and association with horses in funerary and other sacred depositional contexts. A stronger connection between dogs, infants and fertility appears in both the iconographical and osteo-archaeological evidence of the time.

There are not enough examples of human graves containing dogs from Late Romano-British cemeteries for reliable patterns to emerge regarding biases towards age and sex of either the humans or animals in these interments. However, if one includes the data from earlier burials of domestic dogs with human skulls, it is apparent that the association is weighted towards human males. The size of the dogs found with humans in the Romano-British burials appears to have been random.

Figure 18. A 3rd century AD Roman sarcophagus decorated with a small dog peering through a doorway. Photograph © Anne Lever

Chapter 6

Dogs as Symbols in Roman Britain – Images, Visualities and Metonyms

6.1 The Psychology of Symbol Formation

The capacity to create and understand symbols is an integral part of the human psyche. When creating or appreciating a symbol a person chooses to loosen their cerebral grip on practical reality and engage emotionally with the image before them. A symbol like a religious icon or even a national flag can contain such a concentration of ideas that for some people its contemplation can induce a transcendental experience. Of course, a symbol is only as powerful as the reaction it creates in the individual and such responses are influenced by secular experience of the subject and general cultural recognition of stories and beliefs with which the subject is associated (Stevens 1998, 76-89). This chapter examines representations of the domestic dog from Roman Britain and seeks to establish whether its form at that time would have been what Jung termed a 'living symbol' or was its presence in art more often a fashionable artistic flourish. A symbol is 'alive' when it is considered one of the most effective visual triggers of psychological engagement with complex interrelated ideas and beliefs (Stevens 1998, 76-89).

6.2 The Dog as Symbol

To begin to understand how the image of the domestic dog functioned as a symbol, in any given society, one must first of all consider how that population would have experienced the species at a mundane level. A detailed insight into the domestic dog's place in Romano-British life is included in Chapter 3 but it is pertinent at this point to briefly review the available evidence we have to shed light on the matter.

The almost ubiquitous presence of dog bones in the faunal assemblages from Romano-British sites, both towns and rural settlements, is testament to the commonality of the species at this time (Fulford 2001, 199-218, Maltby 1987a, Collis 1968, 18-31, Maltby 1993, 315-339). Evidence suggests that whilst some dogs were pampered others were physically abused (Fulford and Clarke 2002, 364-369, Harcourt 1967, 521-523). The damage by canine gnawing, often visible on the discarded bones of other animal species, and the appearance of dogs' footprints set into ceramic tiles suggests that they were probably allowed to roam quite freely around settlements (Maltby 1987b, 11, Cram 2000, 123-126). It is clear that in domestic domains they were at least as familiar as they are in the Western world today. In this case it is safe to assume that the inclusion of a portrayal of a dog would have contributed to the immediacy with which an observer would have become psychologically involved with a piece of iconography. The following discussion explores where this sense of familiarity might have led the thoughts of a willing surveyor of contemporary symbolism in Roman Britain.

6.3 Hounds and Hunting

6.3.1 The Earthly Reality

Hunting appears to have been a popular sport in Roman Britain. As mentioned in chapter 3, a number of the personal notes on the Vindolanda tablets make enthusiastic references to the chase and associated equipment such as nets and dog collars (A. Birley 2002, 147-151). Besides the iconography, the prevalence of an interest in hunting in Britain is supported by the historical writings of Strabo, who recorded that hunting dogs were a primary export from the island (Strabo *Geography* 4.5.2, Jones 1923, 255). It seems likely that depictions of a dog chasing prey or accompanying a hunter would have elicited a positive response in most of the general populace. Indeed, the image of the hunt appears to have been a very popular motif in Roman Britain. Hunting with canines is believed to be the most widespread and one of the most ancient forms of the activity: it is generally accepted to lie at the root of the evolution of domestic dogs and their relationship with humans (Clutton-Brock 1999, 49-52, Ingold 1980, 66).

6.3.2 Hunter-gods and their Animal Companions

The term 'hound' is sometimes used in this study to refer to a dog that is portrayed as a hunter's companion. In reality, Romano-British dogs sturdy enough to hunt could have been as small as modern terriers or as large as a wolf (Harcourt 1974, 163-166). In the majority of the iconographic images the hounds are somewhere between the two extremes, referred to here as medium or large.

Stone statues and reliefs of what appear to be hunter-gods have been found in various parts of the Britain and hounds accompany a considerable number of them. A fine example was found with several other sculptures of a religious and/or funerary nature, in a Roman timber lined well at Southwark cathedral, London (fig. 26). Coin evidence suggests that the well dates to the late 3rd century AD and that it was probably in-filled sometime in the 4th century (Merrifield 1986, 85-92). Given the considerable body of evidence that supports the theory that the ritual deposition of animals, a practice that clearly took place in Iron Age Britain, was still a widespread practice in Roman times, it is interesting to note that the complete skeletons of a cat and a dog were found together in the basal deposit of the same feature (Fulford 2001, 199-218, Merrifield 1987, 20-57). The hunter god, equipped with a bow and short sword is accompanied by a dog on his left side and a deer on his right side (Merrifield 1986, 85-92). A relief in stone depicting a similar group of figures was found at Chedworth Roman villa, Gloucestershire. In this instance the hunter holds a hare in his right hand above a dog and a deer stands to his left. The exact provenance of this find is uncertain, but given its similarity to other examples of iconography that are certainly religious in nature it is possible that it came from the temple at the site (Webster 1983, 5-20, Goodburn 1979b, 34, Henig 1993, 37). Again, on an altar from Bisley in Gloucestershire a hunter holds a hare out above a dog standing on its hind legs (Clifford 1938, 301). It has been suggested that the anthropomorphic figures on these artefacts represent Silvanus, the Roman god of the woodlands and wildlife (fig. 19) (Henig 1993, 37, Green 1989, 101-106) The only unequivocal British sculpture of Silvanus was found on an inscribed altar from Risingham in Northern Britain, again the hunter stands between a deer and a hound (Green 1989, 101-106). In view of the similarities between all these images, one of which has an inscribed dedication to a deity, it seems reasonable to surmise that these were all hunter-gods and that the beliefs surrounding their associated cults were not very far removed from each other.

A close look at some of the details of the images is one way that we might begin to untangle the underlying spiritual significance of the figures portrayed. One key characteristics of the hunter god scene is the attentiveness of the hound towards its master. As the deity is represented in anthropomorphic form the image works on two levels: the scene symbolises the divine but also illuminates worldly truths. The hound's apparent adoration of its master clearly alludes to human power over the creature, but perhaps also signifies human reverence of the hunter god. The dog's natural instinct to take its place within a pack makes it an ideal emblem for the presence of a hierarchy. The same duplexity of meaning is communicated if we read the dog's attentive demeanour as a symbol of loyalty and protection.

The collar that the dog wears on the sculptures from London and Bath are perhaps a more significant feature than one might at first imagine. Not only do they emphasise the authority of the anthropomorphic figure, but it would perhaps also have been recognisable as a symbol of guardianship: the protection of the hound by his master and the hunter by the propitiated deity. The collar also symbolises control and ferocity. Writing in the 4th century BC, the Greek historian Xenophon described the use of looped collars for the attachment of leads for hunting dogs, which were intended to provide the animal with a degree of protection and allow a lost hound to be identified (Xenophon *Cynegetica* 6, Phillips and Willcock 1999, 146-147). In the 1st century BC the Roman writer Varro, recommended spiked collars for the protection of sheep dogs (Varro *De Re Rustica* II 9 15, Hilzheimer 1932, 411-420). In a number of hound representations from sacred sites in Roman Britain the animals are fettered this way, notably the bronze deerhound from Lydney temple, Gloucestershire (Wheeler 1932, 88-89). It is interesting that when a deer accompanies a hunter god it is not restrained in any way, drawing attention to its freewill and emphasising that a wild beast cannot be owned the way a dog can. The demonstration of ownership of the dog might also invoke a sense of the emotional benefits that people experience from animal companions, so contributing to the positive effects of the iconography (Katcher and Beck 1991, 265-274, Katcher and Beck 1988, 53-73). In a similar vein, the hares that are sometimes held above the hounds might also have been intended to work as a motif for dependency upon and reward for loyalty to the deity. Alternatively, carcasses are used to train hunting hounds and therefore the dead hare held aloft might also contribute to the image of canine control, temptation resisted. At a secular level the hunt is a sport where the hunter and companions pursue a wild animal to its death. In the hunter god images, the hunters and the prey stand together in a united group; of course this is in the realm of the divine. As this is, at best, improbable at an earthly level we should perhaps read this union as a spiritual understanding between the trio in the profane world.

6.3.3 The Hunt as Ritual – Historical Evidence

Although hunting and gathering was not the only means of subsistence in Western Europe from the Neolithic onwards, the veneration of earthly and celestial environmental phenomena, commonly associated with that life-style, pervaded the consciousness of the population during the Iron Age and Roman periods. That the gods were manifest in the forms and forces of nature is a view of the world that they share with societies who do still hunt for subsistence today. That a sympathetic union was felt to exist between hunter and prey in Iron Age and Roman Europe is supported by artistic and written evidence, although there is little physical evidence that wild animals were eaten as part of routine diet. The Strettweg wagon from Austria, dating to the 7th century BC, was found in the tomb of a cremated male. It has been interpreted as a representation of a stag hunt; the disproportionate size of the central figure indicates her divine status and the importance of her influence to the success of the hunt. The smaller humans and prey appear to form a co-operative group and the exaggerated deer antlers are perhaps intended to remind the observer of the importance of the prey within the scheme; these animals are not simply passive game (Green 1996, 115). Arrian, writing late in the 2nd century AD, stated that after a successful season of hunting the Celts always offered thanks to the gods in the form of a sacrifice. This was carried out on the birthday of the goddess who Arrian referred to as Artemis the huntress. On this day hunting hounds were also treated to a celebratory feast and adorned with garlands of flowers. He concluded his record of this tradition by stating that 'I and my fellow hunters follow the Celtic custom: and I can state as fact that nothing that happens without the gods turns out well for men' (Arrian Cynegetica, 33-36, Phillips and Willcock 1999, 125-127). To grasp how this attitude might have made sense in ancient Britain, it is useful to study the attitudes and beliefs of various modern day hunter-gatherer societies towards hunting, their dogs and their prey.

6.3.4 The Hunt as Ritual – An Ethnographic Perspective

In the cosmologies of the hunter-gatherer tribes from Eurasia and North America the kill in a hunt is akin to the sacrifice of a domestic animal by a farmer, the only difference being that a farmer sacrifices an animal to give thanks or seek approval from the gods, whereas in the hunt the hunter observes certain modes of behaviour in order to win the respect of the hunting deities so they will allow the body of an animal to be given up to the hunter. In both cases the death of the animal is perceived as a ritual killing and it is crucial that the animal is believed to comply with the act (Ingold 1986, 243-276). The concept of the willing victim was also an essential element of sacrificial ceremonies in ancient Greece. To achieve the semblance of consent from the chosen animal it would be sprinkled with grain and water and its subsequent shudders and shakes were taken as a sign of acceptance (Detienne 1989, 9). In hunter-gatherer societies from both Eurasia and Africa the prey is perceived as entering into sacred covenant with the hunter, sacrificing its own life to ensure human survival. Throughout the whole process the prey is an object of the utmost respect. The hunter-gatherers' dogs are of intrinsic importance in the hunt and, depending on the tribe, they are either viewed as an actual dispensable extension of their human master/mistress or as a loved companion, the wilful killing of which is treated with the same severity as a homicide (Ingold 1986, 243-276, Morris 1998, 61-119).

To achieve the animal's consent to be killed various different rites have to be observed by the hunter. These can involve such measures as taking specially prepared medicines, abstaining from sex and killing, butchering, cooking and disposing of any waste elements from the prey in a certain way. If the correct procedures are observed hunter-gatherers believe that only the physical body of the animal dies, its soul returns to its divine master or mistress who can then once again send it to earth in another animal's form (Morris 1998, 61-119, Ingold 1986, 243-276). The San Bushmen of the Kalahari desert actually believe that a female eland exercise control over the fertility and prosperity of their whole tribe in her decision to lay down her own life for consumption, or not as the case may be (Saunders 1995, 54-55). Hunter-gatherer tribes perceive the hunt as a spiritual cycle of life, death and regeneration for the animal and for themselves. Bearing this heightened significance in mind it becomes quite feasible to surmise that hunting divinities were not simply regarded as forces to be invoked to promote success in the kill in antiquity, they were also perceived as guardians of both human and animal life (Green 1989, 100-106).

Figure 19. Hunter Gods and their hounds - The Hunter God from Bisley, Gloucestershire (left). Photograph © The British Museum. The Hunter God from Southwark, London (right). Photograph © MoLAS.

6.3.5 The Hounds' Prey

A number of Romano-British hunt scenes convey a sense of harmony between hunters and prey; nevertheless in other instances death is very often present in the form of a captured or lifeless hare. Like the hunter god sculptures, on several Romano-British intaglios captured hares are held out as either a symbol of canine control or perhaps a trophy. On examples from Chester, Cheshire and Wroxeter, Shropshire the hares actually appear to be eviscerated (Henig 1978, 249). A fragmentary and weathered stone relief, dating to the 2nd or 3rd century AD, from Carlisle depicts a hare being pinned to the floor by a large hound and at least eight Romano-British metal knife handles fashioned in the shape of a hound at the heels of a fleeing hare were recorded by Jocelyn Toynbee (fig. 20) (Toynbee 1964, 127, Coulston and Phillips 1988, 176-177). The choice of the hare as the usual victim is interesting for a number of reasons. In the first instance historical writings attest to their special status in ancient Britain: Dio Cassius recorded that Boudicca set a hare free before going into battle against the Roman army, in order to read auspices from its course. Interestingly, it was said that during this ceremony she likened the Romans to hares and foxes attempting to rule over dogs and wolves (Dio Cassius *Roman History* LXII, Cary 1925, 91-93). In the 1st century BC Julius Caesar wrote that eating hare was, for some reason, outlawed by the British (Caesar *De Bello Gallico* V 12-13, Kennedy 1965). In emblematic terms the animal's nocturnal lifestyle and high level of fertility have led to the species being associated with a symbol of feminine fertility cycles, the Moon. When exactly the hare's celestial connection originated is unknown. However, considering disparate cultures across the world have independently seen the shape of a hare rendered in the shadows and craters of the moon it is possible that the linkage is very old indeed (Saunders 1995, 96-97). Therefore it is interesting to note that during the period under discussion the Moon was sacred to the Greek goddess Artemis, another hunter and healer. Like the domestic dog, the hare's part in the hunt also connects it with cyclical activity, as extremely swift and agile prey it perhaps came to represent the fleeting nature of life and ultimately death (Becker 2000, 137-138).

If we accept the historical writings of Arrian as a fair account of hunting practice early in the 1st millennium AD it is clear that what we might refer to as hare coursing was the most popular form of the chase across much of Europe (Arrian *Cynegetica* 1-36 Phillips and Willcock 1999, 93-127). In view of the spiritual approach to hunting at this time and the way that symbol formation occurs i.e. that in the first instance we engage with profane experience of the image subject, if indeed any exists, it seems reasonable that the prolific breeding habits of the hare makes it an ideal motif to represent regenerative aspects of the hunt. One might imagine the creation of a self-fulfilling prophecy, whereby the popularity of hare coursing insured that it was most frequently carried out with adherence to the correct ritual observances and consequently the more fertile the prey appeared to be.

Figure 20. A hound and hare pen-knife handle from Lydney Temple, Gloucestershire. *After* Casey and Hoffman, Antiquity 1999, 129.

There are some exceptions to the portrayal of an alliance between hounds and larger wild animals in Romano British art: a stone relief of a large dog, its jaws locked on to the neck of a stag was found near Bath, Somerset and a fierce hound confronts a lion or bear on a large stone slab from the Roman military fortress at Caerleon, South Wales (Brewer 1986, 41-42, Toynbee 1964, 143). An impressive mosaic from a Romano-British villa at Hinton St Marys, Dorset depicts a number of scenes of stags, and in one instance a hind, being attacked by hounds. These surround the central image of a fair-haired man with a Chi Ro monogram behind him; this figure is believed to represent Christ. In the smaller of the two panels that make-up the pavement, similar hunting scenes surround a representation of Bellerophon from Greek mythology riding Pegasus in pursuit of the three-headed chimaera (Neal 1981, 87-89). Martin Henig has pointed out that since mosaics were costly and intended to be a permanent feature of a homestead, it is highly likely that the chosen images would have held a great deal of significance for the person who commissioned the artwork (Henig 1984b, 174-179). The inclusion of hunting scenes, so popular in pagan Roman Britain, on a Christian mosaic is interesting in that it perhaps suggests that hunting's association with spiritual beliefs about rebirth and regeneration were still being used as a motif for the new religion.

6.3.6 The Goddess Diana and Her Hound

Romano-British hunting imagery was not exclusively masculine: Diana the Roman goddess of the hunt has been identified as the subject of a number of stone sculptures depicting scenes very similar to those of her male counterparts. In fact, due to their weathered condition several of the images are rather androgynous and it has been suggested that they do not necessarily represent Diana at all, but are perhaps more youthful versions of the hunter god archetype (Merrifield 1986, 85-92). Alternatively the representation could be deliberately dual gendered to reflect the liminality of hunting where, similarly to war, fate hangs in the balance. In any case it is reasonable to assume that the significance of the hunting symbolism essentially remained the same whatever the sex of the divinity happened to be. In one androgynous image from London, dating to the 2nd century AD, the figure, equipped with a bow and portrayed drawing an arrow from their quiver, is accompanied by a smallish hound that stares up at their master/mistress, eagerly awaiting the signal to chase (Toynbee 1962, 152). A gemstone from the Thetford Treasure depicts Diana drawing her bow or perhaps just having fired it; the hound next to her appears to already be on the move (Henig 1983, 30-32). The pair also appears on a late issue of Cunobelin's silver coins (De Jersey 2001, 12-13). One might consider that there is a certain historical irony in the fact that during the decades leading up to the Roman conquest the image of a large and imposing canine, that appeared on earlier examples of Cunobelin's coinage, was succeeded by the representation of a clearly subservient hound attending a Classical goddess - particularly when the indigenous ruler's name translates as "Hound of Brilliance" (fig. 22) (De Jersey 2001, 7-9, Ross 1967a, 340, Green 1992b, 30-31).

Figure 21. Diana and hound from shrine of Apollo at Nettleton, Wiltshire. Photograph Courtesy of Bristol's Museums, Libraries and Archives.

In several instances fragments of sculptures have been interpreted as Diana simply because of the presence of an attentive hound with an anonymous figure. The anthropomorphic elements of examples from Maiden Castle, Dorset and Castle Combe, Wiltshire are in truth impossible to identify, although one might expect to find representations of hunting deities in that particular area of the country (Cunliffe and Fulford 1982, 26-27). Scholars have noted that there is a concentration of iconography and inscriptions relating to hunting deities in the South West of England and furthermore this evidence is frequently found at Romano-British shrines where healing practices appear to have been an integral part of the associated cult (Henig 1993, 37-39, Merrifield 1986, 90-91, Clifford 1938, 297-310). These sites include; Chedworth villa and Lydney temple in Gloucestershire, Pagan's Hill temple, Dorset, the temple of Aquae Sulis in Bath and the shrine to Apollo Cunomaglus at Nettleton, Wiltshire.

Interestingly the name Cunomaglus translates as 'Hound Lord' (Webster 1983, Wheeler 1932, Wedlake 1982, Boon 1989, Cunliffe and Davenport 1985). The seemingly incongruous acts of hunting and healing are most likely connected through the perception of the hunt as a regenerative cycle. The attitude of the hunting deities hounds suggests that they are either eagerly awaiting instruction and/or trying hard to contain themselves. The athletic and animated bearing of the dog's perhaps symbolises their place as a moving horizon between domestic and wild realms, the human and animal world and between life and death.

Classically, one of Diana's divine concerns was health issues, particularly ailments peculiar to women (Jenkins 1957, 60-78). As medical complaints could be addressed through propitiation of a hunter god at certain temples it seems fitting that people could seek the help of a hunter goddess for specifically female problems at these same sites; this might also explain the androgyny of the figure interpreted as Diana on the altar from London mentioned above. It is believed that Diana is represented at the healing shrine at Nettleton in Wiltshire. Although only the bottom of a woman's cape remains to identify the figure the presence of the attentive and muscular dog suggests that it was indeed Diana (fig. 21) (Toynbee 1982, 136-137). Likewise, it is believed that Diana once accompanied a stone hound from the temple precinct at Bath, Somerset; in this instance the dog lies beside a bow, eagerly gazing upward at its long departed mistress (Cunliffe 2000, 69). Another stone altar dedicated to Sulis Minerva at Bath features a dog and a snake on two of its sides. As both of these creatures were sacred to Asklepios, the ancient Greek god of healing, it has been suggested that the two figures depicted on the main face of the altar are his mother Coronis, and his son Apollo (Cunliffe and Fulford 1982).

If an earthly subject's symbolism is partly influenced by our experience of that thing at a secular level it seems quite likely that the domestic dog's link to healing was born out of the canine habit of instinctively licking their own wounds and even those of other species given the inclination and opportunity. Dogs have also featured prominently in iconography from healing sites where the hunting emblem is absent. For example, in a number of the stone representations from Fontes Sequanae young pilgrims are portrayed carrying small dogs (Aldhouse-Green 1999a, 11-13). At Mavilly a dog appears in a relief depicting a man holding his hands to his eyes as if drawing attention to a sight disorder and a number of the mother goddesses with lapdogs from Britain, Gaul and the Rhineland were discovered at healing sanctuaries (Green 1992a, 198, Green 1995, 105-116, Wightman 1970, 217). The fact that the animal is independently associated with both hunting and healing perhaps also contributed to the creation of a hunter/healer cult: in terms of motif the dog is undeniably the common thread that cements the two together.

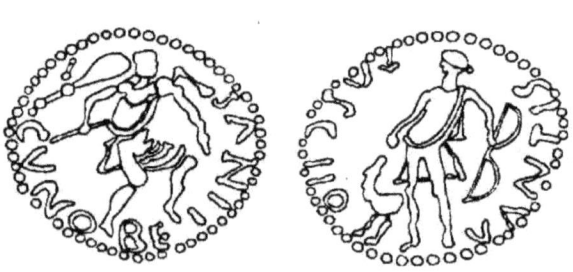

Figure 22. An early issue of Cunobelin's silver coins featuring a large hound (top). Photograph © Chris Rudd. Later issues featuring Diana and hound. After De Jersey, Britannia 2001, 8.

6.3.7 Other Hunting and Hound Images

Representations of dogs from Roman Britain are not always found in religious contexts, although that is not to say that these artefacts were not intended to or did not invoke a deeper level of meaning in some spectators. A lively hunting scene, featuring an athletic hound in pursuit of a hare appeared on number of Castor Ware pots found in *Verulamium*, Hertfordshire dating to between the late 2nd and early 3rd centuries AD (Toynbee 1962, 189-190). A similar chase is depicted on an engraved bowl discovered at a site in Banwell, Somerset and dating to the 4th century AD; here the illustration is complete with a hound, horse, rider and hare. It is also headed with a hearty inscription in a mixture of Latin and Greek which translates as "Long life to you and yours: drink and good health to you", which is perhaps suggestive of a penchant for post-hunt conviviality (Toynbee 1962, 185-186). This work is certainly visual testament to the positive view taken of hunting in Roman Britain and to the integral role the dog played in it as a symbol of vitality.

6.4 Personal Ornamentation Featuring Domestic Dogs

Although not particularly common in Roman Britain ornaments on hairpins, toilet instruments and brooches were sometimes shaped like dogs (Johns 1996, 140-177, Boon 1991, 21-32, Hattatt 1987, 238-240). Enamel brooches like the one depicted below (fig. 23) were generally too small and fragile to have been of much use as fastenings on clothes so they were not merely practical fixtures. Their bright coloured surfaces would have immediately drawn attention to the decoration so one might imagine that as well as having an attractive appearance the images were intended to communicate something of the beliefs and desires of the individual who wore them (Johns 1996, 147). It has been suggested that besides their obvious aesthetic impact the decoration of ancient European military apparel with representations of fierce wild animals was believed to be a way of harnessing the qualities of the animal spirit (Green 1992a, 131-136). It is also clear that Roman intaglios, that frequently depicted animals, were often an expression of the owners' spiritual outlook on the world, therefore we might also consider that the subjects of certain other personal adornments were perceived to have talismanic properties (Henig 1978, Johns 1996, 9-12). Obviously the significance of an amulet, as with any material culture, is entirely dependent on how an individual experiences it. Human reaction to symbols cannot be manufactured or guaranteed. In antiquity the dog symbolism of personal ornamentation would have been far more alive for some people than for others.

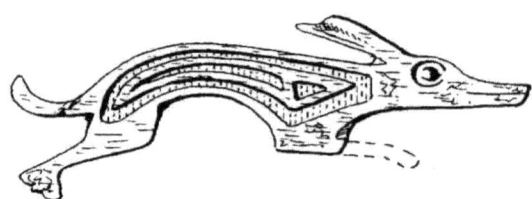

Figure 23. 2nd century AD enamelled dog brooch found in Wiltshire *After* Hattatt 1987, 239-240.

6.5 Statuettes

As mentioned at the beginning of this chapter, British dogs were exported to Rome because of their skill in the hunt (Strabo *Geography* IV. 5.2, Jones 1923, 255). A number of Latin poets also recorded certain attributes of the dogs native to the island: Grattius, writing around the end of the 1st century BC asserted that, although perhaps not the most attractive or charming of creatures, British hounds were hard to beat in terms bravery (Grattius *Cynegetica* 177-188, Duff and Duff 1935, 169). Towards the end of the 3rd century AD, Nemesianus commented on the impressive speed of British dogs (Nemesianus *Cynegetica* 224-227, Duff and Duff 1935, 505). Writing at the beginning of the same century, a Greek poet named Oppian described a type of British scent hound known as *Agassians* as follows:

> *Their size is like that of worthless and greedy domestic table dogs: squat, emaciated, shaggy, dull of eye, but endowed with feet armed with powerful claws and a mouth sharp with close set*

venomous tearing teeth (Oppian *Cynegetica* I, 468-480).

Jocelyn Toynbee speculated that the bronze model, closely resembling a feisty, modern day, border terrier found at site of Coventina's Well in Carrawburgh, Northumberland was perhaps of this ilk (Allason-Jones and McKay 1985, 21, Toynbee 1973, 104-105). Her suggestion that the likeness of the large Irish hounds, sent to the Roman prefect Symmachus by his brother, might be found in the bronze deer hound from Lydney is also a possibility (Symmachus *Epistolae* II, 77, Toynbee 1973, 104-105).

Historical sources may well mention types of British hounds, but it seems unlikely that 'breeds' of dogs' existed in the way that we understand that term today. The bronze model dog found at Kirkby Thore, Westmorland with its generic canine appearance is perhaps more representative of the 'average' Romano-British dog: archaeo-zoological studies have shown that one of the most notable physical characteristics of the species at this time was its variable size (fig. 24) (Toynbee 1962, 150, Harcourt 1974, 151-175, Green 1978, 26). The figurines described are perhaps the most well known from Roman Britain, but it is worth noting that Miranda Aldhouse-Green recorded at least another seven contemporary bronze examples in her corpus of religious material from the civilian areas of the country (Green 1976, 162-232). Besides these examples, at least ten dog figurines and plaques were found at Lydney temple, Gloucestershire, which is discussed fully in the chapter 7. A further four images of dogs, two of which were statuettes, were found amongst a Romano-British hoard of bronze objects at Llys Awel, Abergele in Clwyd (Wheeler 1932, 65-93, Blockley 1991, 117-128) The sympathetic nature of several of these images could be considered testimony to the pleasure some members of the population took from keeping dogs: whilst some of these bronze figures may well have been purpose made votive offerings it would be wrong not to credit the contemporary population with creativity arising out of sentimentality and humour. Even some of the world's poorest societies keep pets simply because they enjoy their entertaining antics, and for many, therapeutic companionship (Serpell 1988, 33-52, Katcher and Beck 1991, 265-264).

Figure 24. Romano-British bronze dog statuette from Kirkby Thore, Westmorland. Photograph © Tullie House Museum and Art Gallery.

6.6 Mother Goddesses and Lapdogs

The images discussed so far have portrayed, if not large dogs, fairly robust looking animals. However, lapdogs have their own place in the iconography of the Western provinces of Rome: they are one of a considerable array of emblems associated with mother goddesses. The majority of the mother goddess with lapdog representations have been found in Gaul and the Rhineland, particularly in the area around Trier. (Green 1995, 105-114, Wightman 1970, 208-227). However, a handful found their way into the British archaeological record. As mentioned in chapter 4, an example from Cirencester, Gloucestershire portrays the goddesses in triplicate, a male infant also accompanies each one and the central goddess also holds a small dog on her lap (fig. 25) (Toynbee 1962, 154-155). Statuettes of a goddess with a lapdogs have been found at a villa site in Dawes Heath, Essex and at Canterbury in Kent (Drury and Wickenden 1982, 239-243, Jenkins 1953, 131-133). The former is thought to have been part of a bigger composition, perhaps similar to the unusual relief of four mother goddesses found in the Roman riverside wall in London, which also portrayed a lapdog as an attribute of one of the divinities (Drury and Wickenden 1982, 239-243, Green 1995, 105-116).

6.6.1 Characteristics of the Mother Goddess Cult

Numerous scholars have discussed the cult of the mother goddesses at length, however, a brief review of their form and interpretations of the beliefs surrounding them is desirable at this time if we are to begin to understand where lapdogs fitted into the bigger picture. The mothers are subject to a fair degree of regional variation: they are portrayed singularly or more often in groups of two or three, in quite naturalistic form. Within the groups, they sit one beside the other and although they are similarly attired in long gowns, age differences between them are portrayed in their physicality; features like hairstyles and ornamentation also distinguish one from the other. They were no doubt intended to appeal to women at any stage in their lives and at the same time represent the cyclical nature of life. They are commonly found at healing shrines and no doubt their help was solicited by pilgrims concerned with feminine health issues: in antiquity pregnancy and childbirth would have been periods of far greater risk than they are today and would have been the cause of great anxiety for all concerned. It is clear from dedications that men also sought the favour of the goddesses: the mother archetype is after all a protector and nurturer of all life. The goddesses were depicted holding or surrounded by a variety of emblems; perhaps the most common being infants, cornucopia, corn and fruit, evidently indicating that their cult was centred around fertility and general domestic well being. However, the presence of their iconography in funerary artwork suggests that their sphere of influence also reached the afterlife. Other objects with which the mothers are associated such as ships' rudders, balance beams and spindles symbolise human fate, the journey through life, which further supports the idea that their powers transcended the earthly realm (Green 1989, 9-44, Green 1995, 105-116).

6.6.2 The Lapdog as a Feature of Mother Goddess Iconography

The lapdog as a mother goddess motif was by no means as widespread as the cornucopia, for example. Nevertheless it was still part of their emblematic repertoire whilst most other animals were not. On a secular level it is perhaps significant that lapdogs appear in the archaeological record of Britain and elsewhere in the Western provinces of Rome for the first time during the Roman period and it seems reasonable to surmise that they were for some time quite a novelty (Luff 1982, 263-264, Harcourt 1974, 151-175). Pliny the Elder recorded that women used 'pretty little dogs' to ease stomach pains, by holding them on their laps (Pliny *Natural History* XXX, Turner 1962, 315-316). As creatures too delicately built to have competed with other dogs for food by scavenging they relied on human care for survival. Affluent householders who had the spare time and resources to keep a dog simply as a pet would have been the most likely members of society to adopt them; in this regard they were an indicator of status and a symbol of material wellbeing that people aspired to or longed to maintain (Creighton 2000, 214). The inclusion of a dog as a cult symbol would have formed a linkage between the human and divine world on a daily basis.

It has been suggested that the domestic dog may have been a metonym for fertility in Europe during Roman rule (Green 1989, 28-30). A knife with a carved ivory handle depicting a dog and a bitch mating was found with one of a number of canine burials at Silchester *Insula IX*. The unusual nature of these deposits suggested that they represented sacrificial offerings; a full description of the evidence is given in chapter 3 (Fulford and Clarke 2002, 364-369, Fulford 2001, 199-218). The considerable number of infant burials found together with dog remains at both sacred and secular sites in Britain might also be indicative of their ritual association with reproduction and regeneration (Anon 1978, 57-60, Fulford and Clarke 2002, 364-369, Scott 1991, 115-121, Alexander and Pullinger 1999, 78-80). This association is discussed in detail in chapter 5.

The duplexity of the anthropomorphic imagery of the mother goddesses is reminiscent of the hunter-gods whereby we can equate the care and affection that the dogs receive with human rewards attainable through veneration of these particular deities; like the larger hounds these dogs can also be interpreted as metonyms for human characteristics like loyalty and trust in the divine. It is notable that the physical tension visible in many of the hunting dogs portrayed in the art of this time is completely absent in the images of lapdogs with mother goddesses. The very peaceful demeanour of the animals illuminates the calming and caring influence of the goddesses.

6.6.3 Therapeutic Aspects of Nurturing – A Link Between Lapdogs and Mother Goddesses?

There appear to be a number of threads that tie lapdogs to the cult of the mother goddess. However, considering the proliferation of mother goddess representations found at healing sanctuaries it is perhaps beliefs in the curative powers of the species that was central to its connection. It might also be significant that the actual act of petting an animal has been found to be psychologically and physiologically beneficial to humans in a number of ways. Modern medical surveys have shown that, amongst other things, petting a dog reduces high blood pressure, their company acts as a positive distraction for many terminally ill people and their demonstrative displays of affection can combat low self-esteem and depression. Their place as a social connector seems to work positively for all concerned and has even led to the establishment of the national charity Pets As Therapy or PAT (Anon 2005, 162-178, Hart 1995). But it is not just specialist academics who have acknowledged these qualities, pet ownership flourishes in some of the world's poorest societies simply because of the sense of wellbeing that comes from having tame animals around: in a survey of communities in the Mulanje and Zomba districts of Africa dog owners explained that one of the reasons for keeping them was that they make the home beautiful (Morris 1998, 41-48, Serpell 1988, 33-52). The need to nurture is a human instinct that is likely to have developed way back in our primate prehistory. Aaron Katcher and Alan Beck have put forward a convincing hypothesis arguing that for the period of an offspring's dependence on its parents to become so extended, as it has in our species, the actual act of nurturing must have had quite considerable physical and social rewards. Human desire to keep and look after pets, which if not universal is certainly very widespread, may be an extension of this evolutionary trait. Characteristics like soliciting play, their seemingly unconditional love and physical neoteny imbue many domestic dogs with a childlike quality that appeals to this part of our nature (Katcher and Beck 1991, 265-274, Katcher and Beck 1988, 53-73). There is no reason to suppose that people in antiquity were unaware of the life enhancing effects of human pet interactions at a caretaking level and as a safe way of engaging with the non-human animal world. In fact there is a considerable amount of historical literature that suggests that early in the 1st millennium AD Europeans were often as besotted with their companion animals as they frequently are today (Toynbee 1973, 101-125). In his treatise on hunting the Greek writer Arrian provides proof that this is as much a male instinct as a female one when he unashamedly asserts that one should take their dog to bed because "a man would notice things that trouble the dog, so as to look after it in the night if it is thirsty or if it has a call of nature" (Arrian *Cynegetica* 9, Phillips and Willcock 1999, 103). As a representation of the mutually beneficial affects of nurturing, the novel and fashionable lapdogs curled up upon a mother archetype was perhaps the ideal motif, second only to a mother with an infant.

Figure 25. Mother goddesses with infants and lapdog from Cirencester, Gloucestershire. Photograph © Corinium Museum, Cirencester, Cotswold District Council.

6.7 Images of the Domestic Dog on Funerary Monuments

As discussed in chapter 5, images of dogs appear on funerary monuments and burial caskets throughout the Roman world. Sometimes the dogs appear alone and on other examples they accompany a stone replica of a deceased human. In either instance one of the most interesting things about these images is that they often appear to represent an animal or relationship between owner and pet that actually existed, rather than solely presenting the dog as the multifaceted metonym it appears to have been (Toynbee 1973, 108-124). A number of sepulchral stones have been found in Britain. A stone relief from Shirva, Dunbartonshire depicts a man reclining on a couch. A lapdog perches playfully on the end of the seat at its master's legs (fig. 26). The image has been interpreted as a scene from a funeral banquet where the deceased is in attendance as if in life (Keppie and Arnold 1984, 41-42). A badly weathered, but nevertheless very animated, hunting scene appears on a gravestone found in Bathford, Somerset. A male figure stands on the right hand side, holding the lead of a large hound that is leaping in pursuit of a hare, fleeing out of the top left of the image (Cunliffe and Fulford 1982). Hunting and feasting would no doubt have been activities that the deceased had enjoyed and in that way these images celebrate past lives as well as encompassing ideas about the after life: the reclining man lives on at his banquet, and hunting, as discussed earlier, was a symbolic trigger for complex ideas about life, death and regeneration. Portraying these social activities with animals that are renowned for their loyalty may also have worked to alleviate any sense of a loved one's isolation in death felt by those left behind; the vitality of the hound and hare image would perhaps also stimulate positive feelings about the hereafter.

Figure 26. Funerary monument depicting a man and a lapdog from Shirva, Dunbartonshire, 3rd century AD. Photograph © Hunterian Museum and Art Gallery, University of Glasgow.

6.8 The Image of the Wolf

Apart from portrayals of Romulus and Remus being nursed by a she wolf, this species is conspicuous only by its relative absence from the native art of Western Europe in both the Iron Age and Roman periods (Toynbee 1973, 101-102, Aldhouse-Green 2004a, 124-126). The beasts whose bodies form the handles of the flagons from Basse-Yutz, Moselle in France, dating to the late 5th - early 4th centuries BC, appear to us as neither definitely dog or wolf; such ambiguity is characteristic of the human, animal and plant images in the art of the area at that time (Green 1992a, 128-161). On occasions when we can say with some degree of certainty that the animal presented is intended to be a wolf the images are not only fierce but to some degree rather monstrous. A number of Iron Age Gallic coins depict wolves as wild creatures with razor sharp teeth and slavering tongues. In one instance a dominating beast rides an almost skeletal horse and on another the wolf appears to devour the moon. It is possible that this latter image is connected to a later mythological tale (Aldhouse-Green 2004a, 124-126). On a British stater from Norfolk, dating from the late 1st century BC, a wolf with bristled hair along its back and huge teeth and jaws replaces the traditional horse motif (fig. 27) (De Jersey 1996, 20-26). The Tarasque of Noves, which dates to 3rd or 2nd century BC, appears to be some sort of demon wolf that is portrayed holding the heads and consuming the limbs of its defeated human adversary or prey (Green 1992a, 150-153). Similarly a huge wolf like creature, depicted seated, with a human arm hanging from its jaws, is the subject of a Romano-British bronze statue from Woodeaton, Oxfordshire (fig. 28) (Henig 1984b, 65).

In antiquity wolves were one of the most globally widespread predators. The writer Columella in his treatise on farming, dating to the 1st century AD, explains that rather than herding skills the most important characteristic of a shepherd dog is its ability to guard flocks against wild animals, particularly the 'stealthy lurking of the wolf' (Columella VII xii 3-9, Forster and Heffner 1941, 309-311). As a threat to domestic livestock and wild herds wolves are still regarded as the enemy by farming and hunter-gatherer communities, whose livelihoods depend on a ready supply of primary and secondary products that their mutually sought after food source provides (Harris 1996, 450-451).

David Gordon White suggests that the reason that wolves have often been demonised throughout history is that, for a number of reasons, they symbolise one of our primal fears. As humans evolved they have strived to create and maintain their own self-serving order on the planet; the original state of the world being perceived of chaos, the return of which is considered terrifying, even apocalyptic. Fear of losing control of our surroundings keeps us perpetually on edge, although we might not be aware of this on a conscious level at all times. Threats to our stability have not been entirely eliminated, forces of nature cannot be controlled and dangerous forms of life still exist literally in the wild. We also fear losing control of ourselves and so to clearly differentiate between sanity and madness we create monsters that live on the periphery of civilisation to enable us to readily identify the nature of our humanity (White 1991, 1-21). Although in reality wolf packs are internally hierarchised and controlled, it is perhaps not difficult to comprehend why wolves have become such symbols of threat when we consider that so many humans share their world with domestic dogs, which are physically reminiscent of wolves but in symbolic terms they commonly represent completely opposite states and qualities. Like chaos, wolves came first and order overcame them when they were tamed and the domestic dog eventually evolved because of this human intervention. The physical similarities of dogs and wolves has drawn attention to their perceived differences and so the species' have become potent metonyms for an array of oppositions; domestic as opposed to wild, protection opposed to threat, healing opposed to destruction and even good opposed to evil. Furthermore, people have perhaps always exaggerated the wicked nature of the wolf because it freely embodies all that we find most unsettling about dogs; when one dog fights another or suddenly turns on a human it is familiar with, it is the wolf in them that we see and are troubled by. Their pack instinct, social hierarchy and sophisticated co-operative survival strategies are also perhaps too close to our own modes of behaviour for comfort; they remind us of our own basically animal nature. In our homocentric way we distinguish ourselves from these, as we see it, wilder, less savoury life forms by making them monstrous. In which case one might consider the fact that the Romans created a myth where a wolf becomes its founder's nursemaid, testament to the great confidence of the Empire.

Figure 27. A Romano-British bronze statue of a canine monster devouring a human limb, Woodeaton, Oxfordshire. Photograph © The British Museum

Figure 28. A 1st century BC stater from Norfolk depicting a wolf-like monster. Photograph © Chris Rudd.

6.9 Summary

Examination of iconography from the Western provinces of Rome suggests that domestic dogs were highly effective symbols, associated with concerns about life, death, fertility, hunting and healing and that these ideas were often inextricably interlinked. The specie's close proximity to humans was perhaps the key contributing factor in the development of their multi-faceted symbolism. For example, their use in hunting appears to have placed them at the forefront of people's imaginations. At this time the sport had a significant spiritual dimension for participants: it was perceived as an act of reciprocity between the hunters, the prey and the numinous forces that were believed to preside over the event. Interestingly, a concentration of hunting and hound images has been found in the South West of England, at temple sites where the cults practised focused to some extent on healing. The link between hounds and healing perhaps stems from the view of the hunt as a regenerative act, as it is perceived by groups of modern day hunter-gatherers whose animistic spirituality is perhaps not dissimilar to pre-Christian Europeans. It is also interesting to note that Romano-British hunting deities are represented as both males and females, and even as rather androgynous figures, as if to appeal to both sexes equally and so encompass all health concerns.

The lapdogs that appear with mother goddesses throughout the Western provinces of Rome are likely to have been emblems of fertility. The passive role of the lapdogs in the iconography, they are usually portrayed curled up upon the mother figure, might also indicate that the therapeutic properties of nurturing was recognised at this time. The existence of such a rich metonymic repertoire suggests that singular hound figurines and their representations in jewellery and other personal items were sometimes considered to have talismanic properties for those who kept them, wore them or offered them as votives.

The domestic dog's association with hunting and consequently cycles of life, death and renewal is also likely to have contributed to their appearance on funerary monuments. However, on several funerary stones from Roman Britain, delicately built dogs are portrayed as pets of the deceased rather than hunting companions. The species may have become linked with death to soften our perception of it: in pet keeping societies dogs can invoke a sense of comfort, companionship and homeliness. Their loyal image stands in stark contrast to monstrous, contemporary portrayals of the wolf that might have arisen out of human perception of the animal as the antithesis of the largely, symbolically benevolent domestic dog, because of its physical likeness to the species.

Chapter 7

Domesticated Dogs – Companions of the God Nodens and Goddess Nehalennia

7.1 Introduction

As discussed in chapter 6, domestic dogs appear in association with a considerable number of divinities in the iconography of Roman Britain and its continental neighbours. They are portrayed as both athletic hounds attending hunting deities and as diminutive lapdogs nursed by mother goddesses (Toynbee 1964, 67-76, Ross 1967b, 339-341, Green 1989, 28-30). However, their place within the core beliefs of religious cults during the Roman period is perhaps most visible in the archaeology from the temple dedicated to the god Nodens at Lydney, Gloucestershire and the remains from the temples to Nehalennia in the Netherlands (Wheeler 1932, Hondius-Crone 1955, Van Aartsen 1971). Evidence from these sites will be discussed in detail in this chapter.

7.2 The Lydney Temple

7.2.1 The Excavators and Proposed Chronology for the Site

Reverend William Hiley Bathurst originally undertook excavations at the hilltop site in the early nineteenth century. Sir Mortimer Wheeler re-examined the Lydney temple and associated artefacts in the 1920s and in 1980-1981 John Casey re-excavated part of the site, concentrating on retrieving evidence that might be used to establish a firm date for the construction of the temple (Bathurst and King 1879, Wheeler 1932, Casey and Hoffman 1999). Their analysis of the coin evidence suggested that the temple was built in the second half of 3rd century AD and was redeveloped in the 4th century AD after part of the original building collapsed into an undetected swallow-hole (Casey and Hoffman 1999, 81-115). In light of the numerous arguments about the dating that have bearing on interpretation of the site (these are discussed in 7.7.1 of this chapter) it is perhaps safest to attribute the temple complex's construction to somewhere between late 3rd century AD and late 4th century AD (Smith 2001, 134-135).

7.2.2 Iron Age and Early Roman Occupation

There is evidence of occupation at the Lydney site dating back to the Iron Age, at which time it was the site of a hillfort. Part of the hillfort's inner bank and ditch and several postholes from a rectangular wooden house are the only structural features remaining from that period. However, further excavation, that was expected to reveal remains of the hillfort rampart, uncovered the bare shaft of an iron mine. A Roman tile found within the clear sequence of layers within the shaft indicated that the mine was in use for several hundred years after the Roman conquest; trial holes and pick marks were still visible in the clay-like walls and ceiling (Wheeler 1932, 4-21).

7.2.3 The Structure and Lay-out of Lydney Temple

The Lydney temple site has a number of structural features that compare favourably with the remains of the continental healing complex Fontes Sequanae at the mouth of the Seine, though the chronologies are very different (fig. 29). Sanctuaries such as these are believed to have been influenced by Mediterranean religious sites known as Asklepieia that were dedicated to the Greek healer god Asklepios (Aldhouse-Green 1999a, 70-76). A guesthouse for visiting pilgrims was the largest building at the Lydney site and this appears to have been connected to a bathhouse with communal hot and cold plunge baths. Adjacent to the baths was a series of rooms that have been interpreted as a dormitory or *abaton* where visitors might undertake a sacred sleep. During this incubation it was hoped the residing deity would appear to the patient and in doing so heal them. Alternatively this building could have perhaps housed commercial outlets supplying various goods to the visitors: the impressive nature of the temple complex suggests that its patrons had wealth to spend (Wheeler 1932, 22-57). However, the former is perhaps the most plausible interpretation: orchestrated processions, with their connotations of cosmic order and demonstration of hierarchical succession were an important element of ritual healing practices at Gallo-Roman shrines. The formality was intended to induce a sense of readiness in the patient (Ghey 2003, 90-93). If one examines Mortimer Wheeler's reconstruction of the layout of the site one can see how a dormitory would fit into a sequence of movement around the temple precinct (fig. 30).

Figure 29. Reconstruction of Lydney temple site, Gloucestershire © Wheeler 1939, Society of Antiquaries of London.

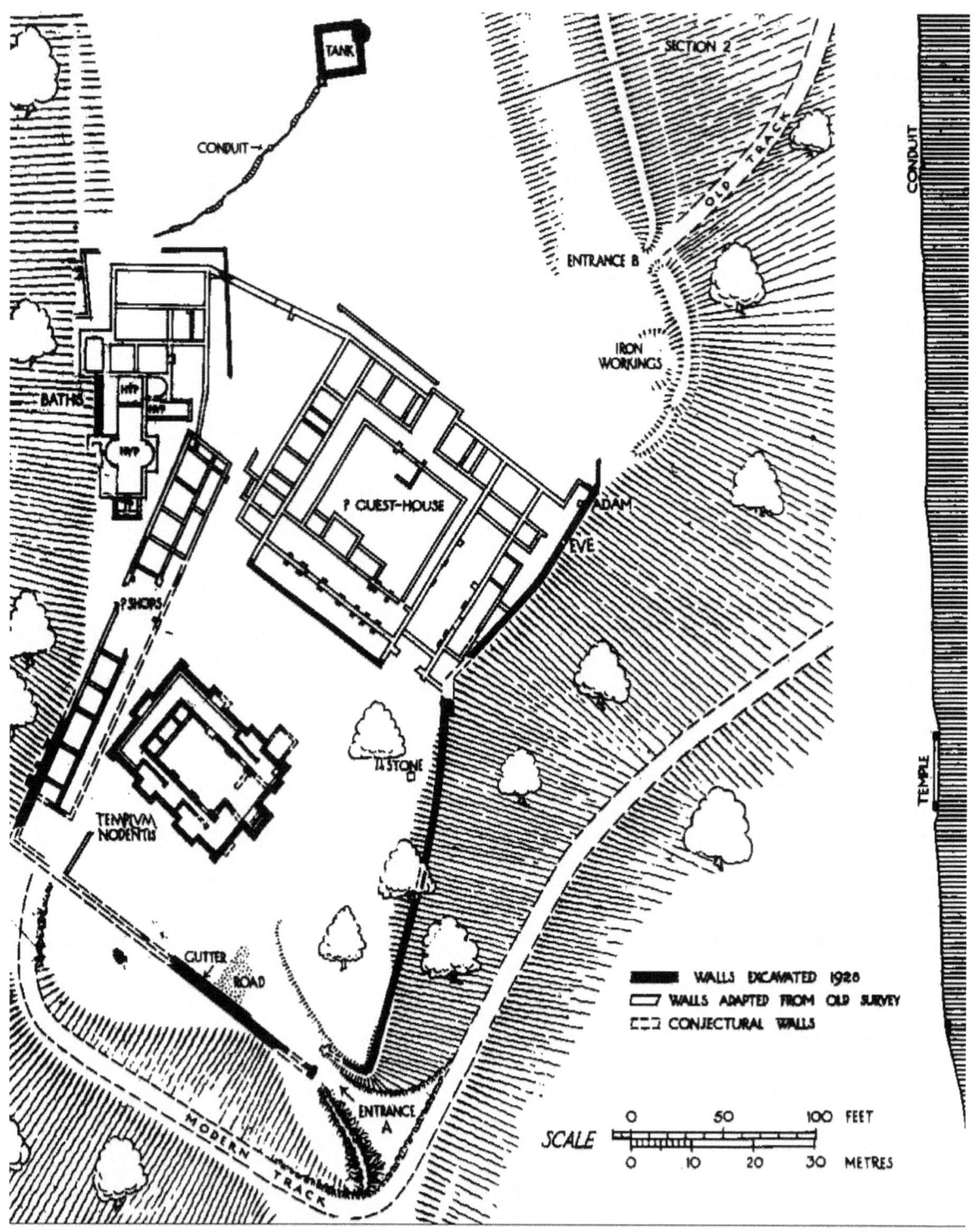

Figure 30. Plan of Lydney Temple site, Gloucestershire.
© Wheeler 1939, Society of Antiquaries of London

In an anti-clockwise direction from the guesthouse pilgrims could have proceeded to the baths, where they would undergo the ritual purification necessary before they could enter the dormitory or *abaton*. After having their prayers answered by Nodens patrons could continue on to the temple to offer their thanks (Wheeler 1932, Plates LI and LII).

A stone stairway led up to the temple itself, which was surrounded by an ambulatory. The far end of the *cella* was divided into three compartments that had perhaps held cult statues of Nodens in different forms. The majority of the artefacts to be examined in this chapter were recovered from the temple area suggesting that they were most likely votive offerings. The floor of the temple was decorated with a mosaic depicting sea-monsters (Wheeler 1932, 23-29). As will be discussed fully later in this chapter, Lydney temple's location overlooking the Severn appears to have had significant bearing on the cult beliefs. It is quite usual to find healing sanctuaries close to natural bodies of water like springs and rivers; there are a number of British examples including the temple to Sulis Minerva at nearby Bath and the shrine of Apollo at Nettleton, Wiltshire, the latter occupying both sides of a river valley (Cunliffe and Davenport 1985, Wedlake 1982, 1-4).

7.3 Ancient and Modern Connections Between Dogs and Healing

As well as the comparative architecture of Lydney temple complex, various artefacts from the site suggest that health was a major concern for visitors. These include oculist stamps, a votive limb with spoon-shaped fingernails indicative of iron deficiency and the bone figure of a naked woman whose abdomen had been incised with lines to draw attention to this area of feminine health concerns like fertility, pregnancy and period pains. Interestingly, at least 10 images of quadrapeds interpreted as dogs have also been found at the site to date (Bathurst and King 1879, 1-16, Wheeler 1932, 39-44, Casey and Hoffman 1999, 81-143). An iconographic connection between dogs and healing during late prehistory and early history is by no means unique to Lydney, as mentioned in chapter 4, images of young pilgrims carrying small dogs were found at the Gallo-Roman healing shrine Fontes Sequanae at the mouth of the Seine (Aldhouse-Green 1999a, 11-13). At a temple to Mars at Mavilly in Burgundy a dog and a raven accompany an image of the deity and a pilgrim: in the Western provinces of Rome Mars was perceived as a healer. Around Trier in the Rhineland numerous representations of mother goddesses depicted with lapdogs have been discovered at temple sites, along with others holding fertility symbols such as swaddled infants and baskets of fruit (Wightman 1970, 208-227, Green 1995, 105-114). In the 2nd century AD the Greek writer Aelian recorded that as many as one thousand sacred hounds were kept at a temple dedicated to a local divinity called Adranus, at a town of the same name in Sicily. Their purpose was to fawn over visitors by day and to lead intoxicated pilgrims home at night (Aelian *De Natura Animalium* 3, 20, Scholfield 1959, 359-389). The great temple to Asklepios at Epidaurus in Greece also housed live dogs that were accorded sacred status because Asklepios was believed to have been suckled by a bitch after he was exposed and left to die by his mother, Coronis (Edelstein and Edelstein 1998, 11-12). The dogs were included in ceremonies involving the distribution of sacrificial cakes and they were also apparently used in curative rituals: there is a record from the sanctuary that a boy's blindness was cured by one of the dogs (*Iamata* IV(2),1.121-2, Stele 1, Edelstein and Edelstein 1998, 292). Wheeler's excavation report on the Lydney temple does not list dogs amongst the species present at the site and recent reanalysis of the bone assemblage for this study confirms this lack of evidence (Watson 1932, 131).

Undoubtedly the canine habit of licking their own wounds and those of others has led people to believe that their saliva had curative properties (Toynbee 1973, 123). This type of reasoning based on straightforward observations of nature appears to be at the root of many mythical and ritual concepts associated with animals; such beliefs very often focus on certain outstanding characteristics of otherwise complex animals (Buxton 1990, 60-79). The link between hounds and healing may not be immediately apparent to many of us in more enlightened times but the association is widespread and enduring. We only have to look at some of the ways that we in the Western world use the species to realise that a manifestation of this connection still exists. Guide dogs for the blind are part of daily life and domestic dogs are sometimes brought into hospitals because of the considerable psychological and physiological benefits that can be experienced by patients through interaction with them: as mentioned in chapter 6 a national charity called Pets as Therapy or PAT has been established for this very reason (Serpell 1995, 162-174, Anon 2005). The healing powers of canine saliva has been clinically tested and scientists have found that there is something in dog saliva that has antibacterial properties that can help prevent the contamination of their own wounds from Escherichia Coli and Streptococcus Canis (Hart and Powell 1990, 383-386). It has also been clinically proven that some dogs can be trained to detect the smell of bladder cancer in human urine and even some untrained dogs have the ability to recognise signs of impending diabetic and epileptic seizures in time to forewarn their humans of the danger (Anon 2004).

Pliny the Elder recorded that dogs might be used in the treatment of a number of physical disorders. For example, it was purported that rubbing the afflicted region with a plant on which a dog had urinated could realign dislocated joints (Pliny *Natural History* XXIV, Turner 1962, 221). Furthermore, it was thought that stomach ailments could be relieved by their transference from the human patient to a lapdog or puppy through close physical contact (Pliny *Natural History* XXX, Turner 1962, 315-316). Other ancient cultures used puppies similarly in healing and purification rituals. The Greeks rubbed a puppy on the sides of a person who needed to be purified and thereby their ills were passed to the animal, which was consequently killed. The Hittites believed that if a puppy was allowed to lick a sick person's body in the afflicted area the dog would absorb the malady and the person would be cured. No explanation as to why a puppy should be used, rather than an adult dog, is given in the historical texts. Puppies perhaps held symbolic spiritual significance that adults did not or in practical terms it could have made better economic sense to kill an animal that had not yet had time and resources expended on it in training (Collins 1992, 1-6, Plutarch *Questiones Romanae* LXVIII, Rose 1924, 148).

In the middle of the 1st millennium BC, Ashkelon in Israel was a busy multicultural seaport under Persian rule but controlled by Phoenicians. Over 700 complete dog skeletons have been found during excavations of a tell dating to this period; each one was carefully arranged and buried in an individual earth pit. None of the dog remains showed signs of butchery and the age range of the animals at death was suggestive of natural fatalities in an urban dog population. The excavator felt that the careful and uniform burials of both adults and puppies suggested that the species may have been considered a sacred animal in that area and that this was possibly due to their role in a healing cult. No direct evidence was found to support this proposal in Ashkelon itself (Stager 1991, 26-42). The interpretation arose from a variety of sources in the Near East that hint at the existence of widespread beliefs in the animals' healing powers. During the 2nd and 1st millennia BC the cult of a goddess known as Gula or Ninisina flourished in various areas of the Near East. Her primary function was healing the sick and the animal sacred to her was the domestic dog. A temple to her actually called the 'Dog House' was excavated in the 1980s. A considerable number of dog images were found at the site along with various representations of humans and other votive offerings; one example depicted a man hugging a dog. Despite this obvious veneration of the species it also appears that dogs were sacrificed to the goddess: 33 dog skeletons were recovered from an earth ramp that led up to the temple (Livingstone 1988, 54-60). In Egypt various parts of domestic dogs were held to have medicinal properties: roasted dog liver was meant to cure a rabies sufferer of the their fear of water and an ointment made of dog dung, along with a number of other unlikely ingredients, was used to relieve pain (Brewer et al. 2001, 44). In the 1st century BC Diodorus Siculus recorded that in Egypt certain dogs were kept in sacred enclosures and had the greatest care and finest foods lavished upon them. When one of these animals died it was embalmed then buried in a consecrated tomb (Diodorus Siculus *Bibliotheca Historia* I 83.2 - I 83.5, Oldfather 1933). An inscription on a plaque from the Phoenician temple to Resheph-Mukol at Kition in Cyprus records that attendants were paid for healing rites involving dogs and puppies performed at the site. Another Phoenician god, Eshmun was conflated with the Greek healing god Asklepios to whom dogs were sacred (Stager 1991, 26-42).

7.4 The Dog Images from Lydney

7.4.1 The Human Faced Quadraped

As mentioned above, it has been recorded that to date at least 10 images of dogs have been recovered from the temple area of the Lydney complex. Undoubtedly the majority of these are portrayals of *canis familiaris,* but others are more ambiguous: one of the animals is represented by no more than a pair of stone paws; the rest of the statue has been lost. Arguably the most unusual image from Lydney is a two-dimensional, human faced, bronze beast that could be canine or feline (fig. 31) (Wheeler 1932, 89, Aldhouse-Green 2004a, 164-170). It has been suggested that there is more to the strange appearance of this creature than abstract artistry: it might be the case that the deity was believed to possess shape-shifting powers, therefore the hybrid may be an illustration of this facet of Nodens' power (Aldhouse-Green 2004a, 164-170). There are no anthropomorphic representations of the god Nodens at the site, but clearly dogs had some degree of sacred status. One bronze hound was found in association with an inscription that provided a direct link between the canine iconography and the god Nodens: a crudely executed yet animated barking dog stands above the words '*Pectillus votum quod promissit deo Nudente m(erito) dedit*', which translates as 'Pectillus hereby gives the vow which he promised to the god Nodens deservedly' (fig. 33) (Wheeler 1932, 89). However, to imagine that Nodens was simply a dog would be to vastly underestimate the complexity of Romano-British religion (Green 1986, 170). From its torso we can see that the animal is undoubtedly a female quadraped and one might ask why a male deity would not maintain the same sex even in different forms. Of course hybrid creatures belong to the realm of the fantastic so to question the specifics of a creation that is beyond logic seems rather pointless.

The idea of healers being aided by spirit helpers, often animals, is widespread across time and space. To make contact with these otherworldly forces is still the intrinsic aim of many shamanic rituals. To encourage this connection between realms, shamans often don animal costumes. Consequently art depicting these ceremonies often include portrayals of therianthropic figures, as if the spirits of the shaman and animal helper are merging into one being. It is certainly possible that linkages between shamanism and healing rites existed in pre-Christian European beliefs. In Iron Age rock carvings from Val Camonica in North Italy human figures wearing animal adornments have been interpreted as ancient shamans. Similarly, the hybrid image from Lydney may represent a healer dressed up in this way during a rite. Alternatively, healing rituals at the temple may have involved living dogs, in which case the hybrid animal may represent an animal being possessed by the deity during the ceremony: unfortunately there is no faunal evidence to support this theory. Whatever the inspiration was for this particular image its unsettling gaze certainly invokes a sense of the supernatural (Aldhouse-Green 2004a, 164-170).

7.4.2 The Lydney Deer Hound

In contrast to the creator of the human-faced quadraped, the craftsperson that modelled a bronze deerhound found at Lydney elegantly and seamlessly merged Roman naturalism with a more stylised form of representation (fig. 32). Although the figurine is unmistakably a hound the muzzle is extended creating a more elegant creature than if it had been an entirely lifelike rendering. Although the hound is recumbent it is clear from its taut musculature that it is anxious to move. This conveyed sense of liminality, between repose and action, is perhaps analogous to the process of healing (Aldhouse-Green 2004a, 140).

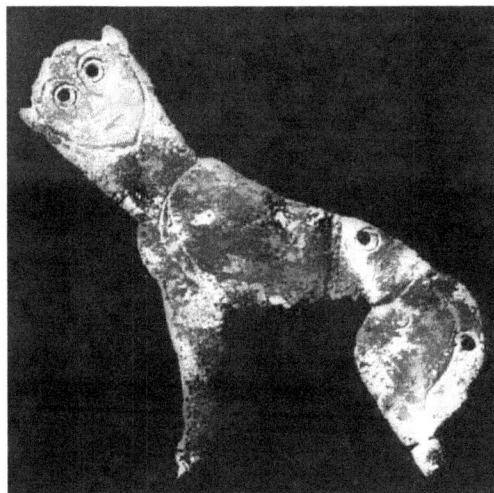

Figure 31. The human faced quadraped from Lydney Temple site, Gloucestershire. Photograph © Wheeler 1939, Society of Antiquaries of London.

Figure 32. Statuette of a bronze deer-hound from Lydney temple, Gloucestershire. Photograph © Wheeler 1939, Society of Antiquaries of London

7.4.3 Other Hound Images from Lydney Temple

One of the dogs from Lydney was found at the bottom of a hole deliberately built into the middle of an inscription on the tessellated floor of the temple, along with 21 Roman coins. This *favissa*, which was approximately 23cm in diameter and lined with a terra-cotta funnel, led straight into the loose earth below (Bathurst and King 1879, 21). This feature was probably intended to receive libations: it would have been considered a channel of communication between this world and the world of the gods. Other bronzes were found close by, several of which exhibited features that indicated they had once been mounted on the walls of the temple or set into a platform of some sort (Wheeler 1932, 39-42).

Although the dog images from Lydney are generally of a quite sympathetic nature they might still represent surrogate sacrificial offerings. There is a substantial amount of evidence to suggest that the domestic dog was a common sacrificial victim in Roman Britain at sacred and secular sites. Although relatively few dog bones have been found within the main temple area of Romano-British sacred sites, articulated skeletons that have been found in these contexts show clear signs of having been used in elaborate ritual ceremonies (Alexander and Pullinger 1999, 78-80). Evidence of dog sacrifice has also been recovered from a healing shrine at Vertault in Burgundy (Meniel et al. 1991, 268-275, Aldhouse-Green 1999a, 73).

Figure 33. Picture (left) and diagram (right) of a bronze plaque bearing an inscription to the god Nodens and an image of a dog. Photograph © Wheeler 1939, Society of Antiquaries of London.

7.5 The Connection between Hunting and Healing in the Western Provinces of Rome

The powerful and lively nature of some of the canine images from Lydney are certainly suggestive of health and vitality, far more so than the small, passive lapdogs that accompany images of mother goddesses from the Western provinces of Rome (Green 1995, 105-114, Green 1989, 28-30). Indeed a number of the Lydney hounds appear quite ready to set off on a hunt. As discussed in detail in chapter 6, hounds and healing are often associated with each other in the iconography from the Roman Empire and in some cases it is clear that ideas about hunting and healing are also interlinked: the themes have been drawn together through context, epigraphy and iconography. For example, Nodens, the deity venerated at Lydney, is epigraphically linked with Silvanus and Mars at the temple site: the former was the Roman god of woodlands and hunting and in Britain and continent the latter was worshipped as a healing god (Wheeler 1932, 100, Green 1992a, 198-200). Although dog bones were not amongst the small faunal assemblage recovered during excavations at Lydney a good deal of antler was present, which could perhaps be interpreted as a contribution to the symbolism of the hunt at the site. As discussed in chapter 6, there is, in fact, a concentration of evidence that draws hunting and healing together at a number of Romano-British temple sites close to Lydney in the South West of England. At the healing shrine of Apollo at Nettleton in Wiltshire an altar is dedicated to Apollo Cunomaglos, which translates as 'Hound Lord'. An incomplete statue of a heavily draped female and an attentive hound from Nettleton suggests that Diana and her canine companion were also present (Toynbee 1982, 135-136). At Pagan's Hill, Somerset the stone torso of a life-size statue of a dog wearing a jewelled collar was found in the upper layers of a Romano-British well. Due to the quality and scale of the figure it has been suggested that it may well have been a main cult statue from the associated temple; similarities between features from this site and Nettleton led to speculation that this site might also have been dedicated to Apollo Cunomaglos (Boon 1989, 201-217). A stone relief of a cloaked hunter-god holding a hare and accompanied by a stag and hound was found at the Chedworth villa complex in Gloucestershire (Webster 1983, 16). Like Lydney, the structural character of the site supports the interpretation that the establishment was a healing sanctuary. The image is unprovenanced, but it is thought that it was found in the temple building (Goodburn 1979b, 34). On a stone found in the temple precinct at Bath a hound was depicted sitting at the feet of, and gazing intently upwards at, a figure holding a bow; the figure has been interpreted as Diana (Cunliffe 2000, 69).

To understand how the seemingly incongruous acts of hunting and healing were related in the beliefs of Romano-British people and their continental neighbours we should perhaps look at the origins of hunting. It is clear from the lack of butchered wild animal bones at habitation sites, like Danebury hillfort in Hampshire, that from at least the Iron Age hunting did not serve any real economic purpose in terms of dietary provision (Grant 1991a, 478). Obviously this was not always the case and acknowledgement of the fundamental importance of hunting in terms of early human survival is perhaps evident in the considerable amount of ceremony surrounding the activity in later times. In the 2nd century AD the Greek historian Arrian wrote that the Celts never embarked on a hunt without first appealing to the gods for their approval (Arrian *Cynegetica* 34-35, Phillips and Willcock 1999, 125-127). For these people hunting was a spiritual act, perhaps symbolising the cycle of life, death and regeneration that essentially the hunt had once been. It is then perhaps feasible to surmise that the hunter-gods, who were often portrayed with their quarry in a harmonious group, were not simply regarded as forces invoked to promote success in the kill, but also as guardians of life and health. Iconographic and epigraphic evidence from the Romano-British temple sites mentioned above certainly suggests that hunting and healing were associated at a spiritual level in Britain. That hunting was a popular activity in Roman Britain is attested by the prolific amount of hunting images in the art of the time: the motif of a dog pursuing its prey appears on everything from penknives like the example found at Lydney temple to grand works of art like the mosaic from Hinton St Mary, Dorset (Casey and Hoffman 1999, 129, Neal 1981, 87-88).

7.6 Solar Imagery at Lydney Temple

Although archaeologists tend to associate domestic dogs with chthonic realms they were occasionally connected with solar imagery in the iconography of the Western provinces of Rome. Dogs were amongst the symbolic motifs of the hammer god Sucellus, particularly in Southern Gaul and Burgundy where his attributes also included solar wheels that clearly signify a celestial connection (Green 1989, 75-86). Interestingly, the swirling hair-growth patterns on the shoulders and haunches of the beautiful bronze deerhound from Lydney are reminiscent of this type of Sun symbolism. To find solar imagery at a temple where healing rituals took place is certainly appropriate as the Sun's eternal fall and rise is suggestive of a return to health from sickness. The decoration on a bronze diadem recovered from the site also has celestial connotations: it depicts a solar deity riding a horse drawn chariot emerging from waves (fig. 34) (Aldhouse-Green 2004b, 208-210). The idea of the sun being carried over the earth this way, before disappearing into the horizon, is an ancient one: a three dimensional bronze representation of horse pulling a cart bearing a large, gold-plated disc, believed to represent the Sun, was found in Trundholm, Denmark and dates to around 1300BC (Green 1991, 112-116).

Figure 34. Bronze diadem from Lydney temple, Gloucestershire. Photograph © Wheeler 1939, Society of Antiquaries of London.

7.6.1 Solar Symbolism and the Treatment of Eye Disorders at Lydney

The Sun is also symbolically associated with eyes: it is shaped like an eye and its rays are reminiscent of our coloured irises. Obviously, it also provides light for us to see (Green 1991, 38-39). Evidence for the treatment of eye disorders at Lydney was found in the form of oculist or collyrium stamps; these were labels for collyria, herbal ointments used as remedies for eye complaints at the time. Their presence suggests that sight related ailments were one of the reasons for pilgrimages to be undertaken. Afflictions such as trachoma and night-blindness appear to have been widespread in the Western Europe during antiquity, possibly due to a diet deficient in Vitamin A and/or unhygienic living conditions. Votive eye plaques and collyrium stamps have been found at numerous healing sanctuaries in this area where artefacts depicting dogs were also present, these include; Mavilly, Burgundy; Fontes Sequanae at the mouth of the Seine and Sainte Sabine, Burgundy (Aldhouse-Green 1999a, 37-40, Boon 1983, 1-12). There is certainly some suggestion in the archaeological record of a connection between hounds and the restoration of eyesight in antiquity. As mentioned above, it was recorded that one of the sacred hounds of Asklepios cured a young blind boy (*Iamata* IV(2),1.121-2, Stele I, Edelstein and Edelstein 1998). It is possible that dogs' natural guiding instinct also contributed to their symbolic role at the Lydney sanctuary and at comparable sites on the continent.

7.6.2 Fertility and Solar Symbolism at Lydney Temple

The passage of the Sun also symbolises life, death and regeneration and consequently fertility, which appears to have been an important issue for visitors to Lydney temple. A number of clearly female figures were recovered during excavations, including an image of a naked woman carved out of bone. She is depicted with long flowing hair and has curved lines incised on her abdomen as if to draw attention to this area of the body. A seated mother goddess holding a cornucopia was also found; unfortunately she now lacks a head (Wheeler 1932, 68). As discussed in detail in chapter 6, mother goddesses were perhaps the most common icons from the Western provinces of Rome and they were often depicted with cornucopia or baskets of fruit and other emblems such as babies, loaves of bread and sometimes, small dogs. It seems likely that their worship was connected with, amongst other things, the preservation of fertility in humans, animals and plants (Green 1995, 105-116). The Lydney temple dogs are far more robust than the lapdogs usually associated with mother goddesses, but it would appear that a facet of domestic dog symbolism in general was associated with reproduction in contemporary Western Europe. Their connection with regeneration through the hunt has been discussed above.

7.6.3 Solar Symbolism and the Significance of Iron at Lydney Temple

Iconography from Western Europe during the Roman period suggests that solar imagery was associated with iron working, therefore it is perhaps significant that Lydney temple was sited in the same area as a large Roman iron mine, the only one still surviving in Britain (Wheeler 1932, 18-22). Although the shafts themselves are now inaccessible, the red ferruginous earth at the site is testament to its rich mineral content and consequently the red tainted water at the site may have been held to have therapeutic powers or it may have been seen as redolent of blood and life-force. There is some evidence to suggest that the presence of iron may have had significance for those who worshipped at the site. A votive bronze arm from the site has odd spoon-shaped fingernails, which is a diagnostic symptom of chronic iron deficiency. On the bronze diadem mentioned above a fish-tailed/ male human hybrid, holding what appear to be two picks, rises out the waves alongside the solar deity. A box of artefacts, including unpublished finds, from the Wheeler excavations was recently returned to the Lydney estate. One of the most interesting finds amongst the repatriated items was a miniature bronze pick that had perhaps been another votive offering to Nodens (Aldhouse-Green 2004b, 208-210). Close examination of the British archaeological record suggests that there is a symbolic linkage between domestic dogs and iconography relating to iron working and perhaps a Smith god, although the pairing is not as frequent or explicit as hounds and hunting deities. At the Chester-le-Street Roman fort, County Durham a foundation deposit was found beneath huge paving stones in one of the towers of the west gate. The deposit contained a face-pot further embellished with a hammer and tongs and the skeleton of a large dog accompanied it. A metalworking furnace was found elsewhere on the site (Goodburn 1979a, 285). A group of rather unusual artefacts were retrieved from a group of two pits and a well in Southwark, London, situated about 20m from and contemporary with a 2nd century smithy. The finds included gemstones, writing tablets, one glass vessel and 42 pottery containers and the near complete skeletons of 20 dogs. One urn was decorated with a hammer, tongs and anvil motif. Large amounts of iron slag and a crucible, which would have been used in bronze working, were recovered from four other nearby pits of a similar age. A pre-Boudican smithy had been replaced by a later workshop in the area so it would seem that these craftsmen had occupied the area for several generations (Drummond-Murray et al. 2002, 97-100, Dennis 1978, 304-307).

As mentioned above, a dog appears as an attribute of the hammer god or Smith god Succellus; this pairing is particularly prominent in Burgundy where the god's association with solar imagery is also marked (Green 1989, 75-86). Two quadrapeds, interpreted as dogs or wolves because they have paws rather than hooves, appear on the Farley Heath sceptre binding along with a hammer, tongs, anvil, a solar wheel and a possible solar deity (Black 1985, 140-142). Ethnographic studies have revealed that in some societies the smithing process in analogous with hunting. The African Gbaya tribe consider both practices to be fraught with danger and success is believed to be in the hands of the gods and accordingly strict customs and taboos are performed and adhered to, to ensure their co-operation (Herbert 1993, 179-180). As mentioned above, it seems likely that fertility was an issue for pilgrims visiting the Lydney temple and it has been suggested that iron working was associated with fertility in Iron Age Britain: at a basic level it was used to make agricultural tools but it may also have been perceived as having regenerative properties because of it mutability. The concepts of fertility and iron working may also have been linked in that the farming equipment that people depended on for their livelihoods could be transformed into iron weapons of death, thus creating a symbolic cycle of life and death (Hingley 1997, 9-18).

7.7 The Lydney Cult

7.7.1 Site Chronology and its Influence on Interpretation

Several academics have disputed the 4th century date for the construction of the Lydney temple complex suggested by Wheeler. One of the arguments for an earlier 3rd century date was based upon the epigraphy on the mosaic floor of the *cella*, which reads (fig. 35):

D(eo) N(odenti) T(itus) Flavius Senilis, pr(aepositus) rel(iquationi), ex stipibus possuit; o [pus cur] ante Victorino inter[prêt]e.

This has been translated as 'To the god Nodens, Titus Flavius Senilis, officer in charge of the supply-depot of the fleet, laid this pavement out of money offerings; the work being in charge of the Victorinus, interpreter on the Governor's staff' (Wheeler 1932, 103). It has been suggested that if this interpretation is correct and indicates the presence of the *Classis Britannica*, then the temple could not date to later than about AD 305 when the Roman Empire had firmly re-established its rule of Britain after Carausius, the commander of the fleet, had seized control of the island (Smith 1994, 28-33). This would supports Casey and Hoffman's conclusion, drawn primarily from coin evidence, that the first temple was constructed in the second half of the 3rd century AD (Casey and Hoffman 1999, 81-115).

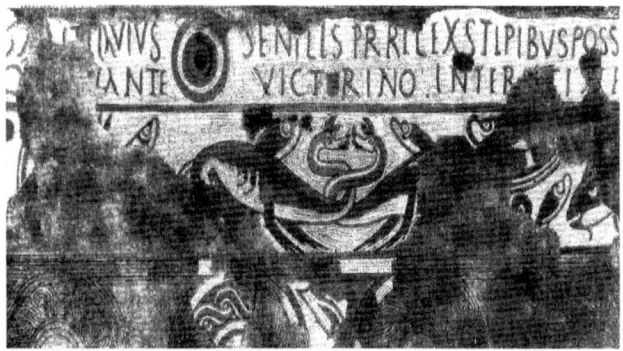

Figure 35. The mosaic from the *cella* floor of Lydney temple, Gloucestershire. Photograph © Wheeler 1939, Society of Antquaries of London.

The phrase, *'o [pus cur] ante Victorino inter[prêt]e'* has also been interpreted as a reference to an 'interpreter of dreams' resident at the site. Furthermore, it has been suggested that the abbreviation *Pr. rel* should be read as *praepositis religionum,* rather than *praefectus reliquiationis,* the former interpretation translates as 'superintendent of religious rites' (Henig 1995, 120). If these alternative interpretations are correct and Senilis was some sort of priest figure at the temple it would certainly explain why he had access to the temple's offering box, if indeed that is what is suggested by 'money offerings' in the epigraphy. If this is the case then a later 4th century date for the construction and redevelopment of Lydney temple could still be correct (Smith 1994, 28-33).

Working with Wheeler's later date in the early 1970s David Shotter speculated that a unit of Roman *barcarii* may have been present in the South West of Britain in the latter half of the 4th century AD, to assist in the country's coastal defence after the attacks of 367AD. Shotter believed that this particular interpretation might explain why archaeology and epigraphy relating to Nodens has only been found near Lancaster, in the North West, and at Lydney in the South West. He suggested that part of the unit *Numerus Barcariorum*, believed to have been stationed in Lancaster, might have been sent south as scouts on the Bristol Channel and Severn Estuary. At Cockersand Moss near Lancaster two statuettes of Nodens were discovered in the early 18th century; sadly these have been lost over time and whether these representations featured dogs remains unknown (Shotter 1973, 206-209). At both Lydney and Cockersand Moss, Nodens is epigraphically linked with the god Mars. If a necessary change from ordinary duties did bring these men to the South West in the latter half of the 4th century AD then their beliefs perhaps influenced the cult practised at Lydney temple. It is known from the discovery of an altar at Halton that the *Numerus Barcariorum* worshipped Mars. Halton-on-Lune is only a little more than six miles up-river from Cockersand Moss where the dedications to Mars Nodens were made, so it would seem likely that Nodens would have been known and perhaps synthesised with Mars in both places (Shotter 1973, 206-209).

7.7.2 Water and Healing Rituals

Whatever Senilis did for a living and whether beliefs in Mars Nodens originated in the North West of England or not, it is clear that the power of water was at the centre of the Lydney deities sphere of influence. The *cella* mosaic would have been expensive and designed to be a permanent feature so it seems likely that sea travel was of utmost importance to Lydney patrons (Henig 1984b, 174-179). Furthermore, a bronze diadem, possibly worn by the resident priest, depicts an assembly of fantastic beings arising out of foaming water. The central figure, a solar deity, is flanked on both sides by two male hybrid figures; one with wings the other with a fishes tail (Wheeler 1932, 90, Aldhouse-Green 2004b, 208-210).

Water was central to the enactment of healing rituals in Roman Europe and consequently most sanctuaries were situated close to natural springs or rivers. Although not all their associated water sources had genuine curative properties bathing in and drinking water, which was perhaps perceived as embodying the essence of the associated deity, was an essential act of lustration at these sites (Aldhouse-Green 1999a, 76-81). In antiquity maladies were believed to occur because of an afflicted individual's transgression or from intrusive impurities and the sacred water at healing sanctuaries was used to rid the patient of these pollutants (Stevens 1998, 277-278). The Severn did not directly feed the baths at Lydney but it is easy to imagine that, with its powerful tides and bores, it was perceived as a manifestation of Nodens' power.

7.7.3 A Symbolic Connection Between Dogs and Water

There appears to have been a linkage between dogs and water in the spiritual beliefs of pre-Christian Europeans: numerous examples of multiple dog deposits in disused wells, ponds and other watery locations exhibit characteristics that cannot be easily explained as the result of ordinary domestic activity (Green 1992a, 111-113). For example, as discussed in chapter 3, a group of seven Romano-British *ollae* were found buried on the Upchurch Marshes, Kent in the 1950s. Each vessel contained the remains of a puppy aged about three weeks old at death and charcoal from burnt twigs and small branches (Noel-Hume 1957, 160-167). During more recent excavations at Shiptonthorpe, West Yorkshire numerous complete pottery vessels and the skulls of a stallion, a bull and two dogs were found in an in-filled waterhole. The dog skulls were of a similar size and appear to have been deliberately placed directly opposite each other on different sides of the pond. Pollen analysis of the infilling also indicated the presence of considerable amounts of mistletoe, which apart from being rare in such contexts was purported by Pliny the Elder to be a sacred plant during this period (Halkon and Millet 2003, 303-309, Pliny *Natural History* XVI 95, Turner 1962).

The aquatically themed images present on the Lydney mosaic and diadem belong to the realms of the imagination. Fantastic sea monsters and hybrids are impossible beings living in a dimension that is essentially uninhabitable to us. The alien creatures embody the chaos and uncertainty of what is in essence another world (Aldhouse-Green 2004a, 149-153). The presence of domestic dogs in the iconography at Nodens' temple temper these alien images with their familiar earthly form. Although the dogs undoubtedly represent liminality, as an animal able to cross thresholds between worlds, they also invoke a sense of security by choosing to ally themselves with humans.

The linkage between dogs and water may simply have arisen from a common association with healing. However, considering domestic dogs' multifaceted metonymic nature it is quite possible that the connection had considerably more depth. Dogs have a somewhat ambivalent place in the world, seeming neither to belong fully to the animal world or the human world whilst maintaining a complex social structure and sense of community amongst their own kind. They occupy a hinterland between wild and domestic realms: in their physical resemblance to wolves and some aspects of their behaviour. As hunters they also represent a moving horizon between life and death. Due to their status as intermediaries between opposing states of being they have come to be viewed as guardians of liminal space in many cultures. Similarly, in the beliefs of numerous societies, past and present, water is an element of the liminal space between this world and the afterlife. In Classical mythology Cerberus the three headed dog guarded the entrance of Hades, allowing the souls of the deceased to enter and cross the River Styx to their resting place (Virgil *The Aeneid* VI 418-425, Day Lewis 1961). In Aztec mythology it is said that owners of a particular type of small, yellow dog would be greeted by them in the afterlife; the animal would look out for them on one side of a broad river and on recognising their master (there is no mention of mistresses) they would jump in the water and swim to them and then carry the deceased back over the river to their final destination. In Huron, native North American, folklore a fierce dog floats on a log on a raging river; it is the final obstacle to negotiate on one's journey to the village of the dead (Schwartz 1997, 93-96).

7.7.4 The Lydney Temple – Features of the Landscape

7.7.4.1 The Promontory Site

Although it is clear that the dogs at Lydney must have been linked with healing aspects of the cult practised at the site, it also seems very likely that their symbolism was somehow connected to maritime issues. To understand how the hounds and aquatic imagery from the site might have complemented each other it is important to know something of the nature of the River Severn. As mentioned above one undeniably impressive feature of the Lydney temple site is the panoramic view of the River Severn afforded by its hilltop location.

7.7.4.2 A Treacherous River

The view of the river itself has remained unchanged since Roman times, as the sea level relative to land is the same. The riverbed is thought to have changed, but overall in terms of tidal phenomena the river itself would have behaved in much the same way as it does today. Although evidence for maritime traffic on the river is sparse, the presence of a Roman quay and a possible dry dock yard for ship maintenance at Gloucester suggests that the waterway was in frequent use (Rowbotham 1978, 4-9).

Above Gloucester the river is very shallow and traders could easily become stranded: barges in recent times have been known to remain stuck, waiting for rainfall, for over two months (Witts 2002, 66). Below Gloucester fierce tides fill the estuary in a few hours, then it drains very

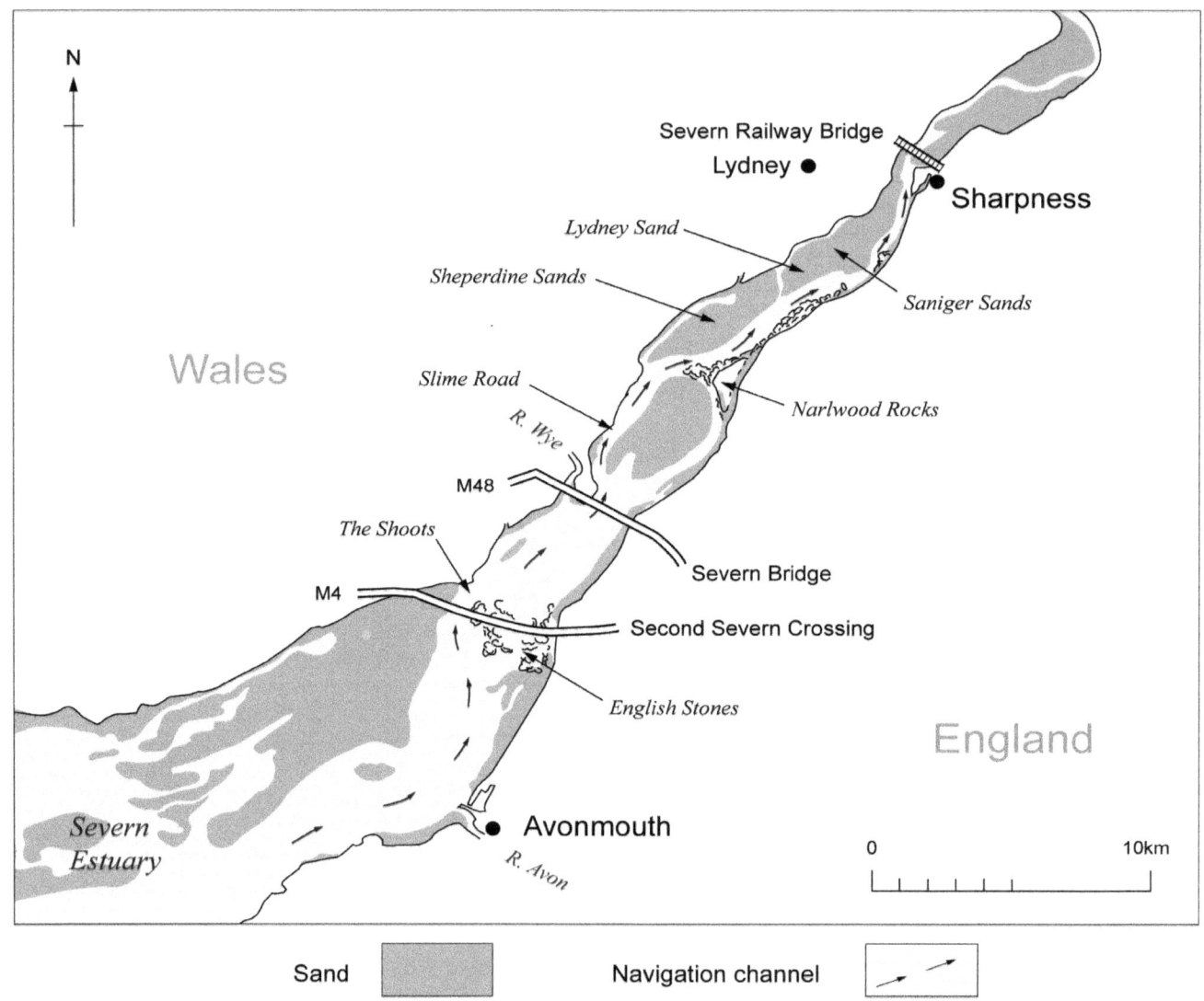

Fig. 36. A map of the Severn Estuary from Avonmouth to Sharpness with navigation channel indicated. *After* Witts 2002. Diagram © Anne Leaver

quickly leaving large ever-changing sandbanks exposed. Boats are prone to grounding on the rivers ebb and can consequently be capsized on the incoming tide. On their journey vessels passing Lydney have to navigate a very narrow course of safe river. When the river was still used as a commercial thoroughfare in the 20th century lights were put in place to guide river traffic past obstacles like the Narlwood rocks; it is unknown whether beacons were lit for this purpose during the Roman period. Even if such a warning system did exist the difficulties involved in steering an accurate course this way, against the strong currents would have made this river passage a sailor's nightmare (fig. 45) (Witts 2002, 66-70).

7.7.4.3 The River Severn Sands

At low water the Lydney Sands may look inviting to walk on. However, the Severn's tide is terrifyingly swift and with hardly any warning one can find oneself waist deep in water, before inevitably being knocked over and carried away by the powerful currents. It is a characteristic of the river that no doubt gave rise to the story of Roman soldiers drowning on the Noose sands not far from Lydney. Legend has it that, in pursuit of Caratacus, Roman forces were goaded into crossing the Severn at low tide by local Britons, only to find themselves cut off beyond hope by the rapid flood tide. However fanciful this tale may be it is true to say that it quite certainly could have happened to the unprepared at any time; unfortunately such accidents still occur all too frequently today (Anon 2000, Wright 2005).

7.7.4.4 The Severn Bore

The biggest differences between the character of the Severn today and in Roman times are the number and size of the famous tidal bores that occur; geological changes within the channel suggest in antiquity they would have been both more frequent and even larger (Rowbotham 1978, 4-9). The first record of the bore dates to around AD800 when historian Nennius wrote *The Wonders of Britain*. Out of the thirteen wonders he described, four are actually different descriptions of the Severn Bore; presumably the author was unaware of his error (Morris 1980, 16-17). Tidal bores in general are very rare: a number of specific tidal and geological features need to be present for a bore to occur. Today, the Severn bore is still amongst the ten largest in the world. Most of the other impressive bores are either in Asia or the Americas, although there are two 'world class' examples in France. The spectacle of the Severn Bore is awe-inspiring today and through the eyes of pre-Christian Europeans who venerated nature, whether familiar with the phenomena or not, it was undoubtedly perceived as an intense manifestation of numinous power (fig. 37). From the Lydney temple the view of the Severn Bore would not have been at its most dramatic in terms of wave height but it would have overlooked the first point where it becomes clearly visible, just after it passes Lydney and the river narrows at Sharpness (Rowbotham 1983, 19-20).

Figure 37. The Severn Bore. Photograph: Fred Rowbotham

7.7.4.5 The Symbolic Linkage Between Dogs and Water Through Liminality

Water is by far the most abundant liminal element between the bodies of *terra firma* where we humans are physically most at home. As discussed above, it seems likely that dogs were viewed as symbolic guardians of liminal space in the spiritual beliefs of Roman Europe and it perhaps follows that they were perceived as a symbol of protection on waterborne journeys.

Dogs are our self-appointed allies and like us naturally earth dwelling, but they are also very strong swimmers; these facts together with their guiding abilities strengthens their position as a symbol of safe passage. This interpretation draws the two main themes of the iconography at Lydney temple together. However, in case this argument sounds rather too contrived it is worthwhile considering the iconography associated with another deity from the Western provinces of Rome that clearly supports this theory.

7.8.1 Nehalennia and Her Hound

In a considerable proportion of the representations of the goddess she is accompanied by a medium to large sized hound. The dog is usually pictured gazing intently at its mistress and in certain instances there is physical contact between them: on one altar from Domburg the dog's nose is touching Nehalennia's knee (Hondius-Crone 1955, 48-49). The dog is portrayed as her close companion rather than simply an associated emblem and the adoration and expectancy with which the hound looks at its divine mistress perhaps reflects human veneration of the deity (fig. 38). In other forms of iconography from the Western Provinces of Rome, like that of the hunter-god discussed fully in chapter 6, the hound works to bridge the gap between the human world and the divine by appearing to be a part of both.

Figure 38. Nehalennia and her hound on an altar found at Colijnsplaat, Netherlands. Photograph courtesy of Rijksmuseum van Oudheden, te Leiden.

7.8.2 Nehalennia, Hercules and Neptune

Numerous altars from Nehalennia's temple at Domburg also depicted the Greco-Roman gods Hercules and Neptune. In a cult concerned with seafaring it is no surprise to find reference to Neptune, ruler of the ocean realms but the reason for the presence of Hercules is perhaps not as obvious, although as the prodigy of a divine and mortal coupling his presence might represent synergy between natural and super-natural realms. Hondius-Crone suggested that the god might represent safety for traders over land where the majority of his adventures took place (Hondius-Crone 1955, 106-107). However, in mythology Hercules was also said to have erected a pair of pillars, situated opposite each other on the coasts of Spain and Africa. Sailors would offer thanks to the god when they returned safely from a voyage between the two continents. It is also said that he narrowed these straits to deter whales and sea-monsters (Graves 1960, 495-497).

Both Hercules and Neptune appear on the altars at Domburg in their traditional Classical guises, complete with trident in the case of the former and with a club and lion skin in the latter; their divine status is unmistakable (Hondius-Crone 1955). In contrast to these Greco-Roman gods the mortal style of Nehalennia in her robes, which quite likely represents the fashion of the time and locality, lends an altogether more earthbound dimension to the iconography.

7.8.3 Nehalennia's Motifs

It was the role of Nehalennia and her animal companion to ensure a safe return journey to their homes for traders and mariners. The importance of 'home' is also apparent from other motifs with which she is connected. For example, she is frequently depicted with fruit, particularly apples and cornucopia. Interestingly, it has been noted that when the cornucopia is present the dog is absent, as if the two attributes were interchangeable. These emblems were common to mother goddesses from all over the Western provinces of Rome and are suggestive of abundance and wellbeing. However, this symbolic repertoire also works on a deeper level. For example, fruit motifs also represent fertility invoking ideas about life cycles (Green 1989, 10-16, Green 1995, 176-180). Nehalennia is also portrayed with her foot on the prow of a boat, which is often perceived as the soul of the ship: during Classical antiquity eyes were often painted on ships' prows or they were adorned with figureheads to physically represent this concept. Nehalennia's iconography also included a ship's rudder suggesting that she could provide some sort of guidance on waterborne journeys and perhaps also on one's voyage through life: after all a rudderless vessel is out of control and at the mercy of the elements (Green 1989, 10-16, Green 1995, 176-180, Stevens 1998, 292-294). A sea voyage can also be a metonym for our final journey to the afterlife.

7.9 Summary

As we have seen throughout this study the domestic dog was associated with numerous deities who were believed to have a wide-ranging sphere of influence and were associated with numerous spiritual concepts in antiquity. This is particularly evident in the iconography from the Western provinces of Rome. Their association with the divine during this period is perhaps most striking at the temple to Nodens in Lydney, Gloucestershire in the altars dedicated to Nehalennia's from the Netherlands.

The Lydney temple shares a number of structural features in common with contemporary continental, healing sanctuaries. It is believed that their forms were influenced by temples to the Classical Greek god Asklepios, who significantly was said to have been raised by domestic dogs and viewed the animal as sacred. An examination of academic literature carried out for this study reveals that a connection between dogs and healing appears to have arisen independently in numerous societies throughout the world and in fact, still exists in Western culture today.

It was noted that the representations of dogs from the Lydney temple are of quite robust creatures, rather like hunting hounds, as opposed to the passive lapdogs that sometimes appear with mother goddesses in iconography from the Western provinces of Rome. The linkage between hunting and healing has been discussed in detail throughout this study and evidence from historical texts, epigraphy, iconography, structured deposition of their faunal remains and ethnographic analogy has been used to support the theory that the now demonized sport was at one time considered to be a spiritual act associated with fertility and regeneration.

It would appear that geological features of the site and the location of the Lydney temple in the landscape contributed to the establishment of a cult centre in the area, and the same factors may also have led to the selection of the domestic dog for the most prominent cult symbol. The mineral rich soil at the site, which was a Roman iron mine prior to the establishment of the sanctuary was perhaps believed to have curative properties: votives from the site, including a miniature bronze pick, seem to support this. Furthermore, on a number of significant occasions in the Romano-British archaeological record dog images and dog remains have been found in association with objects related to iron working. Solar symbolism, which is present at the Lydney site, and images of dogs are brought together in other examples of contemporary iconography connected with smith gods, whose sphere of influence encompassed fertility and wellbeing.

Both Noden's temple site at Lydney and the sanctuaries to Nehalennia in the Netherlands are, or were, situated close to large bodies of water and it is apparent that safe passage on voyages was a primary concern of visiting pilgrims. The domesticated dog is perhaps not the first creature that one might associate with sea travel but as they appear to have been perceived as guardians of liminal space it would seem fitting that their protection might be sought during transit between landmasses. Furthermore, as the journey to a final resting place was across a river in Roman belief, the dogs association with the afterlife is perhaps also alluded to by their appearance in the iconography from these sites.

Chapter 8

Conclusion

8.1 The Domesticated Dog in the Art and Archaeology of Iron Age and Roman Britain

The identification of ritual activities involving animals in antiquity has been an area of increasing archaeological interest during the last few decades. Extensive research in this area has established that in Britain domestic dogs appear in 'special deposits' from Iron Age grain storage pits at settlement sites in statistically notable numbers, compared to other domestic species. However, in a survey of the faunal assemblages from Iron Age sites of a recognisably sacred nature, carried out for this study, dog bones were all but non-existent and most that were found showed no indication of having been ritually deposited. The only exception was the recent discovery of a complete dog skeleton within the entrance of a boundary feature at the East Leicestershire hoard site. The structured deposition of dogs within boundaries and entrance ways during the Iron Age is certainly quite notable: as well as the East Leicestershire specimen, unusual interments of domestic dogs have been found within the earthworks of three hillforts in Southern Britain. The role of the domestic dog as an earthly guard no doubt contributed to its symbolic role as a supernatural guardian but perception of the animal as an occupier of liminal space, for example, between human and animal worlds, might have added a more transcendental level to an otherwise straightforward symbolic linkage. Unfortunately, there isn't any Iron Age iconography from Britain that can help support this interpretation.

Dog remains are also uncommon in British Iron Age funerary contexts. In a survey of Iron Age cremation and inhumation cemeteries from Southern Britain the only dog bones recorded were a single canine tooth in a grave at King Harry Lane cemetery and the complete skeleton of a lapdog in the infill of a woman's grave at Mill Hill, Deal in Kent. Dog remains are also conspicuous by their absence in the 'Arras' burials from East Yorkshire and Durotrigian burials of Southern Dorset. As such an overwhelming negative feature we may consider that dogs were an inappropriate presence in these contexts. As only a handful of examples of humans buried with dogs have been found dating to the British Iron Age no distinct patterns could be identified in this data set. However, it is perhaps worth noting that, to date, more men than women have been found buried with dogs and the animals that were buried with women were notably small. A number of the dogs buried with humans were buried in positions that could perhaps be interpreted as subservient to the people; although their distribution across time and space is far to broad to suggest this is anything other than coincidence. These arrangements could still be independently arising reflections of human perception of the animal's place in society.

There is ample evidence, in the form of cut and chop marks on their bones, that dogs were eaten in Iron Age Britain. They were also eaten during the Romano-British period but it would appear, far less frequently. Despite this concession, life for the average Romano-British dog does not seem to have been particularly comfortable. Pathologies, indicative of quite severe physical abuse are often visible on their skeletons. It is perhaps worth noting at this point that the physique of the average domestic dog in Roman Britain was a far cry from the elegant, greyhound like creatures frequently portrayed in the iconography of the time. However dogs were regarded in life did not preclude them from receiving quite remarkable burials. Michael Fulford recently noted that they were a common feature of unusual 'ritual' interments found at Romano-British settlement sites in Southern Britain. A survey of numerous sites in the same area, carried out for this study, supported these findings. Archaeo-zoologists have tended to interpret the large numbers of dogs and puppies found in pits and wells at settlements as evidence of population control. However, it is my contention that practical motivation does not preclude ritual enactment. It has been suggested that this depositional activity may well have developed out of Iron Age practice of placing special animal deposits in disused grain storage pits, mentioned above. Spatial analysis of the special animal deposits and human burials from the Iron Age and Roman phases of the settlement site at Winnall Down, Hampshire revealed that interments from the later phase directly overlay earlier examples, which suggests that the presence and significance of such deposits had been communicated over a considerable period of time.

The survey of Romano-British settlement sites carried out for this study has highlighted a number of characteristics of dog burials, most notably their association with infant burials and human skulls. Interestingly, the connection between these finds also occurs at sacred sites, like the temple complexes at Springhead in Kent and in the ritual shafts at Ridgeons Gardens, Cambridge and Folly Lane, St Albans. It seems likely that, despite the increase in areas of constructed sacred space in the Romano-British period, comparable sacrificial ceremonies, frequently involving dogs, were being carried out at shrine and settlement sites: purpose dug shafts containing numerous votive animal offerings were found at a farmstead at Keston in Kent.

The association between interments of dogs and infants is perhaps suggestive of their use in fertility rituals. Both dogs and infants are a motif of the mother goddess iconography from the Western provinces of Rome and their sphere of influence was centred on fertility and regeneration. It seems possible that these symbolic linkages were not only portrayed in contemporary iconography but also played out in rituals involving the actual physical manifestations of these emblems. However, there is perhaps another reason for the recurrent association between child and dog burials. I have suggested that both infants and dogs may have been the most suitable surrogates for an adult human sacrifice during the periods under discussion. The rate of child mortality was high in Roman Britain and there is evidence that infanticide was practised. An infant's life, although probably regarded as superior to an animal, was not valued as highly as that of an adult humans and therefore it was perhaps expendable in times when a powerful sacrificial offering was deemed necessary. In the case of the domestic dog, its close proximity to, and relationship with humans probably gave the species a certain status over other domestic animals that cannot be measured in economic terms. Furthermore, in a number of the unusual dog burials, dating to both the Iron Age and Romano-British periods, the animals appear to have suffered a degree of overkill and/or their bodies have been restrained in some way and this is highly reminiscent of the treatment meted out to numerous humans in contemporary burials found in unusual contexts. It is also possible that the restraint of the animals was intended to symbolise human control over nature: robust collars are a prominent characteristic of hound images from Roman Britain.

Dogs were connected to ideas about regeneration during the Roman period because of the part they played in the hunt. There is considerable iconographic and epigraphic evidence from Roman Britainto support this theory. The original role of the hunt, killing prey to support life, gave the sport a spiritual dimension, which is mentioned in historical texts and is still common amongst hunter-gatherer tribes today. Hunters, having asked hunting deities for their blessing, would view a successful hunt as confirmation of divine approval; it became an act symbolising the eternal cycle of life, death and rebirth. In one area of South West England there is a notable concentration of hunter-god images and references to hunting deities at sites that were associated with healing further supporting their association with regeneration. Alternatively hunting and healing could be linked as a result of their shared association with the domestic dog: passive lapdogs as well as hounds were portrayed in iconography found at healing shrines in the Western provinces of Rome. Like many symbolic associations, the domestic dog's linkage with healing perhaps grew out of observation of one of its natural habits, namely licking wounds; the connection has arisen independently in a large number of cultures across time and space.

The spiritual significance that hunting held in pagan antiquity might also be visible in the structured deposition of human and animal remains from Iron Age and Roman Britain: for example, the burial of a dog within the earthworks at Blewburton Hill, hillfort, Dorset was accompanied by a horse and rider. A similar trio were found beneath the remains of a feature interpreted as a monument plinth at a Roman cemetery in York. A dog, a deer and a horse were also found buried together, nose to tail, in a pit in a Romano-British cemetery in East London. The funerary contexts of these interments is interesting because it perhaps further supports the existence of a symbolic connection between hunting and positive ideas about regeneration discussed above. The circular arrangement of the East London burial is perhaps also part of hunting/ life-cycle symbolism: a number of other animal burials involving dogs have been found similarly arranged in Roman Britain.

Some of the most interesting associations between images of dogs and other iconographic emblems have been found at the Romano-British temple site in Lydney, Gloucestershire. In structure, the site compares favourably with a number of Late Iron Age and Roman healing shrines in Gaul, which are thought to have originally been inspired by Greek Asklepia. The representations of hunting hounds and references to Silvanus, the Roman god of the woodlands, connect hunting and healing. Solar and water imagery are also prominent characteristics of the archaeology from Lydney. The linkage between solar imagery and dogs may have arisen through a shared association with healing. However, faunal and iconographic evidence from the Romano-British archaeological record suggests that there may be more than one bond between these two emblems. In several notable instances dog skeletons have been found in association with Romano-British iconography symbolising iron working. It has been suggested that the recyclable nature of iron and its use in production of agricultural tools led to its symbolic linkage with regeneration and fertility in antiquity. Interestingly, the Lydney temple was built on the site of a Roman iron mine and characteristics of several artefacts from the temple site indicate that the mineral rich earth may have been held to have therapeutic properties. A shared connection with fertility and healing perhaps explains the presence of iron-working and dog symbolism at Lydney and their contextual associations elsewhere in the Romano-British archaeological record.

The mosaic on the *cella* floor of the Lydney temple suggests that aquatic concerns were central to the cult practiced at the site. Healing sanctuaries from Roman Europe were commonly built close to bodies of water, which were believed to embody the spirit of the divine. Furthermore, the navigation of the River Severn in the Lydney area is particularly treacherous, as it would have been during the Roman period and perhaps significantly the awesome Severn Bore does not become visible on the river until it has just passed the stretch of water overlooked by the temple. Dogs and water were perhaps symbolically connected through a common association with healing. However, the two are perhaps also metaphysically intertwined. As mentioned above, the perception of the domestic dog as guardian of earthly thresholds seems to have led to their being associated with liminal space at a supernatural level. In Iron Age and Roman Britain this linkage is identifiable in their quite frequent appearance in structured deposits made at the time of the foundation or termination of a town, settlement or building or placement within their boundary features. As water is the liminal space between bodies of land, dogs may have been perceived as guardian of this realm and therefore protectors of humans passing through an environment naturally alien to them. This idea is further supported by the iconography of the Netherlands goddess, Nehalennia who was patroness of seafarers: the most dominant emblem in her associated symbolic repertoire was her attentive hound. Interestingly, in the art from the Western provinces of Rome, hounds are quite commonly portrayed craning their necks to gaze upwards at their divine companion; this is perhaps reflective of human veneration of these deities.

In the myths and beliefs of numerous cultures, journeys by sea are often used as analogies for of our journey through life and similarly a person's final journey to the afterlife often involves crossing a body of water. This is perhaps another reason why dogs appear to have had an aquatic connection: the species has a widespread and enduring association with death and the hereafter, which certainly seems to be manifested in the archaeological record of Roman Britain. In the first instance they are portrayed as the vehicles of death in examples of hunting iconography, particularly in their pursuit of hares. The association is perhaps more explicit when they are featured on funerary monuments, although it is not always clear whether these animals are portraits of dogs that actually existed or generic motifs. The species' association with hunting and lifecycles and perception of the animal as a guardian/occupier of liminal space and transitory states will have no doubt contributed to its symbolic association with death. However, it is my contention that for many people the almost subconscious uncertainty of sharing living space with an animal that resembles a wolf and is a natural born killer is comparable to the constant yet repressed fear of death that many humans experience. That both death and dogs are unpredictable threats that form part of everyday life might also have generated a linkage between the two. A wariness of the domestic dog's darker side is perhaps visible in Iron Age and Roman iconography depicting wolves: they were portrayed as monstrous with notable regularity. Their untamed nature perhaps represented an uncontrollable part of a world that humans have always striven to order.

The remains of dogs found with humans in Romano-British funerary contexts and elsewhere in the archaeological record share some particularly interesting characteristics. Although human sacrifice was outlawed under Roman rule the amount of mutilated human skulls found in unusual deposits, frequently accompanied by dog skeletons, might indicate that such ceremonies were still being carried out, perhaps under the guise of judicial punishments. If this was the case the associated dog remains were perhaps interred to act as symbolic guardians over spirits deemed dangerous because of how they lived their lives or because of the manner of their death. The animals may have belonged to the deceased and been perceived as a part of their identity that needed to be destroyed with them or they were perhaps intended to represent spirit guides, like animals in shamanic rituals. The association between domestic dogs and human skulls is confined mainly to between the 1st to the late 3rd centuries AD, however dogs appear with decapitated corpses and mutilated human bodies in formal cemeteries quite frequently later in the Roman period. It cannot be said for certain whether the earlier and later practises are related but it is certainly possible that these examples of symbolic expression shared a common root. No patterns emerged in the Romano-British record in terms of preference of size or sex of the animals used in structured deposits or human burials but it is perhaps worth noting that far more dogs were found buried with men than women.

8.2 Suggestions for Future Research

It would be interesting and hopefully rewarding to extend the chronological parameters of this study to include archaeology from either earlier or later periods in British prehistory/history in an attempt to discover whether human perception of domesticated dogs changed over time.

During my research for this study a great deal of art and archaeology dating to the Iron Age and Roman periods was examined. Although my study was centred around domestic dogs it was quite clear that there is a wealth of information about other animals available that could yield useful insights into the way ancient Britons and their continental neighbours viewed the natural world around them. Arguably some of the most notable zoo-archaeological finds involved the structured deposition of horses during both periods. However, the presence of bovine skeletons and skulls, in significant locations and in unusual features, at a number of Romano-British temple sites was a more unexpected phenomenon that perhaps merits further investigation.

Bibliography

ALCOCK, L. 1973. *'By South Cadbury is that Camelot...' - The Excavation of Cadbury Castle 1966-1970.* London: Book Club Associates.

ALDHOUSE-GREEN, M. J. 1999a. *Pilgrims in Stone – Stone Images from the Gallo-Roman Sanctuary of Fontes Sequanae.* Oxford: British Archaeology Reports - International Series 754.

ALDHOUSE-GREEN, M. J. 1999b. Religion & Deities. *In:* R. TURNER ed. *Excavations of an Iron Age Settlement and Roman Religious Complex at Ivy Chimneys, Witham, Essex 1978-83.* East Anglian Archaeology, pp. 255-258.

ALDHOUSE-GREEN, M. J. 2001. *Dying for the Gods – Human Sacrifice in Iron Age and Roman Europe.* Stroud: Tempus Publishing Ltd.

ALDHOUSE-GREEN, M. J. 2004a. *An Archaeology of Images - Iconography and Cosmology in Iron Age and Roman Europe.* London: Routledge.

ALDHOUSE-GREEN, M. J. 2004b. Gallo-British Deities and their Shrines. *In:* M. TODD ed. *A Companion to Roman Britain.* Oxford: Blackwell Publishing Ltd.

ALEXANDER, J. and PULLINGER, J. 1999. Roman Cambridge – Excavations on Castle Hill 1956-1988. *Proceedings of the Cambridge Antiquarian Society,* **Vol. LXXXVIII**.

ALLASON-JONES, L. and MCKAY, B. 1985. *Coventina's Well - A Shrine on Hadrian's Wall.* Oxford: Oxbow Books.

ANDREWS, P. April 2003. *Personal Communication.*

ANON 1962. *An Inventory of the Historical Monuments in the City of York.* Norwich: Her Majesty's Stationery Office.

ANON 1975. Ilchester Inhumation Cemetery. *Current Archaeology,* **50**, p. 83.

ANON 1978. The Cambridge Shrine. *Current Archaeology,* **61**, pp. 57-60.

ANON 2000. *The Severn Bore - Severn Tides.* [Web Page]. www.severnbore.direct.co.uk (1 February 2005).

ANON 2005. *Pets as Therapy.* [Web Page]. www.petstherapy.org (24 April 2005).

ASHBY, T., HUDD, A. and KING, F. 1910. Excavations at Caerwent, Monmouthshire, on the Site of the Romano-British City of Venta Silurum, in the Year 1908. *Archaeologia,* **Vol. 86**, pp. 1-20.

BARBER, B. and BOWSHER, D. 2000. *The Eastern Cemetery of Roman London.* London: Museum of London Archaeology Service.

BATHURST, W. H. and KING, C. W. 1879. *Roman Antiquities at Lydney Park, Gloucestershire.* London: Longmans, Green & Co.

BAXTER, I. 21 March 2002. *Personal Communication.*

BECKER, U. 2000. *The Continuum Encyclopedia of Symbols.* London: Continuum International Publishing Group Inc.

BEDWIN, O. 1980. Excavations at Chanctonbury Ring, Wiston, West Sussex 1977. *Britannia,* **11**, pp. 192-193.

BIDDLE, M. 1967. Two Flavian Burials from Grange Road, Winchester. *The Antiquaries Journal,* **XLVII**, pp. 224-250.

BIRLEY, A. 2002. *A Band of Brothers - Garrison Life at Vindolanda.* Stroud: Tempus Publishing Ltd.

BIRLEY, R. 17 October 2002. *Personal Communication.*

BLACK, E. 1985. A Note on the Farley Heath Sceptre-Binding. *Surrey Archaeological Collections,* **76**, pp. 140-142.

BLACK, E. W. 1983. Ritual Dog Burials from Roman Sites. *Kent Archaeological Review,* **71**, pp. 20-22.

BLOCKLEY, K. 1991. The Romano-British Period. *In:* J. MANLEY, S. GRENTER and F. GALE eds. *The Archaeology of Clwyd.* Clwyd: Clwyd County Council.

BOON, G. 1983. Potters, Oculists and Eye Troubles. *Britannia,* **XIV**, pp. 1-12.

BOON, G. 1989. A Roman Sculpture Rehabilitated: The Pagans Hill Dog. *Britannia,* **XX**, pp. 201-217.

BOON, G. 1991. Tonsor Humanus - Razor and Toilet-knife in Antiquity. *Britannia,* **22**, pp. 21-32.

BOOTH, P., CLARK, K. and POWELL, A. 1996. A Dog Skin from Asthall. *International Journal of Osteoarchaeology,* **6**, pp. 382-387.

BOWLER, D. 1983. Rangoon Street. *Popular Archaeology,* pp. 13-18.

BREWER, D., CLARK, T. and PHILLPS, A. 2001. *Dogs in Antiquity*. Warminster: Aris & Phillips.

BREWER, R. J. 1986. *Corpus of Sculpture of the Roman World - Wales*. Oxford: Oxford University Press.

BROOKES, A. 2004 *The Visible Dead - A New Approach to the Study of Late Iron Age Mortuary Practice in South-Eastern Britain*. University of Wales, Newport: Unpublished Ph.D. Thesis.

BROTHWELL, D. 1995. The Special Animal Pathology. *In:* B. CUNLIFFE ed. *Danebury an Iron Age Hill Fort in Hampshire - A Hill Fort Community in Perspective*. Vol. 6. Oxford: Council for British Archaeology, pp. 207-233.

BROWN, D. and WICHBOLD, D. 1991. *Evaluation and Salvage Recording at King's School (St Alban's), Worcester - Report 41*. Worcestershire County Council Archaeological Service.

BRUNAUX, J. L. 1988. *The Celtic Gauls: Gods, Rites & Sanctuaries*. London: B. A. Seaby Ltd.

BUDGE, E. A. W. 1930. *Amulets and Superstitions*. London: Humphrey Milford - Oxford University Press.

BUXTON, R. 1990. Wolves and Werewolves in Greek Thought. *In:* J. BREMMER ed. *Interpretations of Greek Mythology*. London: Routledge, pp. 60-79.

CARY, E. 1925. *Dio's Roman History*. London: William Heinemann.

CARY, M., DENNINGTON, J. D., WRIGHT DUFF, J., NOCK, A. D., ROSS, W. and SCULLARD, H. H. (eds.) 1961. *The Oxford Classical Dictionary*. Oxford: The Clarendon Press.

CASEY, P. J. and HOFFMAN, B. 1999. Roman Temple Excavations, Lydney Park, Gloucestershire 1980-81. *Antiquaries Journal,* **79**, pp. 81-143.

CHAMPION, S. 1975. Andover, Portway Industrial Estate. *In: Archaeological Excavations, 1974*. London: Her Majesty's Stationery Office, pp. 22-23.

CHAPMAN, A. 2000. Excavation of an Iron Age Settlement and a Middle Saxon Cemetery at Great Houghton, Northampton, 1996. *Northamptonshire Archaeological Journal,* **29**, pp. 1-41.

CLARK, K. 13 November 2002. *Personal Communication*.

CLARK, P. 1998. *Zoroastrianism - An Introduction to an Ancient Faith*. Brighton: Sussex Academic Press.

CLARKE, G. 1979. *Winchester Studies 3 Pre-Roman & Roman Winchester - Part II The Roman Cemetery at Lankhills*. Oxford: Clarendon Press.

CLIFFORD, E. M. 1938. Roman Altars in Gloucestershire. *Transactions of the Bristol and Gloucestershire Archaeological Society,* **59**, pp. 297-310.

CLUTTON-BROCK, J. 1999. *A Natural History of Domesticated Animals*. 2nd edn. Cambridge: Cambridge University Press.

COLLINS, A. E. P. 1952. Excavations on Blewburton Hill, 1948 and 1949. *The Berkshire Archaeological Journal,* **53**, pp. 21-64.

COLLINS, B. J. 1992. The Puppy in Hittite Ritual. *Oriental Institute,* **136**, pp. 1-6.

COLLIS, J. R. 1968. Excavations at Owslebury, Hants - An Interim Report. *The Antiquaries Journal,* **XLVIII**, pp. 18-31.

COLLIS, J. R. 1998. *The European Iron Age*. London: Routledge.

COTTON, M. A. 1957. Weycocks Hill, 1953. *Berkshire Archaeology Journal,* **105**, pp. 48-68.

COTTRELL, B. 1994. *Thresholds Between Worlds*. Oxford: Abzu Press.

COULSTON, J. C. and PHILLIPS, E. J. 1988. *Corpus of Sculpture of the Roman World - Great Britain: Hadrian's Wall West of the North Tyne, and Carlisle*. Oxford: Oxford University Press.

COWLEY, L. F. 1946. Report on the Animal Bones. *In:* C. FOX ed. *A Find of the Early Iron Age from Llyn Cerrig Bach, Anglesey*. Cardiff: National Museum of Wales, p. 97.

CRAM, L. 2000. Foot-Impressed Tiles. *In:* M. FULFORD and J. TIMBY eds. *Late Iron Age and Roman Silchester - Excavations on the Site of the Forum-Basilica 1977, 1980-86*. London: Society for the Promotion of Roman Studies, pp. 123-126.

CREIGHTON, J. 2000. *Coins & Power in Late Iron Age Britain*. Cambridge: Cambridge University Press.

CROCKFORD, S. 2000. *Dogs Through Time - An Archaeological Perspective*. Oxford: British Archaeology Reports.

CRUMMY, P. 1984. *Colchester Archaeological Report 3: Excavations at Lion Walk, Balkerne Lane, and Middleborough, Colchester, Essex*. Colchester: Colchester Archaeological Trust Ltd.

CUNLIFFE, B. 1971. Danebury, Hampshire - The First Interim Report on the Excavation, 1969-70. *The Antiquaries Journal,* **LI**, pp. 240-252.

CUNLIFFE, B. 1983. *Danebury - Anatomy of an Iron Age Hill Fort.* London: B T Batsford Ltd.

CUNLIFFE, B. 1984. *Danebury: An Iron Age Hill Fort in Hampshire.* Oxford: Council for British Archaeology.

CUNLIFFE, B. 1992. Pits, Preconceptions & Propitiation in the British Iron Age. *Oxford Journal of Archaeology,* **11** (1), pp. 69-83.

CUNLIFFE, B. 2000. *Roman Bath Discovered.* 4th edn. Stroud: Tempus Publishing Ltd.

CUNLIFFE, B. and DAVENPORT, P. 1985. *The Temple of Sulis Minerva at Bath.* Oxford: Oxford University Committee for Archaeology.

CUNLIFFE, B. and FULFORD, M. G. 1982. *Corpus of Sculpture of the Roman World - Bath and the Rest of Wessex.* Oxford: Oxford University Press.

DAVIES, S. M., STACEY, L. C. and WOODWARD, J. 1985. Excavations at Alington Avenue, Fordington, Dorchester, 1984/85: Interim Report. *Proceedings of the Dorset Natural History and Archaeological Society,* **49**, pp. 101-110.

DAVIS, S. 1989. Animal Remains from the Iron Age Cemetery. *In:* I. STEAD and V. RIGBY eds. *Verulamium - The King Harry Lane Site.* London: British Museum Publications, pp. 250-252.

DAVIS, S. J. M. 1987. *The Archaeology of Animals.* London: B T Batsford Ltd.

DAVIS, S. J. M. and VALLA, F. R. 1978. Evidence for Domestication of the Dog 12,000 Years Ago in the Natufian of Israel. *Nature,* **276**, pp. 608-610.

DAY LEWIS, C. 1961. *The Aeneid of Virgil.* London: The Hogarth Press.

DE JERSEY, P. 1996. *Celtic Coinage in Britain.* Princes Risborough: Shire Publications Ltd.

DE JERSEY, P. 2001. Cunobelin's Silver. *Britannia,* **32**, pp. 1-44.

DE VIDAS, A. A. 2002. A Dogs Life Among the Teenek Indians (Mexico) – Animal's Participation in the Classifications of Self and Other. *The Journal of the Royal Anthropological Institute,* **8** (3), pp. 531-550.

DENNIS, G. 1978. *Southwark Excavations 1972-1974 - 1-7 St Thomas Street.* London: Southwark & Lambeth Archaeological Excavation Committee.

DETIENNE, M. 1989. Culinary Practices and the Spirit of Sacrifice. *In:* M. DETIENNE and J. VERNANT eds. *The Cuisine of Sacrifice Among the Greeks.* London: University of Chicago Press, pp. 1-20.

DOBNEY, K. M. and JACQUES, S. D. 1995. The Mammal Bones. *In:* R. J. WILLIAMS, P. J. HART and A. T. L. WILLIAMS eds. *Wavendon Gate – A Late Iron Age and Roman Settlement in Milton Keynes.* Aylesbury: The Buckinghamshire Archaeological Society, pp. 203-236.

DOWN, A. 1989. *Chichester Excavations VI.* Chichester: Phillimore & Co Ltd.

DRUMMOND-MURRAY, J., THOMPSON, P. and COWAN, C. 2002. *Settlement in Roman Southwark - Archaeological Excavations (1991-1998) for the London Underground Ltd Jubilee Line Extension.* London: Museum of London Archaeology Service.

DRURY, P. J. and WICKENDEN, N. P. 1982. Four Bronze Figurines from the Trinovantian Civitas. *Britannia,* **13**, pp. 239-243.

DUFF, J. W. and DUFF, A. M. 1935. *Minor Latin Poets.* London: William Heinemann Ltd.

DUNCAN, H. 15 October 2002. *Personal Communication.*

EDELSTEIN, E. J. and EDELSTEIN, L. 1998. *Asclepius and Interpretation of the Testimonies.* London: John Hopkins University Press.

ELLIS-DAVIDSON, H. 1982. *Pagan Scandinavia.* London: Thames and Hudson.

ESMONDE CLEARY, S. 2000. Putting the Dead in Their Place: Burial Location in Roman Britain. *In:* J. PEARCE, M. MILLET and M. STRUCK eds. *Burial, Society and Context in the Roman World.* Oxford: Oxbow Books.

EVERTON, R. 1988. The Dog Skeletons from Pit XLIV. *Somerset Archaeology and Natural History,* **132**, pp. 54-55.

EVERTON, R. F. 1982. The Human Remains. *In:* P. LEACH ed. *Ilchester Excavations 1974-1975.* Vol. 1. Bristol: Western Archaeological Trust.

FASHAM, P. 1985. *The Prehistoric Settlement at Winnall Down, Winchester: Excavations of MARC3 Site R17 in 1976 and 1977.* Winchester: Hampshire Field Club in association with the Trust for Wessex Archaeology.

FINN, T. M. 1997. *From Death to Rebirth – Ritual and Conversion in Antiquity.* New Jersey: Paulist Press.

FORSTER, E. S. and HEFFNER, E. H. 1941. *Lucius Junius Moderatus Columella on Agriculture.* London: William Heinemen Ltd.

FORSTER, E. S. and HEFFNER, E. H. 1954. *Lucius Junius Moderatus Columella on Agriculture.* London: William Heinemann Ltd.

FOX, C. 1946. *Find of the Early Iron Age from Llyn Cerrig Bach, Anglesey.* Cardiff: National Museum of Wales.

FRANCE, N. E. and GOBEL, B. M. 1985. *The Romano-British Temple at Harlow, Essex.* Gloucester: West Essex Archaeological Group.

FRAZER, J. G. 1929. *The Fasti of Ovid.* London: MacMillan & Co. Ltd.

FRERE, S. S. 1986. Roman Britain in 1985. *Britannia,* **XXVI**, p. 397.

FULFORD, M. 2001. Links with the Past: Pervasive 'Ritual' Behaviour in Roman Britain. *Britannia,* **22**, pp. 199-218.

FULFORD, M. and CLARKE, A. 2002. Silchester - A Crowded Late Roman City. *Current Archaeology,* **XV** (9), pp. 364-369.

GHEY, E. 2003 *Beyond the Temple: Establishing a Context for Gallo-Roman Sanctuaries.*

GOODBURN, R. 1978. Roman Britain in 1977. *Britannia,* **IX**.

GOODBURN, R. 1979a. Roman Britain in 1978. *Britannia,* **10**, pp. 267-356.

GOODBURN, R. 1979b. *The Roman Villa - Chedworth.* Hatfield: The Stellar Press.

GOTTLIEB, A. 1968. Dog: Ally or Traitor? - Mythology, Cosmology and Society Amongst the Beng of the Ivory Coast. *American Ethnologist,* **13**, pp. 447-499.

GRANT, A. 1984a. Animal Husbandry. *In:* B. CUNLIFFE ed. *Danebury – An Iron Age Hill Fort in Hampshire, Excavations 1969 – 1978, Vol. 2 – The Finds.* London: Council for British Archaeology Research Report, pp. 496-548.

GRANT, A. 1984b. Survival or Sacrifice? A Critical Appraisal of Animal Burials in Britain in the Iron Age. *In:* C. GRIGSON and J. CLUTTON-BROCK eds. *Animals & Archaeology: 4. Husbandry in Europe.* Oxford: British Archaeology Reports - International Series 227, pp. 221-227.

GRANT, A. 1985. The Animal Bones. *In:* B. CUNLIFFE and P. DAVENPORT eds. *The Temple of Sulis Minerva at Bath – Volume 1 The Site.* Oxford: Oxford University Committee for Archaeology, pp. 164-173.

GRANT, A. 1989. Animals in Roman Britain. *In:* M. TODD ed. *Research on Roman Britain - 1960-1989.* London: Society for the Promotion of Roman Studies, pp. 135-146.

GRANT, A. 1991a. Animal Husbandry. *In:* B. CUNLIFFE and C. POOLE eds. *Danebury – An Iron Age Hill Fort in Hampshire – Volume 5.* Oxford: Council for British Archaeology, pp. 447-487.

GRANT, A. 1991b. Economic or Symbolic? Animals and Ritual Behaviour. *In:* P. GARWOOD, D. JENNINGS, R. SKEATES and J. TOMS eds. *Sacred & Profane.* Oxford: Oxbow Books, pp. 109-114.

GRAVES, R. 1960. *The Greek Myths - Complete Edition.* London: Penguin Books Ltd.

GREEN, H. J. M. 1977. *Godmanchester.* Cambridge: Oleander Press.

GREEN, H. J. M. 1986. Religious Cults at Roman Godmanchester. *In:* M. HENIG and A. KING eds. *Pagan Gods and Shrines of the Roman Empire.* Oxford: Oxford University Committee for Archaeology, pp. 29-55.

GREEN, M. J. 1976. *A Corpus of Religious Material from the Civilian Areas of Roman Britain.* Oxford: British Archaeology Reports - British Series 24.

GREEN, M. J. 1978. *A Corpus of Small Cult-Objects from the Military Areas of Roman Britain.* Oxford: BAR Publishing. British Arch. Reports British Series 52.

GREEN, M. J. 1989. *Symbol and Image In Celtic Religious Art.* London: Routledge.

GREEN, M. J. 1991. *The Sun-Gods of Ancient Europe.* London: B T Batsford Ltd.

GREEN, M. J. 1992a. *Animals in Celtic Life and Myth.* London: Routledge.

GREEN, M. J. 1992b. *Dictionary of Celtic Myth and Legend.* London: Thames & Hudson Ltd.

GREEN, M. J. 1995. *Celtic Goddesses - Warriors, Virgins & Mothers.* London: British Museum Press.

GREEN, M. J. 1996. *Celtic Art.* London: George Weidenfeld & Nicolson Ltd.

GREGORY, T. and GURNEY, D. 1986. *Excavations at Thornham, Warham, Wighton and Caistor St. Edmund.* Norfolk: Norfolk Archaeological Unit & Norfolk Museum Services.

HALKON, P. and MILLET, M. 2003. East Riding: An Iron Age and Roman Landscape Revealed. *Current Archaeology,* **187**, pp. 303-309.

HALL, H. 1982. Report on the Human and Animal Bone. *In:* W. J. WEDLAKE ed. *The Excavation of the Shrine of Apollo at Nettleton, Wiltshire, 1956-1971.* London: Thames & Hudson Ltd.

HAMILTON, J. 2000. The Animal Bones. *In:* B. CUNLIFFE and C. POOLE eds. *The Danebury Environs Programme – The Prehistory of a Wessex Landscape - Houghton Down, Stockbridge, Hants 1994.* Vol. 2 pt. 6. Oxford: English Heritage and University of Oxford Committee for Archaeology, pp. 131-146.

HARCOURT, R. A. 1967. Osteoarthritis in a Romano-British Dog. *Journal of Small Animal Practice,* **8**, pp. 521-523.

HARCOURT, R. A. 1974. The Dog in Prehistoric and Early Historic Britain. *Journal of Archaeological Science,* **1**, pp. 151-175.

HARCOURT, R. A. 1979b. The Dog Bones. *In:* G. CLARKE ed. *Winchester Studies 3 Pre-Roman & Roman Winchester - Part II The Roman Cemetery at Lankhills.* Oxford: Clarendon Press, pp. 244-245.

HARMAN, M., MOLLESON, T. I. and PRICE, J. L. 1981. Burials, Bodies & Beheadings in Romano British & Anglo-Saxon Cemeteries. *Bulletin of the British Museum of National History(Geology),* **35** (3), pp. 145-188.

HARRIS, D. R. 1996. Domesticatory Relationships of People, Plants and Animals. *In:* R. F. ELLEN, K. ed. *Redefining Nature.* Oxford: Berg, pp. 437-463.

HARRIS, E. and HARRIS, J. 1965. *The Oriental Cults in Roman Britain.* Leiden: E J Brill.

HARRIS, M. 1991. *Cannibals and Kings.* New York: Vintage Books.

HART, B. L. and POWELL, K. L. 1990. Antibacterial Properties of Saliva: Role in Maternal Periparturient Grooming and in Licking Wounds. *Physiology and Behaviour,* **48** (3), pp. 383-386.

HART, L. 1995. Dogs as Human Companions: A Review of the Relationship. *In:* SERPT ed. *The Domestic Dog - Its Evolution, Behavious and Interactions with People.* Cambridge: Cambridge University Press.

HARVEY, D. 1996. A Roman Cemetery in Newarke Street, Leicester - Roman Ceramic Material. *Transactions of the Leicester Archaeological and Historical Society,* **70**, pp. 73-74.

HATTATT 1987. *Brooches of Antiquity.* Oxford: Oxbow Books.

HENIG, M. 1978. *A Corpus of Roman Engraved Gemstones from British Sites.* 2 edn. Oxford: BAR Publishing. British Archaeological Reports British Series 8.

HENIG, M. 1983. The Gemstones. *In:* C. JOHNS and T. POTTER eds. *The Thetford Treasure.* London: British Museum Press.

HENIG, M. 1984a. Amber Amulets. *Britannia,* **XIV**, pp. 243-246.

HENIG, M. 1984b. *Religion in Roman Britain.* London: B T Batsford Ltd.

HENIG, M. 1993. *Corpus of Sculpture of the Roman World, Great Britain - Roman Sculpture from the Cotswold Region with Devon and Cornwall.* Oxford: Oxford University Press.

HENIG, M. 1995. *The Art of Roman Britain.* London: B T Batsford Ltd.

HERBERT, E. W. 1993. *Iron, Gender & Power - Rituals of Transformation In African Socieities.* Bloomington & Indianapolis: Indiana Univeristy Press.

HEY, G. 1991. Yarnton, Worton Rectory Farm. *South Midlands Archaeology*, pp. 86-92.

HILL, J. D. 1995. *Ritual and Rubbish in the Iron Age of Wessex - A Study on the Formation of a Specific Archaeological Record.* Oxford: British Archaeology Reports - British Series 242.

HILL, J. D. 1996. The Identification of Ritual Deposits of Animals. A General Perspective from a Specific Study of 'Special Animal Deposits' from the Southern English Iron Age. *In:* S. ANDERSON and K. BOYLE eds. *Ritual Treatment of Human and Animal Remains.* Oxford: Oxbow Books, pp. 17-32.

HILL, J. D. 23 September 2003. *Personal Communication.*

HILZHEIMER, M. 1932. Dogs. *Antiquity,* **VI**, pp. 411-420.

HINGLEY, R. 1997. Iron, Ironworking and Regeneration: A Study of the Symbolic Meaning of Metalworking in Iron Age Britain. *In:* A. GWILT and C. HASELGROVE eds. *Reconstructing Iron Age Societies.* Oxford: Oxbow Monograph 71, pp. 9-18.

HONDIUS-CRONE, A. 1955. *The Temple of Nehalennia at Domburg.* Amsterdam: J. M. Meulenhoff.

HUNTINGTON, R. and METCALF, P. 1979. *Celebrations of Death - The Anthropology of Mortuary Ritual.* Cambridge: Cambridge University Press.

INGOLD, T. 1980. *Hunters, Pastoralists and Ranchers.* Cambridge: Cambridge University Press.

INGOLD, T. 1986. *The Appropriation of Nature.* Manchester: Manchester University Press.

JACKSON, D. A. 1975. The Iron Age Site at Twywell, Northamptonshire. *Northamptonshire Archaeological Journal,* **10**, pp. 31-95.

JACOBI, R. 25 March 2004. *Personal Communication.*

JENKINS, F. 1953. A Note on a Clay Figurine. *Archaeologia Cantiana,* **LXV**, pp. 131-133.

JENKINS, F. 1957. The Role of the Dog in Romano-Gaulish Religion. *Collection Latomus,* **XVI**, pp. 60-78.

JOHNS, C. 1996. *The Jewellery of Roman Britain - Celtic and Classical Traditions.* London: UCL Press Ltd.

JONES, H. L. 1923. *The Geography of Strabo - English Translation.* London: William Heinemann Ltd.

JOPE, E. M. 2000. *Early Celtic Art in the British Isles - Text.* Oxford: Clarendon Press.

KATCHER, A. H. and BECK, A. M. 1988. Health and Caring for Living Things. *In:* A. ROWAN ed. *Animals and People Sharing the World.* London: University Press of New England.

KATCHER, A. H. and BECK, A. M. 1991. Animal Companions - More Companion than Animal. *In:* M. ROBINSON and L. TIGER eds. *Man & Beast Revisited.* London: Smithsonian Institution Press, pp. 265-274.

KENNEDY, M. 1965. *Caesar - De Bello Gallico, V.* Cambridge: Cambridge University Press.

KENNEDY, M. 2002. *Knife Twists - Mystery of Dog Burials.* [Web Site]. Newspaper Article. <http://www.guardian.co.uk/uk_news/story/0,3604,626325,00.html> (8 January 2002).

KENT, R. 1938. *Varro - On the Latin Language.* London: William Heinemann Ltd.

KENT, S. 1981. The Dog: an Archaeologist's Best Friend or Worst Enemy - the Spatial Distribution of Faunal Remains. *Journal of Field Archaeology,* **8**, pp. 367-372.

KEPPIE, L. J. F. and ARNOLD, B. 1984. *Corpus of Sculpture of the Roman World, Great Britain - Scotland.* Oxford: Oxford University Press.

KING, A. and SOFFE, G. 1998. Internal Organisation at the Iron Age Temple on Hayling Island. *Proceedings of the Hampshire Field Club Archaeological Society,* **53**, pp. 35-41.

KIRK, G. S. and FITZGERALD, R. 2004. *The Iliad - Oxford World's Classics.* Oxford: Oxford University Press.

KUCHLER, S. 1997. Sacrificial Economy and Its Objects. *Journal of Material Culture,* **2**, pp. 39-60.

KVIDELAND, K. 1993. Boundaries and the Sin-Eater. *In:* H. ELLIS-DAVIDSON ed. *Boundaries and Thresholds.* Bath: The Thimble Press, pp. 84-90.

LAMBRICK, G. 1985. Stanton Harcourt - Gravelly Guy. *South Midlands Archaeology,* **XV**, pp. 107-110.

LARSSON, L. 1991. Symbolism and Mortuary Practice: Dogs in Fractions - Symbols in Action. *Archaeology and Environment,* **11**, pp. 33-38.

LAST, J. 2001. *Thorley - Draft Publication.* Hertfordshire Archaeological Trust.

LAST, J. 14 May 2002. *Personal Communication.*

LEGGE, A. J. 1995. A Horse Burial and other Grave Offerings. *In:* K. PARFITT ed. *Iron Age Burials from Mill Hill, Deal.* London: British Museum Press.

LEVITAN, B. 1989. The Vertebrate Remains from Chichester Cattlemarket. *In:* A. DOWN ed. *Chichester Excavations.* Vol. VI. Chichester: Phillimore & Co Ltd, pp. 242-267.

LEVITAN, B. 1993. Vertebrate Remains. *In:* A. WOODWARD and P. LEACH eds. *The Uley Shrines – Excavation of a Ritual Complex on West Hill, Uley, Gloucestershire: 1977-79.* London: English Heritage, pp. 257-301.

LINCOLN, B. 1979. The Hell Hound. *Journal of Indo-European Studies,* **7**, pp. 273-285.

LIVERSIDGE, J. 1977. Roman Burials in the Cambridge Area. *Proceedings of the Cambridge Antiquarian Society,* **LXVII**, pp. 15-38.

LIVINGSTONE, A. 1988. The Isin 'Dog House' Revisited. *Journal of Cuneiform Studies,* **40**, pp. 54-60.

LOCKER, A. 1999. The Animal Bone. *In:* B. PHILP, P. PARFITT, J. WILLSON and W. WILLIAMS eds. *The Roman Villa Site at Keston, Kent - Second Report (Excavations 1967 and 1978-1990).* Kent: Kent Archaeological Rescue Unit.

LORENZ, K. Z. 1964. *Man Meets Dog.* Harmondsworth: Penguin Books Ltd.

LUFF, R. M. 1982. *A Zooarchaeological Study of the Roman North-Western Provinces.* Oxford: BAR Publishing. British Archaeological Reports Int. Ser. 137.

LUFF, R. M. 1992. The Faunal Remains. *In:* N. P. WICKENDEN ed. *The Temple and Other Sites in the North-Eastern Sector of Caesaromagus.* Chelmsford: Chelmsford Museum Service & Council for British Archaeology Report 75, pp. 166-174.

MACDONALD, J. L. 1979. Religion. *In:* G. CLARKE ed. *Winchester Studies 3 Pre-Roman & Roman Winchester - Part II The Roman Cemetery at Lankhills.* Oxford: Clarendon Press.

MACKEY, R. 1999. The Welton Villa - A View of Social and Economic Change During the Roman Period in East Yorkshire. *In:* P. HALKON ed. *Further Light on the Parisi - Recent Research in Iron Age and Roman East Yorkshire.* Hull: East Riding Archaeological Research Trust, East Riding Archaeological Society, Department of History, University of Hull, pp. 21-32.

MALTBY, M. 1978. *Animal Bones from the Roman Site at Little Somborne, Hampshire.* Ancient Monuments Laboratory Report, AML Report 2644. English Heritage.

MALTBY, M. 1985. The Animal Bones. *In:* P. J. FASHAM ed. *The Prehistoric Settlement at Winnall Down, Winchester: Excavations of MARC3 Site R17 in 1976 and 1977.* Winchester: Hampshire Field Club in association with the Trust for Wessex Archaeology.

MALTBY, M. 1987a. *The Animal Bones from the Excavations at Owslebury, Hant. An Iron Age and Early Romano-British Settlement.* Ancient Monuments Laboratory Reports, AML Report 6/87. English Heritage.

MALTBY, M. 1987b. *The Animal Bones from the Later Roman Phases from Winchester Northern Suburbs: The Unsieved Samples from Victoria Road Trenches X-XVI.* Ancient Monuments Laboratory Report, AML Report 125/87. English Heritage.

MALTBY, M. 1988. *The Animal Bones from the 1984/85 Excavations at Alington Ave, Dorchester, Hampshire.* Ancient Monuments Laboratory Reports, English Heritage.

MALTBY, M. 1993. The Animal Bones. *In:* P. J. WOODWARD, S. M. DAVIES and A. H. GRAHAM eds. *The Excavations at the Old Methodist Chapel and Greyhound Yard, Dorchester, 1981-1984.* Dorchester: Dorset Natural History and Archaeological Society, pp. 315-339.

MATTHEWS, C. L. 1981. A Romano-British Inhumation Cemetery at Dunstable. *Bedfordshire Archaeological Journal,* pp. 1-73.

MAYS, S. 1993. Infanticide in Roman Britain. *Antiquity,* **67**, pp. 883-888.

MAYS, S. and STEELE, J. 1995. A Mutilated Human Skull from Roman St Albans, Hertfordshire, England. *Antiquity,* **70**, pp. 155-161.

MAYS, S. and STEELE, J. 1996. A Mutilated Human Skull from Roman St Albans, Hertfordshire, England. *Antiquity,* **70**, pp. 155-161.

MCKINLEY, J., SMITH, P. and FITZPATRICK, A. P. 1997. Animal Bone from Burials and other Cremation-related Contexts. *In:* A. P. FITZPATRICK ed. *Archaeological Excavations on the Route of the A27 Westhampnett Bypass, West Sussex, 1992.* Vol. 2. Salisbury: Wessex Archaeology.

MEANEY, A. L. 1981. *Anglo-Saxon Amulets and Curing Stones.* Oxford: British Archaeology Reports.

MEATES, G. W. 1974. Farningham Roman Villa II. *Achaeologia Cantiana,* **LXXXVIII**, pp. 1-12.

MENACHE, S. 1997. Dogs: God's Worst Enemies? [Web Site]. http://www.psyeta.org/sa/sa5.1/menache.html (16 December 2002).

MENIEL, P. 1987. *Chasse et Elevage chez les Gaulois.* Paris: Editions Errance.

MENIEL, P. 1989. Les Animal dans les Religieuses des Gaulois. *In:* J. D. VIGNE ed. *L' Animal dans les Pratiques Religieuses: les Manifestations Materielles.* Paris: Anthropozoologica Troisieme Numero Special, pp. 87-97.

MENIEL, P., MANGIN, J. M. and MANGIN, M. 1991. Les Depots D'animaux de Vertault (Cote d'Or): Les Sanctuaires Celtiques et les Monde Mediterraneen. *Archeologie d'Aujhourdhui: Dossiers de Protohistoire,* **3**, pp. 268-275.

MERRIFIELD, R. 1986. The London Hunter God. *In:* M. HENIG and A. KING eds. *Pagan Gods and Shrines of the Roman Empire.* Oxford: Oxford University Committee for Archaeology, pp. 85-92.

MERRIFIELD, R. 1987. *The Archaeology of Ritual and Magic.* London: B T Batsford.

MILES, D. 1984. *Archaeology of Barton Court Farm, Abingdon, Oxon.* Oxford: Oxford Archaeological Unit and Council for British Archaeology.

MILLER, T. 1995. The Romano-British Temple at Great Chesterford, Essex. *Proceedings of the Cambridge Antiquarian Society,* **LXXXIV**, pp. 15-57.

MORRIS, B. 1998. *The Power of Animals - An Ethnography.* Oxford: Berg.

MORRIS, E. 1988. The Iron Age Occupation at Dibbles Farm, Christon. *Somerset Archaeology and Natural History,* **132**, pp. 23-81.

MORRIS, J. 1980. *British History and the Welsh Annals (c. 800AD).* London: Phillimore.

NEAL, D. S. 1981. *Roman Mosaics in Britain.* London: Society for Promotion of Roman Studies.

NIBLETT, R. 1999. *The Excavation of a Ceremonial Site at Folly Lane, Verulamium.* London: Society for the Promotion of Roman Studies –Britannia Monograph Series No. 14.

NOEL-HUME, I. 1957. Ritual Burials on the Upchurch Marshes. *Achaeologia Cantiana,* **LXX**, pp. 160-167.

O'CONNOR, T. 2000. *The Archaeology of Animal Bones.* Stroud: Sutton Publishing.

OLDFATHER, C. H. 1933. *Diodorus Siculus - Library of History.* Cambridge MA: Harvard University Press.

OLOWO OJADE, J. 1994. Nigerian Cultural Attitudes to the Dog. *In:* R. WILLIS ed. *Signifying Animals - Human Meaning in the Natural World.* London: One World Archaeology, pp. 215-221.

PARFITT, K. 1995. *Iron Age Burials from Mill Hill, Deal.* London: British Museum Press.

PAYNE, G. 1897. The Roman Villa at Darenth. *Achaeologia Cantiana,* **XXII**.

PENN, W. S. 1958. The Romano-British Settlement at Springhead, Excavation of the Watling Street, Shop and Pedestal, Site B. *Achaeologia Cantiana,* **LXXIII**, pp. 77-110.

PENN, W. S. 1961. Springhead: Temples III and IV. *Achaeologia Cantiana,* **LXXIV**, pp. 113-140.

PENN, W. S. 1964. Springhead: The Temple Ditch Site. *Achaeologia Cantiana,* **LXXIX**, pp. 170-190.

PERRY, B. T. 1982. Excavations at Bramdean, Hampshire, 1973-1977. *Proceedings of the Hampshire Field Club Archaeological Society,* **38**, pp. 57-74.

PHILLIPS, A. and WILLCOCK, M. 1999. *Xenophon & Arrian on Hunting.* Warminster: Aris & Phillips Ltd.

PHILP, B., PARFITT, P., WILLSON, J. and WILLIAMS, W. 1999. *The Roman Villa Site at Keston, Kent - Second Report (Excavations 1967 and 1978-1990).* Kent: Kent Archaeological Rescue Unit.

PHILPOTT, R. 1991. *Burial Practices in Roman Britain - A Survey of Grave Treatment and Furnishings AD 43-410.* Oxford: British Archaeology Reports - British Series 219.

PIERCY FOX, N. 1963. Reports from Local Secretaries and Groups - Bromley. *Archaeologia Cantiana,* **LXXVIII**, pp. 1-1i.

PIERCY FOX, N. 1968. The Ritual Shaft at Warbank, Keston. *Achaeologia Cantiana,* **LXXXII**, pp. 184-190.

PORTER, J. R. 1993. Thresholds in the Old Testament. *In:* H. ELLIS-DAVIDSON ed. *Boundaries and Thresholds.* Bath: The Thimble Press, pp. 65-75.

POULTNEY, J. W. 1959. *The Bronze Tables of Iguvium.* Oxford: B H Blackwell Ltd.

PRESTON DAY, L. 1984. Dog Burials in the Greek World. *American Journal of Archaeology,* **88**, pp. 21-32.

PRICE, N. 2001. *The Archaeology of Shamanism.* London: Routledge.

PRIEST, V. 2003. *Archaeological Evaluations on a Ritual Site in East Leicestershire.* University of Leicester.

PRYOR, F. 2001. *The Flag Fen Basin: Archaeology and Environment of a Fenland Landscape.* Swindon: English Heritage.

RAHTZ, P. and HARRIS, L. The Temple Well and Other Buildings at Pagans Hill, Chew Stoke, North Somerset. *Somerset Archaeology and Natural History Society,* **101/2**, pp. 15-51.

REYNOLDS, P. J. 1980. *Iron Age Agriculture Reviewed.* Petersfield: Archaeological Research.

ROSE, H. J. 1924. *The Roman Questions of Plutarch.* Oxford: Clarendon Press.

ROSKAMS, S. 1980. GPO Newgate Street, 1975-79 - the Roman Levels. *London Archaeologist,* **III** (15), pp. 403-407.

ROSS, A. 1967a. *Pagan Celtic Britain.* London: Routledge & Kegan Paul Ltd.

ROSS, A. 1967b. *Pagan Celtic Britain - Studies in Iconography and Tradition.* London: Routledge & Kegan Paul Ltd.

ROSS, A. 1968. Shafts, Pits, Wells - Sanctuaries of the Belgic Britons? *In:* J. M. COLES and D. D. A. SIMPSON eds. *Studies in Ancient Europe - Essays Presented to Stuart Piggott.* Leicester: Leicester University Press.

ROWBOTHAM, F. W. 1978. The River Severn at Gloucester with Particular Reference to its Roman and Medieval Channels. *The Gloucester and District Archaeological Research Group Review,* **12**, pp. 4-9.

ROWBOTHAM, F. W. 1983. *The Severn Bore.* London: David & Charles.

ROWSOME, P. 1983. 119-121 Cannon St, 1-3 Abchurch Yard, 14 Sherborne Lane. *London Archaeologist,* **IV** (10), p. 277.

RUSHTON FAIRCLOUGH, H. 1918. *Virgil - Volume 1.* London: William Heinemann Ltd.

RYKWERT, J. 1976. *The Idea of a Town.* London: Faber and Faber.

SAUNDERS, N. J. 1995. *Animal Spirits - The Shared World Sacrifice, Ritual and Myth, Animal Souls and Symbols.* London: MacMillan.

SAVOLAINEN, P., ZHANG, Y., LOU, J., LUNDEBERG, J. and LEITNER, T. 2002. Genetic Evidence for an East Asian Origin for Domestic Dogs. *Science,* **298**, pp. 1610-1613.

SAVORY, H. N. 1980. *Guide Catalogue of the Bronze Age Collections.* Cardiff: National Museum of Wales.

SCHOLFIELD, A. F. 1959. *Aelian - On the Characteristics of Animals.* London: William Heinemann Ltd.

SCHWARTZ, M. 1997. *A History of Dogs in the Early Americas.* London: Yale University Press.

SCOTT, E. 1991. Animals and Infant Burials in Romano-British Villas: A Revitalization Movement. *In:* P. GARWOOD, D. JENNINGS, R. SKEATES and J. TOMS eds. *Sacred & Profane.* Oxford: Oxbow Books, pp. 115-121.

SCOTT, E. 1999. *The Archaeology of Infancy and Infant Death.* Oxford: British Archaeology Reports - International Series 819.

SERPELL, J. 1988. Pet- Keeping in Non-Western Societies: Some Popular Misconceptions. *In:* A. ROWAN ed. *Animals and People Sharing the World.* London: University Press of New England, pp. 33-52.

SERPELL, J. 1995. *The Domestic Dog - Its Evolution, Behaviour and Interactions with People.* Cambridge: Cambridge University Press.

SHOTTER, D. C. A. 1973. Numeri Barcariorum: A Note on RIB 601. *Britannia,* **IV**, pp. 206-209.

SMITH, A. 2001. *The Differential Use of Constructed Sacred Space in Southern Britain from the Late Iron Age to the 4th Century AD.* Oxford: British Archaeology Reports - British Series 318.

SMITH, S. 1994. A Reassessment of the Dating Evidence for the Lydney Temple Site. *Dean Archaeology,* 7.

SOREN, D. and SOREN, N. 1995. What Killed the Babies of Lugnano? *Archaeology,* (September/October), pp. 43-48.

SOREN, D. and SOREN, N. 1999. *A Roman Villa and a Late Roman Infant Cemetery - Excavation at Poggio Gramignano Lugnano in Teverina.* Rome: L'Erma di Bretschneider.

STAGER, L. E. 1991. Why Were Hundreds of Dogs Buried at Ashkelon? *Biblical Archaeological Review,* (May/June), pp. 26-42.

STEAD, I., BOURKE, J. B. and BOTHWELL, D. (eds.) 1986. *Lindow Man - The Body in the Bog.* London: British Museum Publications.

STEVENS, A. 1998. *Ariadne's Clue - A Guide to the Symbols of Humankind.* Princeton: Princeton University Press.

STRATHERN, A. 1982. Witchcraft, Greed, Cannibalism and Death. *In:* M. BLOCH and J. PARRY eds. *Death and the Regeneration of Life.* Cambridge: Cambridge University Press, pp. 111-133.

TOYNBEE, J. M. C. 1962. *Art in Roman Britain.* London: Phaidon.

TOYNBEE, J. M. C. 1964. *Art in Britain Under the Romans.* Oxford: The Clarendon Press.

TOYNBEE, J. M. C. 1971. *Death and Burial in the Roman World.* London: Thames and Hudson.

TOYNBEE, J. M. C. 1973. *Animals in Roman Life and Art.* London: Thames & Hudson.

TOYNBEE, J. M. C. 1982. The Inscribed Altars; Statuary; Terracottas; Intaglios; and Special Bronze Objects. *In:* W. J. WEDLAKE ed. *The Excavation of the Shrine of Apollo at Nettleton, Wiltshire, 1956-1971.* London: Thames & Hudson Ltd.

TURNBULL, V. 1975. The Animal Bones - Excavations at Bourton Grounds, Thornborough. *Records of Buckinghamshire,* **XX** (1), pp. 49-51.

TURNER, H. W. 1971. *Living Tribal Religions.* London: Ward Lock Educational Ltd.

TURNER, P. 1962. *Selection from The History of the World Commonly Called The Natural History of C. Plinius Secundus.* London: Centaur Press Ltd.

TURNER, R. 1999. *Excavations of an Iron Age Settlement and Roman Religious Complex at Ivy Chimneys, Witham, Essex 1978-1983.* Chelmsford: East Anglian Archaeology.

TURNER, R. C. and BRIGGS, C. S. 1986. The Bog Burial of Britain and Ireland. *In:* I. STEAD, J. B. BOURKE and D. BROTHWELL eds. *Lindow Man - The Body in the Bog.* London: British Museum Publications Ltd, pp. 144-161.

UCKO, P. 1969. Ethnography and the Archaeological Interpretation of Funerary Remains. *World Archaeology,* **1**, pp. 262-280.

VAGO, T. 1991. Dogs Used for Parchment. *Biblical Archaeological Review,* **17** (6), p. 18.

VAN AARTSEN, J. 1971. *Deae Nehalenniae.* Middelburg: Rijksmuseum van Oudheden.

WAINWRIGHT, G. 1979. *Gussage All Saints - An Iron Age Settlement in Dorset.* London: Her Majesty's Stationery Office.

WAIT, G. 1985. *Ritual & Religion in Iron Age Britain.* Oxford: British Archaeology Reports - British Series 149.

WATERER, J. W. 1976. Leatherwork. *In:* D. STRONG and D. BROWN eds. *Roman Crafts.* London: Gerald Duckworth and Co Ltd, pp. 179-194.

WATSON, D. M. S. 1932. Bones. *In:* R. E. M. WHEELER ed. *Report on the Excavation of the Prehistoric, Roman and Post-Roman Site in Lydney Park, Gloucestershire.* Oxford: Oxford University Press, p. 131.

WEBSTER, G. 1983. The Function of Chedworth Roman 'Villa'. *Transactions of the Bristol and Gloucestershire Archaeological Society,* **101**, pp. 5-20.

WEBSTER, G. 1986. *The British Celts and Their Gods Under Rome.* London: Batsford.

WEDLAKE, W. J. 1982. *The Excavation of the Shrine of Apollo at Nettleton, Wiltshire, 1956-1971.* London: Thames & Hudson Ltd.

WESTWOOD, J. 2001. Friend or Foe? Norfolk Traditions of Shuck. *In:* H. ELLIS-DAVIDSON and A. CHAUDRI eds. *Supernatural Enemies.* Durham: Carolina Academic Press, pp. 101-116.

WHEELER, R. E. M. 1932. *Report on the Excavation of the Prehistoric Roman, and Post-Roman Site in Lydney Park, Gloucestershire.* Oxford: Oxford University Press.

WHEELER, R. E. M. 1943. *Reports of the Research Committee of the Society of Antiquaries of London, No XII - Maiden Castle, Dorset.* Oxford: Oxford University Press.

WHEELER, R. E. M. and WHEELER, T. V. 1936. *Verulamium - A Belgic and Two Roman Cities.* Oxford: Oxford University Press.

WHIMSTER, R. 1981. *Burial Practices in Iron Age Britain - A Discussion and Gazetteer of the Evidence c. 700 BC - AD 43.* Oxford: British Archaeology Reports.

WHITE, D. G. 1991. *Myths of the Dog Man.* London: Chicago University Press.

WHYTEHEAD, R. 1986. The Excavation of an Area within a Roman Cemetery at West Tenter Street, London E1. *London & Middlesex Archaeological Society,* **37**, pp. 23-124.

WIGHTMAN, E. 1970. *Roman Trier and the Treveri.* London: Rupert Hart-Davis.

WILLIS, R. 1994. *Signifying Animals - Human Meaning in the Natural World.* London: One World Archaeology.

WILSON, B. 1992. Considerations for the Identity of Ritual Deposits of Animal Bones In Iron Age Pits. *International Journal of Osteoarchaeology,* **2**, pp. 341-349.

WILSON, D. R. 1970. Roman Britain in 1969. *Britannia,* **1**, pp. 302-303.

WITTS, C. 2002. *Disasters on the Severn.* Stroud: Tempus Publishing Ltd.

WOODWARD, A. 1992. *Shrines and Sacrifice.* London: B. T. Batsford Ltd.

WOODWARD, A. and WOODWARD, P. J. 2004. Dedicating the Town: Urban Foundation Deposits in Roman Britain. *World Archaeology,* **36** (1), pp. 68-86.

WOODWARD, P. J., DAVIES, S. M. and GRAHAM, A. H. 1993. *Excavations at the Old Methodist Chapel and Greyhound Yard, Dorchester, 1981-1984.* Dorchester: Dorset Natural History & Archaeological Society.

WOOLF, A. 1997. At Home in the Long Iron Age - A Dialogue Between Households and Individuals In Cultural Reproduction. *In:* J. MOORE and E. SCOTT eds. *Invisible People and Processes - Writing Gender and Childhood into European Archaeology.* London: Leicester University Press, pp. 68-74.

WRIGHT, D. 2005. *Severn Bore - Myths and Legends.* [Web Page]. http://tidal-bore.tripod.com/england/severn_myths.html (1 March 2005).